Disaster Communications in a Changing Media World

THE BUTTERWORTH-HEINEMANN HOMELAND SECURITY SERIES

Other titles in the Series

- **Emergency Management and Tactical Response Operations** (2008)
  ISBN: 978-0-7506-8712-6
  Thomas D. Phelan, Ed.D.
- **Nuclear Safeguards, Security, and Nonproliferation** (2008)
  ISBN: 978-0-7506-8673-0
  James E. Doyle
- **Biosecurity and Bioterrorism** (2008)
  ISBN: 978-0-7506-8489-7
  Jeffrey R. Ryan & Jan F. Glarum
- **Maritime Security** (2008)
  ISBN: 978-0-12-370859-5
  Michael McNicholas
- **Introduction to Emergency Management, Third Edition** (2008)
  ISBN: 978-0-7506-8514-6
  George Haddow et al.
- **Terrorism and Homeland Security: An Introduction with Applications** (2007)
  ISBN: 978-0-7506-7843-8
  Philip P. Purpura
- **Introduction to Homeland Security, Third Edition** (2008)
  ISBN: 978-1-85617509-8
  Jane Bullock et al.
- **Emergency Response Planning for Corporate and Municipal Managers, Second Edition** (2006)
  ISBN: 978-0-12-370503-7
  Paul Erickson

Other related titles of interest:

- **Introduction to Security, Eighth Edition** (2008)
  ISBN: 978-0-7506-8432-3
  Robert J. Fischer, Edward P. Halibozek, and Gion Green
- **The Corporate Security Professional's Handbook on Terrorism** (2008)
  ISBN: 978-0-7506-8257-2
  Edward P. Halibozek et al.
- **Design and Evaluation of Physical Protection Systems, Second Edition** (2008)
  ISBN: 978-0-7506-8352-4
  Mary Lynn Garcia
- **Vulnerability Assessment of Physical Protection Systems** (2006)
  ISBN: 978-0-7506-7788-2
  Mary Lynn Garcia
- **Introduction to International Disaster Management** (2007)
  ISBN: 978-0-7506-7982-4
  Damon Coppola
- **Risk Analysis and the Security Survey, Third Edition** (2006)
  ISBN: 978-0-7506-7922-0
  James F. Broder
- **High-Rise Security and Fire Life Safety, Second Edition** (2003)
  ISBN: 978-0-7506-7455-3
  Geoff Craighead

Visit **http://elsevierdirect.com/security** for more information on these titles and other resources.

Disaster Communications in a Changing Media World

By

George D. Haddow and Kim S. Haddow

AMSTERDAM • BOSTON • HEIDELBERG • LONDON
NEW YORK • OXFORD • PARIS • SAN DIEGO
SAN FRANCISCO • SINGAPORE • SYDNEY • TOKYO

Butterworth-Heinemann is an imprint of Elsevier

ELSEVIER

Butterworth-Heinemann is an imprint of Elsevier
30 Corporate Drive, Suite 400, Burlington, MA 01803, USA
Linacre House, Jordan Hill, Oxford OX2 8DP, UK

Library of Congress Cataloging-in-Publication Data
Haddow, George D.
    Disaster communications in a changing media world / by George D. Haddow
and Kim S. Haddow.
        p. cm. — (Butterworth-Heinemann homeland security series)
    Includes bibliographical references and index.
    1. Emergency management.   2. Disasters—Press coverage—Planning.
I. Haddow, Kim.   II. Title.
    HV551.2.H25 2008
    363.34′6--dc22   2008034720

British Library Cataloguing-in-Publication Data
A catalogue record for this book is available from the British Library.

ISBN: 978-1-8561-7554-8

For information on all Butterworth–Heinemann publications
visit our Web site at www.elsevierdirect.com

Printed in the United States of America

08 09 10 11 12 13 10 9 8 7 6 5 4 3 2 1

To Douglas and Owen

Table of Contents

Acknowledgement

We would like to acknowledge the emergency management and communications professionals who contributed their "Other Voice" to this book: Jane Bullock, John Copenhaver, Kim Fuller, Holly Harrington, Eric Holdeman, Greg Licamele, Rocky Lopes, Bob Mellinger, Ann Patton, and JR Thomas. Their generosity in sharing their experiences and lessons learned is greatly appreciated.

Many thanks to Orli Cotel.

Introduction

"Providing clear and consistent direction to citizens before, during, and following disasters is key to emergency preparedness and an effective response."
–Florida Governor Jeb Bush[1]

Communications is core to the success of disaster mitigation, preparedness, response, and recovery. The ability to disseminate accurate information to the general public, to elected officials and community leaders, and the media reduces risk, saves lives and property, and speeds recovery. It is no longer an afterthought or a luxury—communications is now as important as logistics or the pre-deployment of materials. Planning and controlling the flow of information before, during, and after a disaster will define credibility, trustworthiness, authority, and effectiveness of your efforts (Figure FM.1).

The emergence of new media—online news sites, e-mail, blogs, text messaging, cell phone photos, and the increasing role played by "first informers"—witnesses who now have the ability to transmit information immediately from the event—are redefining the roles of government and media.

The government's historical role as gatekeeper is now an anachronism. Traditional media's role as the sole conduit of reliable and officially sanctioned information has been eclipsed by the increasing use and influence of new media. The tools and rules of communications are evolving and disaster communications must evolve to capitalize on these changes and exploit the opportunities they provide—imagine being able to deploy an army of bloggers to help convey an evacuation order or report on the locations of new shelters as they open.

Finally, even though the means to the end are evolving, the goals, the values, and the underlying principles of effective disaster communication—the need for transparency, increased accessibility, trustworthiness and reliability, and to create partnerships with the media—have not changed and need to be embraced along with the practical ability to convey information effectively.

---

[1] Assessing Your Disaster Public Awareness Program: A guide to strengthening public education. 2006. Emergency Management Accreditation Program, The Council of State Governments Through Support from the Alfred P. Sloan Foundation, October 2006.

FIGURE FM.1 Tallahassee, FL, August 16, 2004—Gov. Jeb Bush provides information to the media at the state Emergency Operation Center as FEMA and other state officials look on. FEMA Photo/George Armstrong.

The purpose of this textbook is to define the principles of effective communications before, during, and after disasters. It examines the challenges to communicating in a world altered by the emergence and evolution of new media, the impact of "first informers" on disaster communications, and the changing roles of the government and traditional media as information gatekeepers. The book contains practical information and advice on communications staffing and planning, working with the media, and real world examples of good and bad communication strategies and tactics.

Chapter 1 examines the critical role communications plays in a successful emergency management operation and throughout all four phases of emergency management—mitigation, preparedness, response, and recovery. This chapter defines the mission of an effective disaster communications strategy and outlines five critical assumptions that serve as the foundation for such a strategy. Examples of effective communications in disaster events and promoting disaster reduction efforts are included in this chapter; examples of ineffective communications and the effect these failures had on disaster response operations are also included.

Chapter 2 looks at disaster communications in a changing media world. Much has changed in the past 20 years in the media world, including the advent of cable news and 24/7 coverage, the rise of the Internet, and the emergence of "first informers." This chapter tracks the increasing use and influence of new media in successive disasters since the September 11 attacks in 2001 and how these changes have affected overall coverage of disasters, how disaster-related messages are presented to the public, and what these changes mean to emergency management professionals in their efforts to communicate with their partners and the public.

Chapter 3 presents a set of basic principles for a successful communications strategy. Discussion and examples are provided in the areas of accuracy, accessibility, transparency, customer focus, leadership commitment, the role of communications in disaster planning, developing a partnership and trust with the media, and creating an emotional connection with the public.

Chapter 4 provides guidance on how emergency managers can develop and implement effective communication plans based on the principles discussed in Chapter 3 in all four phases of emergency management—mitigation, preparedness, response, and recovery. While the types of information to be communicated and the means for collecting, analyzing, and sharing this information may vary to some degree from one phase to the other, the basic principles of focusing on customer needs, leadership commitment to communications, and including communications in all planning and operations cross all phases. The timing and the delivery of the information may vary between mitigation and response, but the need for the delivery of timely and accurate information that individuals and communities can act on is constant. Many of the delivery mechanisms are also the same, including television, radio, print and the Internet, and new media.

Chapter 5 examines what it takes for emergency officials to communicate and work together with these four primary audiences—the general public, elected officials and community leaders, partners and stakeholders (i.e. first responders, volunteers, non-governmental organizations, etc.), and the media. Communicating with these four primary audiences is no longer a one-way street for emergency officials. It is now a cooperative venture that requires new skills, protocols, and technologies to be employed to design, build, and maintain effective disaster communications. The emergence of the new media has created a cadre of ordinary citizens as "first informers" providing first hand accounts of conditions where they live in real time. The new media must also be enlisted in getting information back out from emergency officials to local populations through their networks and contacts.

Chapter 6 examines the wide variety of new communication mechanisms available to collect disaster information and disseminate disaster communications. New technologies allow emergency officials to speed the flow of disaster information; increase the means and odds that people can access and share disaster information; humanize the crisis; expand the community; enlarge the perspective; and enrich, expand, and enhance disaster coverage, as Figure FM.2 shows. Topics covered in this chapter include how citizen journalists are working with traditional media outlets in disasters by making contributions to traditional media, establishing formal partnerships with traditional media, and replacing traditional media with online news sites. The relationship between the new media and the government is examined and definitions for new media functions are included in this chapter.

Chapter 7 examines how newsrooms and operations work. Topics discussed include the never-ending news cycle; how reporters now are expected to write their

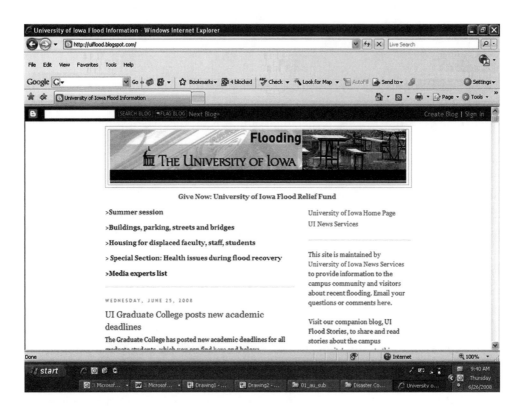

FIGURE FM.2 University of Iowa Web page on flooding (http://uiflood.blogspot.com/).

story, do a Web version, blog, and post audio and video; how the traditional media mine online content; and how news rooms decide what is news several times a day. Information is provided on how a news room functions, how to prepare for interviews, building relationships with reporters, who's who in a newsroom, and how to pitch story ideas to news departments.

Chapter 8 discusses the challenges of having the truth heard in a cluttered, chaotic world where everyone is a reporter and turning that trend to your advantage. This chapter examines the fact that emergency management organizations must establish partnerships with both the traditional media outlets and the new media in order to meet their primary communications mission of providing the public with timely and accurate information before, during, and after a disaster. These new partnerships must be based on the communications principles detailed in this book and take full advantage of the various information sources, networks, and messengers available to emergency management organizations. The purpose of this chapter is to detail the seven elements that we believe will comprise an effetive disaster communications capability in the future. These seven elements include: Communication Plan; Information Coming In; Information Going Out; Messengers; Staffing; Training and Exercises; and Monitor, Update, and Adapt.

Finally, the Resources Section of the book contains a wealth of information concerning all aspects of disaster communications complete with Web links and references to information sources, research papers, and support materials for use by emergency officials seeking to establish an effective disaster communications capability. Information is included in the following categories: Glossary of Terms, Disaster-Related Newsletters, Disaster Web sites, Bloggers, Special Needs Populations, Preparedness Messages, Research Reports, Communication Plans, Case Studies, and National Media Outlets.

Disaster communications is vitally important to effective emergency management. Traditional and new media play significant roles in disaster communications. Our hope is that this book will inform and guide emergency management professionals on how they can best work with these media outlets to provide timely and accurate information to the public before, during, and after a disaster.

1

Communications: The Critical Function

Communications has become an increasingly critical function in emergency management. The dissemination of timely and accurate information to the general public, elected and community officials, and the media plays a major role in the effective management of disaster response and recovery activities. Communicating preparedness, prevention, and mitigation information promotes actions that reduce the risk of future disasters. Communicating policies, goals, and priorities to staff, partners, and participants enhances support and promotes a more efficient disaster management operation. In communicating with the public, establishing a partnership with the media is key to implementing a successful strategy.

Communicating with the Public

"Communicating with residents is one of the most important tasks that elected officials perform in the wake of a disaster. The public needs concise, accurate, timely information to know what to do, and to be reassured that local government is responding appropriately."

Source: *City of San Jose Memorandum*, August 6, 2007, http://www.sanjoseca.gov/clerk/Agenda/082007/082007_01.pdf

Information sharing and its corollaries—collaboration and coordination—are key to effective, sustainable, timely, and participatory post-disaster recovery. "Unimpeded communication and the free flow of information are cornerstones of any post-disaster relief framework...."[1]

When that coordination doesn't occur it hinders response and recovery efforts. "...[O]ne of the central facts documented in the aftermath of Katrina: the importance of maintaining a timely and accurate flow of information in a disaster zone. When information was neither timely nor accurate, people suffered."[2]

---

[1] D. Gillmor (2006). *We the Media: Grassroots Journalism by the People, for the People*. O'Reilly Media Inc.

[2] A. L. May (2006). *First Informers in the Disaster Zone: The Lessons of Katrina*. The Aspen Institute.

Communication failures by government responders in Hurricane Katrina were noted in the report prepared by the United States House of Representatives that stated, "The lack of a government public communications strategy and media hype of violence exacerbated public concerns and further delayed relief." The House report also asked "why coordination and information sharing between local, state, and federal governments was so dismal. . . . Why situational awareness was so foggy, for so long. . . . Why unsubstantiated rumors and uncritically repeated press reports—at times fueled by top officials—were able to delay, disrupt, and diminish the response."[3]

This chapter defines the mission of an effective disaster communications strategy and outlines five critical assumptions that serve as the foundation for such a strategy. Examples of effective communications in disaster events and promoting disaster reduction efforts are included in this chapter; examples of ineffective communications and the effect these failures had on disaster response operations are also included.

Mission

The mission of an effective disaster communications strategy is to provide timely and accurate information to the public in all four phases of emergency management:

- *Mitigation*—to promote implementation of strategies, technologies, and actions that will reduce the loss of lives and property in future disasters.
- *Preparedness*—to communicate preparedness messages that encourage and educate the public in anticipation of disaster events.
- *Response*—to provide to the pubic notification, warning, evacuation, and situation reports on an ongoing disaster.
- *Recovery*—to provide individuals and communities affected by a disaster with information on how to register for and receive disaster relief.

Assumptions

The foundation of an effective disaster communications strategy is built on the following five critical assumptions:

- Customer Focus
- Leadership Commitment
- Inclusion of Communications in Planning and Operations
- Situational Awareness
- Media Partnership

---

[3] Select Bipartisan Committee to Investigate the Preparation for and Response to Hurricane Katrina, 2006, *A Failure of Initiative: Final Report of the Special Bipartisan Committee to Investigate the Preparation for and Response to Hurricane Katrina*, Government Printing Office, February 15, 2006, http://www.gpoaccess.gov/congress/index.html.

□ □ □ ██

Five Critical Assumptions for a Successful Communications Strategy

1. *Customer Focus*—Understand what information your customers and your partners need and build communication mechanisms that deliver this information in a timely and accurate fashion.
2. *Leadership Commitment*—The leader of the emergency operations must be committed to effective communications and must participate fully in the communications process.
3. *Inclusion of Communications in Planning and Operations*— Communications specialists must be involved in all emergency planning and operations to ensure that communicating timely and accurate information is considered when action decisions are being considered.
4. *Situational Awareness*—Effective communication is based on the timely collection, analysis, and dissemination of information from the disaster area in accordance with basic principles of effective communications, such as transparency and truthfulness, to be discussed in greater detail in Chapter 3.
5. *Media Partnership*—The media (i.e. television, radio, Internet, newspapers, etc.) are the most effective means for communicating timely and accurate information to the public. A partnership with the media involves understanding the needs of the media and employing trained staff who work directly with the media to get information to the public. And now that citizen journalists and new media technologies (cell phones, laptops, digital cameras) have become more vital and accepted sources of information and imaging from the front lines of a disaster, methods for incorporating this data and information must also be implemented.

██ □ □ □

Customer Focus

An essential element of any effective emergency management system is a focus on customers and customer service. This philosophy should guide communications with the public and with all partners in emergency management. A customer service approach includes placing the needs and interests of individuals and communities first, being responsive and informative, and managing expectations. In the 1990s, when disaster communications was valued, the Federal Emergency Management Agency (FEMA) emergency information field guide illustrates the agency's focus on customer service and its strategy of getting messages out to the public as directly as possible. The introduction to the guide states the following:

"As members of the Emergency Information and Media Affairs team, you are part of the frontline for the agency in times of disaster. We count on you to be ready and able to respond and perform effectively on short notice. Disaster victims need to know their government is working. They need to know where and how to get help.

They need to know what to expect and what not to expect. Getting these messages out quickly is your responsibility as members of the Emergency Information and Media Affairs team."[4]

The guide's Mission Statement reinforces this point further:

"To contribute to the well-being of the community following a disaster by ensuring the dissemination of information that:

- is timely, accurate, consistent, and easy to understand;
- explains what people can expect from their government; and
- demonstrates clearly that FEMA and other federal, state, local, and voluntary agencies are working together to provide the services needed to rebuild communities and restore lives.[4]"

The customers for emergency management are diverse. They include internal customers, such as staff, other federal agencies, states, and other disaster partners. External customers include the general public, elected officials at all levels of government, community and business leaders, and the media. Each of these customers has special needs, and a good communications strategy considers and reflects their requirements (see Fig. 1.1).

FIGURE 1.1 Camilla, GA, February 14, 2000—Vice President Al Gore, Senator Max Cleland, Congressman Sanford Bishop, FEMA Director James Lee Witt, FEMA Region 4 Director John Copenhaver, and other officials express concern and pledge federal assistance for the victims of Monday's devastating tornado. Photo by Liz Roll/FEMA News Photo.

[4] FEMA (1998). *FEMA Emergency Information Field Guide* (condensed). Washington, DC. FEMA.

Leadership Commitment

Good communication starts with a commitment by the leadership of the emergency management organization to sharing and disseminating information both internally and externally. One of the lessons learned from Hurricane Katrina according to a report authored by Donald F. Kettl of the Fels Institute of Government at the University of Pennsylvania in the report entitled *The Worst is Yet to Come: Lessons from September 11 and Hurricane Katrina* is "We need public officials to lead. Communicating confidence to citizens and delivering on promises are both critical in crises."[5]

☐ ☐ ☐

Lessons for State and Local Officials

"Create a single public face to encourage citizens' confidence—citizens need a voice of confidence from the scene. In the 1979 accident at the Three Mile Island nuclear plant, near Harrisburg, PA, Governor Dick Thornburgh and Harold Denton, from the Nuclear Regulatory Commission, brought unified command (UC) and consistent communications with citizens. Mayor Rudolph Giuliani underlined that lesson with his steady leadership following the September 11 terrorist attacks. One of the things that worsened Katrina's aftermath was the sense that no one was in charge because the public did not have steady communications from an official who should speak confidently about what was being done."

Source: D. F. Kettl. *The Worst is Yet to Come: Lessons from September 11 to Hurricane Katrina*. Fels Institute of Government. University of Pennsylvania. September 2005.

☐ ☐ ☐

The leader of any disaster response and recovery effort must openly endorse and promote open lines of communications among the organization's staff, partners, and public in order to effectively communicate. This leader must model this behavior in order to clearly illustrate that communications is a valued function of the organization.

Recent examples of leadership commitment to effective disaster communications include the efforts of California Governor Arnold Schwarzenegger during the 2007 wildfires in southern California. The Governor participated in multiple planned and unplanned press conferences and availabilities in order to deliver timely and accurate information to the public on the progress of response and recovery efforts during the wildfires. The Governor was credited with assuring the public and ensuring that the response was properly handled (see Fig. 1.2).

---

[5] D. F. Kettl (2005). *The Worst is Yet to Come: Lessons from September 11 to Hurricane Katrina*. Fels Institute of Government, University of Pennsylvania, September 2005.

FIGURE 1.2 San Diego, CA, October 30, 2007—California Governor Arnold Schwarzenegger, San Diego Mayor Jerry Sanders and FEMA Administrator David Paulison address the media at a press briefing in San Diego following the Southern California wildfires. Photo by Andrea Booher/FEMA.

Governor's Star Turn Masks Work Ahead

"Governor Arnold Schwarzenegger's constant, reassuring presence throughout the firestorm that lit up Southern California has won him praise even from opposition Democrats and a firefighters union that had been one of his harshest critics.

The Republican governor, a former bodybuilder and actor who relishes action outside the office, took command at news conferences and public appearances, political veterans of both parties agreed.

Behind the scenes, he had a more personal impact during hours spent mingling or posing for pictures with thousands of displaced residents huddled in evacuation centers, his aides said."

Source: J. P. Sweeney. Copley News Service. November 5, 2007. http://www.signonsandiego.com/uniontrib/20071105/news_1n5firegov.html

In the 1990s, FEMA Director James Lee Witt was a strong advocate for keeping FEMA staff informed of agency plans, priorities, and operations. Director Witt characterized a proactive approach in communicating with FEMA's constituents. His accessibility to the media was a significant departure from previous FEMA leadership

FIGURE 1.3 Laguna Canyon, CA, February 26, 1998—Federal Emergency Management Agency Director, James Lee Witt, addresses the questions of the media at the site of the Laguna Canyon mud flows that led to at least one death, and caused a great deal of damage. Photo by Dave Gatley/FEMA.

(see Fig. 1.3). Director Witt exhibited his commitment to effective communications in many ways:

- He held weekly staff meetings with FEMA's senior managers and required that his senior managers hold regular staff meetings with their employees.
- He published an internal newsletter to employees entitled "Director's Weekly Update" that was distributed to all FEMA employees in hard copy and on the agency electronic bulletin board that updated employees on agency activities.
- He made himself and his senior staff available to the media on a regular basis, especially during a disaster response, to answer questions and to provide information.
- During a disaster response, he held media briefings daily and sometimes two to three times a day.
- He would held special meetings with victims and their families.
- He led the daily briefings among FEMA partners during a disaster response.
- He devoted considerable time to communicating with members of Congress, governors, mayors, and other elected officials during both disaster and non-disaster times.

- He met four to five times per year with the State Emergency Management Directors, FEMA's principal emergency management partners.
- He gave speeches all over this country and around the world to promote better understanding of emergency management and disaster mitigation.

Through his leadership and commitment to communications, FEMA became an agency with a positive image and reputation. Communications led to increased success in molding public opinion and garnering support for the agency's initiatives in disaster mitigation.

Inclusion of Communications in Planning and Operations

The most important part of leadership's commitment to communications is inclusion of communications in all planning and operations. This means that a communications specialist is included in the senior management team of any emergency management organization and operation. It means that communication issues are considered in the decision-making processes and that a communications element is included in all organizational activities, plans, and operations.

In the past, communicating with external audiences, or customers, and in many cases internal customers, was not valued or considered critical to a successful emergency management operation. Technology has changed that equation. In today's world of 24-hour television and radio news and the Internet, the demand for information is never-ending, especially in an emergency response situation. Emergency managers must be able to communicate critical information in a timely manner to their staff, partners, the public, and the media.

To do so, the information needs of the various customers and how best to communicate with these customers must be considered at the same time that planning and operational decisions are being made. For example, a decision process on how to remove debris from a disaster area must include discussion of how to communicate information on the debris removal operation to community officials, the public, and the media.

During the many major disasters that occurred in the 1990s, FEMA Director Witt assembled a small group of his senior managers who traveled with him to the sites of disasters and worked closely with him in managing FEMA's efforts. This group always included FEMA's Director of Public Affairs. Similarly, when planning FEMA's preparedness and mitigation initiatives, Director Witt always included staff from Public Affairs in the planning and implementation phases. Every FEMA policy, initiative, or operation undertaken during this time included consideration of the information needs of the identified customers and a communications strategy to address these needs.

Again the response to Hurricane Katrina clearly illustrates the downside of failing to include consideration of communications issues in conducting a response operation. The Lessons Learned report prepared by White House Homeland Security Advisor Francis Townsend noted, "The lack of communications and situational awareness had a debilitating effect on the Federal response."[6]

---

[6] F. F. Townsend (2006). *The Federal Response to Hurricane Katrina Lessons Learned*. The White House.

☐ ☐ ☐ ▬▬▬▬▬▬▬▬▬▬▬▬▬▬▬▬▬▬▬▬▬▬▬▬▬▬▬▬▬

Lessons Learned from Hurricane Katrina

"The Department of Homeland Security (DHS) should develop an integrated public communications plan to better inform, guide, and reassure the American public before, during, and after a catastrophe. The Department of Homeland Security should enable this plan with operational capabilities to deploy coordinated public affairs teams during a crisis."

Source: F. F. Townsend, February 2006. *The Federal Response to Hurricane Katrina Lessons Learned*. The White House.

▬▬▬▬▬▬▬▬▬▬▬▬▬▬▬▬▬▬▬▬▬▬▬▬▬▬▬▬▬ ☐ ☐ ☐

One reason for this failure is the fact that the information centers were established late in the recovery process, as noted in the White House report:

"The DHS Public Affairs Office established a Joint Information Center (JIC) in Baton Rouge on Wednesday, September 6, to provide accurate and timely information on the Federal response and relief efforts as well as to counter misinformation. The formation of a second facility in New Orleans three days later improved the flow of accurate information back to the Baton Rouge JIC. These JICs helped to stem the spread of rumors and unsubstantiated reports that had plagued public information efforts during the first week after landfall."[5]

These JICs were established on September 6 in Baton Rouge and September 9 in New Orleans. Hurricane Katrina made landfall on August 29. These JICs should have been established long before 8 and 11 days after the storm made landfall.

One positive development recently is the inclusion of Public Information as one of five objectives that guided the planning for the Department of Homeland Security's Top Officials 4 (TOPOFF 4) Full-Scale Exercise in October 2007.

☐ ☐ ☐ ▬▬▬▬▬▬▬▬▬▬▬▬▬▬▬▬▬▬▬▬▬▬▬▬▬▬▬▬▬

Planning Objectives for TOPOFF 4 Full Scale Exercise— October 2007

"• **Prevention:** To test the handling and flow of operational and time-critical intelligence between agencies to prevent a terrorist incident.

• **Intelligence/Investigation:** To test the handling and flow of operational and time-critical intelligence between agencies prior to and in response to a linked terrorist incident.

• **Incident Management:** To test the full range of existing procedures for domestic incident management of a terrorist WMD event and to improve top officials' (federal/state/local) capabilities to respond in partnership in accordance with the National Response Plan (NRP) and National Incident Management System (NIMS).

Continued

• **Public Information:** To practice the strategic coordination of media relations and public information issues in the context of a terrorist WMD incident or incident of national significance.
• **Evaluation:** To identify lessons learned and promote best practices."

Source: *After Action Quick Look Report. National Exercise Program. Top Officials 4 (TOPOFF 4) Full-Scale Exercise*, October 15–20, 2007. November 19, 2007. http://www. fema.gov/pdf/media/2008/t4_after%20action_report.pdf

□ □ □

Situational Awareness

Situational awareness is key to an effective disaster response. Knowing the number of people killed and injured, the level of damage at the disaster site, the condition of homes and community infrastructure, and current response efforts provide decision makers with the situational awareness necessary to identify needs and appropriately apply available resources. The collection, analysis, and dissemination of information from the disaster site are the basis for an effective communications operation in a disaster response. This is also true during the disaster recovery phase, especially early in the recovery phase when the demand for information from the public, and therefore the media, is at its highest. Developing effective communication strategies to promote community preparedness and/or mitigation programs requires detailed information about the nature of the risks that impact the community and how the planned preparedness programs will help individuals and communities to be ready for the next disaster and the mitigation programs will reduce the impacts of future disasters.

Sharing this information is all important and this will require creating a culture among emergency officials where information sharing is valued. Information available to citizens at times of crises—man-made or natural—is often inadequate, biased, incorrect, or late. "Studies show that the problem lies not with the technologies (or lack thereof) but with the culture of information sharing. The access, dissemination, and archiving of information is often controlled by government agencies, institutions who have a parochial interest in controlling its flow—what gets out where, to whom, how, and when."[1]

The government culture can get in the way. The government officials uniformly said that they would not abandon the public information apparatus that is engrained in the governmental culture and hierarchy. "Responsibilities are limited and decided with specificity, and you do not get out of your lane," said Chet Lunner, 9 DHS director participating in the Aspen Institute's Katrina debrief. "You do not get to be a GS-14 or GS-15 by going on television, by upstaging your boss. That is a very big cultural issue."[2]

A glaring lack of situational awareness was identified as a severe hindrance to the government response to Hurricane Katrina.

☐ ☐ ☐

Situational Awareness in Hurricane Katrina

"While authorities recognized the need to begin search-and-rescue missions even before the hurricane winds fully subsided, other aspects of the response were hindered by a failure to quickly recognize the dimensions of the disaster. These problems were particularly acute at the federal level. The Homeland Security Operations Center (HSOC)—charged with providing reliable information to decision-makers including the Secretary and the President—failed to create a system to identify and acquire all available, relevant information, and as a result situational awareness was deeply flawed. With local and state resources immediately overwhelmed, rapid federal mobilization of resources was critical.

Yet, reliable information on such vital developments as the levee failures, the extent of flooding, and the presence of thousands of people in need of life-sustaining assistance at the New Orleans Convention Center did not reach the White House, Secretary Chertoff, or other key officials for hours, and in some cases more than a day. FEMA Director Michael Brown, then in Louisiana, contributed to the problem by refusing to communicate with Secretary Chertoff opting instead to pass information directly to the White House staff. Moreover, even though senior DHS officials did receive on the day of landfall numerous reports that should have led to an understanding of the increasingly dire situation in New Orleans, many indicated they were not aware of the crisis until sometime Tuesday morning.

DHS was slow to recognize the scope of the disaster or that FEMA had become overwhelmed. On the day after landfall, DHS officials were still struggling to determine the "ground truth" about the extent of the flooding despite the many reports it had received about the catastrophe; key officials did not grasp the need to act on the less-than-complete information that is to be expected in a disaster. DHS leaders did not become fully engaged in recovery efforts until Thursday, when in Deputy Secretary Michael Jackson's words, they "tried to kick it up a notch"; after that, they did provide significant leadership within DHS (and FEMA) as well as coordination across the federal government. But this effort should have begun sooner.

The Department of Defense (DOD) also was slow to acquire information regarding the extent of the storm's devastation. DOD officials relied primarily on media reports for their information. Many senior DOD officials did not learn that the levees had breached until Tuesday; some did not learn until Wednesday. As DOD waited for DHS to provide information about the scope of the damage, it also waited for the lead federal agency, FEMA, to identify the support needed from DOD. The lack of situational awareness during this phase appears to have been a major reason for DOD's belated adoption of the forward-looking posture necessary in a catastrophic incident."

Source: Senate Committee on Homeland Security and Governmental Affairs, 2006. *Hurricane Katrina: A Nation Still Unprepared*. S. Rept. 109–322, Government Printing Office, May, 2006.

☐ ☐ ☐

The U.S. Senate report on the Hurricane Katrina response listed the following findings regarding situational awareness:

- The HSOC failed to take timely steps to create a system to identify and acquire all available, relevant information.
- The HSOC failed in its responsibility under the NRP to provide "general situational awareness" and a "common operational picture," particularly concerning the failure of the levees, the flooding of New Orleans, and the crowds at the Convention Center.
- On the day of landfall (Monday), senior DHS officials received numerous reports that should have led to an understanding of the increasingly dire situation in New Orleans, yet they were not aware of the crisis until Tuesday morning.
- Louisiana was not equipped to process the volume of information received by its emergency operations center after landfall.
- Lack of situational awareness regarding the status of deliveries created difficulties in managing the provision of needed commodities in Louisiana and Mississippi.[7]

Situational Awareness and Media Stories

"Without sufficient working communications capability to get better situational awareness, the local, state, and federal officials directing the response in New Orleans had too little factual information to address—and, if need be, rebut—what the media were reporting. This allowed terrible situations—the evacuees' fear and anxiety in the Superdome and Convention Center—to continue longer than they should have and, as noted, delayed response efforts by, for example, causing the National Guard to wait to assemble enough force to deal with security problems at the Convention Center that turned out to be overstated."

Source: Select Bipartisan Committee to Investigate the Preparation for and Response to Hurricane Katrina, 2006, *A Failure of Initiative: Final Report of the Special Bipartisan Committee to Investigate the Preparation for and Response to Hurricane Katrina*, Government Printing Office, February 15, 2006, http://www.gpoaccess.gov/congress/index.html

FEMA's National Incident Management System (NIMS) includes a section on Public Information in its Incident Command System (ICS) component (see Fig. 1.4). One of the three top command staff reporting to the Incident Commander (IC) in ICS is the Public Information Officer (PIO).

---

[7] Senate Committee on Homeland Security and Governmental Affairs (2006). *Hurricane Katrina: A Nation Still Unprepared*. S. Rept. 109-322, Government Printing Office.

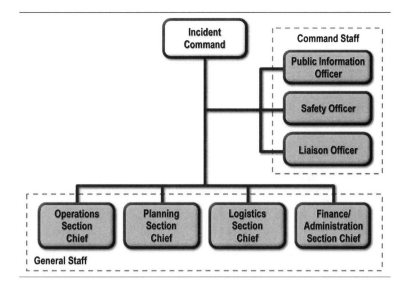

FIGURE 1.4 Incident Command System: Command Staff and General Staff (Source: FEMA. National Incident Management System: *FEMA 501/Draft*, August 2007).

Public Information in the National Incident Management System (NIMS)

"Public Information consists of the processes, procedures, and systems to communicate timely, accurate, and accessible information on the incident's cause, size, and current situation to the public, responders, and additional stakeholders (both directly affected and indirectly affected). Public information must be coordinated and integrated across jurisdictions and across agencies/organizations; among Federal, State, tribal, and local governments; and with the private sector and NGOs. Well developed public information, education strategies, and communications plans help to ensure that lifesaving measures, evacuation routes, threat and alert systems, and other public safety information is coordinated and communicated to numerous audiences in a timely and consistent manner. Public Information includes processes, procedures, and organizational structures required to gather, verify, coordinate, and disseminate information."

Source: FEMA. *National Incident Management System: FEMA 501/Draft.* August 2007.

According to the most recent version of NIMS, "The PIO gathers, verifies, coordinates and disseminates accurate, accessible, and timely information on the incident's cause, size, and current situation; resources committed; and other matters of general interest for both internal and external use."[8] Fig. 1.5 shows a PIO in action.

---

[8] FEMA (2007). *National Incident Management System: FEMA 501/Draft, August 2007.* Washington, DC: FEMA.

FIGURE 1.5 New Orleans, St. Bernard, LA, February 27, 2006—FEMA Public Affairs Officer Dave Passey talks to reporters in front of the cruise ships Ecstasy and Sensation about the progress of relocating residents into land-based temporary housing. FEMA is helping victims living on the cruise ships find long-term housing before the ships' contract expires March 1st and the ships set sail. Marvin Nauman/FEMA photo.

The duties of the PIO are defined as follows:

The PIO supports the Incident Command structure as a member of the Command staff. The PIO advises Incident Command on all public information matters relating to the management of the incident. The PIO handles inquiries from the media, the public, and elected officials, emergency public information and warnings, rumor monitoring and response, media monitoring, and other functions required to gather, verify, co-ordinate, and disseminate accurate, accessible, and timely information related to the incident, particularly regarding information on public health, safety, and protection. PIOs are able to create coordinated and consistent messages by collaborating to:

- identify key information that needs to be communicated to the public;
- draft messages that convey key information and are clear and easily understood by all, including those with special needs;
- prioritize messages to ensure timely delivery of information without overwhelming the audience;
- verify accuracy of information through appropriate channels; and
- disseminate messages using the most effective means available.[7]

During a disaster response, an effective information management system involves three critical elements:

1. **Collection of information at the disaster site**—This effort may involve numerous groups including local first responders (police, fire, and emergency

medical technicians), local and state emergency management staff, Federal damage assessment teams, the local Red Cross chapter and other voluntary organizations on the ground, community leaders, and individuals. Increasingly, the public has been using online tools to share directly or through the traditional media information and images from the front lines and information from "First Informers" needs to be acknowledged and included.

2. **Analysis of information**—This effort is undertaken to identify immediate response support needs and early recovery phase needs and is used by decision makers to match available resources to these identified needs.

3. **Dissemination of information**—This involves sharing of this information internally with all stakeholders in a timely fashion and externally with the media and through the media with the public.

In the Incident Command System (ICS) as defined by FEMA, this information is collected, evaluated, and disseminated by the Planning Section.

□ □ □ ■■■

Planning Section Responsibilities in the Incident Command System (ICS)

"The Planning Section collects, evaluates, and disseminates incident situation information and intelligence to IC/UC and incident management personnel. The Planning Section then prepares status reports, displays situation information, maintains the status of resources assigned to the incident, and prepares and documents the Incident Action Plan (IAP) based on Operations Section input and guidance from IC/UC.

The Planning Section is normally responsible for gathering and disseminating information and intelligence critical to the incident, unless IC/UC places this function elsewhere. The Planning Section is also responsible for assembling the IAP. The IAP includes the overall incident objectives and strategies established by Incident Command. In the case of UC, the IAP must adequately address the mission and policy needs of each jurisdictional agency, as well as interaction between jurisdictions, functional agencies, and private organizations. The IAP also addresses tactics and support activities required for the planned operational period, generally 12–24 hours."

Source: FEMA. *National Incident Management System: FEMA 501/Draft*, August 2007.

■■ □ □ □

Media Partnership

The media plays a primary role in communicating with the public. No government emergency management organization could ever hope to develop a communications network comparable to those networks already established and maintained by television, radio, newspapers, and online news outlets across the country. To effectively provide timely disaster information to the public, emergency managers must establish a partnership with their local media outlets. (See Eric Holdeman's "Another Voice")

□ □ □

Another Voice: Eric Holdeman

Eric Holdeman, former director of the King County (WA) Office of Emergency Management, is a principal with ICF International.

The Media is My Friend

Here in the 21st Century we are living in the information age. Media in all its forms dominates our lives. Old media in the form of newspapers, magazines, television, and radio is being challenged by "new media" in the form of the internet, podcasts, wikis, and blogs. Trust in the traditional media is at a historical low as people are using new media to get their news and evaluate the "truthiness" of what traditional media is telling them. In this internet age there are intense pressures to be first with the story and to verify all the facts later. It is interesting to note that the very first media call we received at the King County Emergency Operations Center (EOC) following the Nisqually Earthquake in 2001 came from Australia.

Into this mix come emergency management professionals who are seeking to provide disaster public education before an event, and then warnings and disaster public information to tell the story of disaster response and recovery once a disaster has come and passed.

Generally, emergency managers recognize that they cannot have an effective program without interacting with the media, but because of mistrust of the media in all its forms they avoid contact and treat the media as the enemy.

I believe that the media is a critical partner in your efforts to educate, inform, and warn the public. Like all relationships, they are best built before an event occurs. Initiating contact with all types of media representatives will enable them and you to begin building a relationship that acknowledges the role of the media while still being a person who they know they can trust. Hence you can either provide them with information or, failing that, refer them to other reliable and knowledgeable sources that can provide information and commentary on what is happening.

News rooms like EOCs are 24/7 enterprises that may never sleep. After all, it is drive time sometime everywhere. In order to be of use to the media you must first be accessible. Providing reporters, assignment editors, and news rooms all of your contact information, including your home phone number, is perhaps the one single thing that you can do to be responsive to their needs. You must realize that if they don't talk to you, they will talk to someone since they need to fill their news with content. It only makes sense that you should be that resource to them.

Disasters don't respect our artificial and man made jurisdictional boundaries. Therefore, when a large scale disaster strikes, it is typically a regional event.

Continued

Media cannot have staff at the multitude of EOCs that activate to respond to an event. They will gravitate to scenes that have graphic images and to EOCs that are prepared to share information in a consolidated manner, that paints the big picture for their audiences. To accommodate media getting the story it is important that technology systems and operating methodologies are put in place before an event that enables them to get the story. When building the Regional Communications and Emergency Coordination Center (RCECC) we invited television and radio engineering representatives to participate in the design process to ensure that we could provide them with space, connections, power, and other tools that would enable them to efficiently get the story from our center.

Katrina showed that even the media can be impacted by a disaster. Television and radio stations had damaged facilities, lost power, and went off the air. Recognizing that an earthquake in the Pacific Northwest will have the same effect on our local media they were invited to become signatories to the Regional Disaster Response Plan. This will enable them to share resources between media companies if they choose to do so, and it also provides a legal instrument for the sharing of government resources to the media that might enable them to continue broadcasting during a disaster.

There are other things that can be done to improve the media's ability to get the story. For instance, the primary warning radio station in the Central Puget Sound Emergency Alert System (EAS) Network has pre-positioned a portable "radio station in a box" which would enable a remote broadcast from the King County EOC should the situation warrant its use.

In the end, the media has been shown to be a critical partner in the preparation for a future disaster. Instead of looking at the media as the enemy, it is time we start thinking of the media as a friend. If you are having trouble with this concept, just repeat, "The media is my friend" over and over to yourself. Then, get out there and start building working relationships.

□ □ □

The goal of a media partnership is to provide accurate and timely information to the public in both disaster and non-disaster situations. The partnership requires a commitment by both the emergency manager and the media to work together, and it requires a level of trust between both parties.

Traditionally, the relationship between emergency managers and the media has been strained. There is often a conflict between the need of the emergency manager to respond quickly and the need of the media to obtain information on the response so it can report it just as quickly. This conflict sometimes results in inaccurate reporting and tension between the emergency manager and the media. The loser in this conflict is always the public, which relies on the media for its information.

It is important for emergency managers to understand the needs of the media and the value they bring to facilitating response operations. An effective media partnership provides the emergency manager with a communications network to reach the public with vital information. Such a partnership provides the media with access to the disaster site, access to emergency managers and their staff, and access to critical information for the public that informs and ensures the accuracy of their reporting.

An effective media partnership helps define the roles of the emergency management organizations to manage public expectations and to boost the morale of the relief workers and the disaster victims. All these factors can speed the recovery of a community from a disaster event and promote preparedness and mitigation efforts designed to reduce the loss of life and property from the next disaster event.

Improving Disaster Communications

Moderator of the Aspen Institute's discussion about communications before, during and after Hurricane Katrina, Charles Firestone, "divided the ideas for improvement—all trust-building notions—into three broad categories: first, more *openness*, including more accessibility by the media to decision makers and experts and more transparency in government for the media and the public; second, greater *collaboration* between government and the media, between the various forms of media, and between the media and the community; and, third, enhanced *exchanges* between all of the above.

The following are the highlights of the proposals that surfaced:

Openness

- Centralized communications centers in the disaster zone that are pre-announced and staffed quickly by local, state, and federal responders.
- A premium on communication as part of the job descriptions of disaster officials, taking a page from the public diplomacy effort.
- Enhancing transparency by providing more information on disaster-related Web sites that incorporate techniques for making this information easier to find.

Collaboration

- Pre-planning among media to share information dissemination facilities, including transmitters that offer wireless hotspots to the public.
- Suspension of proprietary and competitive urges to create distributive networks that share content across media platforms.
- An experiment to bring together traditional media and new media for crisis planning, including BarCamps (to use the latest Internet jargon).

Exchanges

- Finding teachable moments when media and government can best seize public attention to communicate with citizens to enhance individual preparedness.

Continued

- A national effort in which media entities band together for a public education campaign to stimulate personal preparedness.
- Participation by journalists, including representatives of new media, in tabletop exercises and other drills that simulate government and media response in a crisis."

Source: A. L. May (2006). *First Informers in the Disaster Zone: The Lessons of Katrina.* The Aspen Institute, Communications and Society Program. Washington, DC.

Communicating in the Era of Homeland Security

Communicating with the public is an area that needs to be improved if the nation is going to have a truly effective homeland security system. To date, the Department of Homeland Security (DHS) has shown little interest in communicating with the public, and when it has the results have not always been positive—the "duct tape and plastic" fiasco serves as a classic example. FEMA's failed communications in

FIGURE 1.6 New Orleans, LA, August 13, 2007—U.S. Department of Homeland Security Secretary Michael Chertoff addresses the news media after reviewing Louisiana's emergency preparedness plans with commander, Eighth Coast Guard District, Rear Adm. Joel R. Whitehead; Federal Emergency Management Agency Administrator R. David Paulison; Louisiana National Guard Major Gen. Bennett C. Landreneau, The Adjutant General; Louisiana Governor Kathleen Blanco; Governor's Office of Homeland Security Acting Director Col. Jeff Smith; Lt. Gov. Mitch Landrieu and Gulf Coast Principal Federal Official Gil Jamieson. The presentation and press conference were at the Eighth Coast Guard District Offices on Lake Ponchartrain. Photo Manuel Broussard/FEMA.

Hurricane Katrina is another (see Fig. 1.6). DHS and its State and local partners need to address three factors to improve its communications with the American people.

First, there must be a commitment from the leadership, not only at DHS and its State and local partners, but at all levels of government, including the executive level, to communicate timely and accurate information to the public. This is especially important in the response and recovery phases to a terrorist incident.

In a disaster scenario, the conventional wisdom that states information is power, and that hoarding information helps to retain such power, is almost categorically reversed. Withholding information during disaster events generally has an overall negative impact on the well-being of the public, and on the impression the public forms about involved authorities. In practice, sharing of information is what generates authority and power, when that information is useful and relates to the hazard at hand. Two shining examples of this fact are the actions of former FEMA Director James Lee Witt and former New York City Mayor Rudy Giuliani. Both leaders went to great lengths to get accurate and timely information to the public in a time of crisis, and their efforts both inspired the public and greatly enhanced the effectiveness of the response and recovery efforts they guided.

To date, DHS leadership and the political leadership have been reluctant to make this commitment to share information with the public. This is something that must change if they expect the American people to fully comprehend the homeland security threat and to become actively engaged in homeland security efforts. Few citizens have any idea of what actual terrorism risks they face, and fewer can actually relate those risks in any comparable fashion to the risks they face every day without notice.

Second, homeland security officials at all levels must resolve the conflict between sharing information with the public in advance and in the aftermath of a terrorist incident that has value for intelligence or criminal prosecution purposes. This is directly linked to the commitment issue discussed in the previous paragraphs and has been repeatedly cited by homeland security officials as reasons for not sharing more specific information with the public.

This is a very difficult issue that, in the past, DHS has tried to ignore. However, the continued frustration among the public and State and local officials with the Homeland Security Advisory System (HSAS) is just one sign that this issue will not solve itself nor just go away.

Also at issue is the question of when to release relevant information to the public without compromising intelligence sources and/or ongoing criminal investigations. This is an issue that rarely, if ever, confronts emergency management officials dealing with natural and unintentional man-made disasters. Therefore, there is little precedent or experience for current homeland security officials to work with in crafting a communications strategy that balances the competing need for the public to have timely and accurate information with the need to protect intelligence sources and ongoing criminal investigations. To date, the needs of the intelligence and justice communities have clearly been judged to outweigh those of the public—but at a cost.

Withholding information leaves the public vulnerable and suspicious of the government. Lucy Dalglish, executive director of the Reporters Committee for Freedom of the Press, & Paticipant in the Aspen Institute's debrief on Hurricane Katrina, said her task, and the task of journalists, was to convince government officials that, over the long run, transparency can build trust and save lives: "The same information that a terrorist can use to do great damage can possibly give families information about which escape route to use to get away from a nuclear power plant. I think we're going to find that if we have a flu pandemic, the information that can be used to terrorize and scare people can also be used to save their lives. I think what we have to do is work very hard at convincing people that access to information is ultimately going to be our friend.[2]"

Members of Congress and DHS Secretary Michael Chertoff have spoken often about reworking the HSAS. This would be a critical first step in reestablishing trust with the public for the warning system. From this starting point, if the commitment is there among the homeland security leadership, additional communications mechanisms can be developed to ensure that the public gets timely and accurate information both in advance of any terrorist incident and during the response and recovery phases in the aftermath of the next terrorist attack.

Third, more effort must be invested by Federal departments and agencies to better understand the principal terrorist threats that our nation faces (i.e., biological, chemical, radiological, nuclear, and explosives), and to develop communications strategies that educate and inform the public about these threats with more useful information. The 2001 Washington, DC, anthrax incident is a perfect example of uninformed or misinformed public officials sharing what is often conflicting and, in too many instances, wrong information with the public.

The nation's public officials must become better informed about these principal risks and be ready and capable of explaining complicated information to the public. As the anthrax incident made clear, this is not a luxury, but a necessity if the response to similar incidents in the future is to be successful.

Decades of research and a new generation of technologies now inform emergency managers as they provide information about hurricanes, tornadoes, earthquakes, and hazardous materials incidents to the public. A similar research effort must be undertaken for these five new terrorist risks and communications strategies that will ensure that homeland security officials at all levels are capable of clearly explaining to the public the hazards posed by these threats.

These communications strategies must consider how to communicate to the public when incomplete information is all that is available to homeland security officials. In the vast majority of cases, this partiality of information is probable. A public health crisis will not wait for all the data to be collected and analyzed, nor will the public. Homeland security officials must develop strategies for informing the public effectively, as the crisis develops, by forming effective messages that are able to explain to the public how what is being said is the most accurate information available based on the information that, likewise, is available—despite its incomplete nature. Clearly, this is not an easy task, but it is not impossible. The public will increasingly expect such communications efforts, so the sooner such a system is in place, the better the next incident will be managed.

Conclusion

Whether dealing with the media, the public, or partners, effective communication is a critical element of emergency management. Media relations should be open and cooperative, the information stream must be managed to provide a consistent, accurate message, and officials need to be proactive about telling their own story before it is done for them. A customer service approach is essential to communicate with the public, a collaborative approach should be taken to promoting programs, and great care should be given as to how and when risk is communicated to citizens. Multiple agencies and unclear lines of responsibility make communications among partners a challenge; political skill and acumen are needed to overcome such hurdles, and efforts are under way to improve communications in this area.

2

Disaster Communications in a Changing Media World

Introduction

Working with the media before, during, and after a disaster is a fact of life for an emergency management official. The media remains the single most effective means for communicating timely and accurate information to the public. Historically, emergency managers have shied away from talking to the media, especially during a disaster response. That day is over. As we noted in Chapter 1, emergency managers or other government officials involved in disaster response can no longer ignore the media. The same is true for communicating with the public during the recovery phase and in promoting preparedness and mitigation messages to the public. Developing a partnership with the media should now be standard operating procedure for any and all emergency management operations in this country and around the world.

However, the media is constantly changing and emergency managers must keep up with these changes to have an effective communications operation. Disaster preparedness information used to be exclusively published in brochures and pamphlets that were distributed in post offices and courthouses around the country. In the 1950s, Civil Defense workers went directly to communities to dispense information on nuclear preparedness in town hall meetings. Years later, representatives from the National Flood Insurance Program (NFIP) held similar meetings in communities around the country to inform residents about flood insurance.

Over time, the radio has become an integral part of communicating warning messages to the public before the next tornado or hurricane strikes. In turn, radio has often been the sole source of information in the immediate aftermath of a massive disaster that cuts off electricity to the disaster area for days at a time because of the availability of transistor and crank radios that do not require electricity.

Television has become a big part of disasters in the past 50 years. The pictures and stories that are generated by disaster events are a natural fit for television. It was the size of the satellite photo of Hurricane Floyd on television coupled with evacuation warnings from local, state, and federal officials transmitted by television that prompted 3 million residents in Florida, Georgia, and South Carolina to evacuate their homes as the storm threatened the Eastern Seaboard. It is also the television that graphically communicated the sad events that occurred in New Orleans after Hurricane Katrina.

Over time, television has changed considerably. Once there were only three national networks and usually three or four local stations in any given community. Now there are hundreds of channels available nationwide. There are 24/7 news channels and the Weather Channel and they are available across the country.

The rise of the Internet as a source for disaster and emergency-related information and news has been spectacular in the past 15 years. A survey conducted in April 2008 by the Canadian Centre for Emergency Preparedness (CCEP) found that the Internet has overtaken newspapers on the list of emergency information sources used by the Canadian public. Television and radio are ranked first and second on this list but it may not be long before the Internet grabs even more of the public's attention, especially as older and low-to-moderate income individuals and families gain access to the Internet.

The media continues to change with the advent of "first informers," ordinary citizens armed with a cell phone who can take pictures and/or video at the disaster site and add commentary and post their submissions on the Internet or provide them to CNN, MSNBC, or other news outlets. Some of the first, if not the first, photos and commentaries coming out of the Asian Tsunami disaster in 2004 were filed by these "first informers" who were there when the tsunami struck and survived to provide information and images of the damage and destruction.

Just as the reporting and information flow during a disaster response and aftermath are being impacted by the changing media, so too the mechanisms used to promote preparedness and mitigation messages are changing. The Internet is a wonderful source of information but it can also be used to organize a community preparedness program and promote individuals' involvement in community hazard mitigation efforts.

The purpose of this chapter is to examine the various forms of media that emergency managers have historically relied on and the new forms of media that are changing how disaster news and information is shared with the public and what this means for emergency managers seeking to partner with the media. We will examine the various historical uses of media in all four phases of emergency management and new media in this changing media world.

Historical Uses of Media

Civil Defense

Some the first disaster preparedness materials were developed by the Civil Defense Administration. In 1950 an animated movie entitled *Duck and Cover* and starring Bert the Turtle delivered the message that "whenever danger threatened him he never got hurt, he knew just what to do, duck and cover ... he did what we all must learn to do, duck and cover." The film's narrator echoed this message at the film's end saying,

"Be sure and remember what Bert the Turtle just did friends because we must all remember to do the same thing . . . duck and cover." (You can view this short film at http://www.youtube.com/watch?v=AN-4kH7fpTg)

Numerous other film strips and training materials were developed by Civil Defense for use in grade school education programs and "duck and cover" drills and at Civil Defense fairs held around the country. An assortment of these films is available for viewing at the Military.com Web site at http://www.military.com/Content/MoreContent1/?file=cw_media.[1]

In 1980, the Federal Emergency Management Agency (FEMA) published a series of pamphlets concerning the design and construction of home fallout shelters.[2] A Civil Defense poster from the 1950s proclaimed this preparedness message, "The best way to survive the hazards of radioactive fallout, or any other threat an enemy may use against us, is to be prepared—know the facts—learn what to do, now!"[1] Figure 2.1 shows art work from a 1950s Civil Defense pamphlet.

FIGURE 2.1 Art from a popular Civil Defense pamphlet from the 1950s. Source: Military.com, http://www.military.com/Content/MoreContent1/?file=cw_index

[1] Military.com 2008. http://www.military.com/Content/MoreContent1/?file=cw_index

[2] Trinity Atomic Web Site (2008). http://www.cddc.vt.edu/host/atomic/civildef/#Burt

□ □ □

Duck and Cover

"The pamphlet *Duck and Cover* was produced for the Federal Civil Defense Administration (FCDA) in 1951. In addition to the 20 million copies of this pamphlet distributed by the FCDA, *Duck and Cover* was also released as an animated film, a record album, and a radio program. This civil defense program was designed specifically to help educate and organize the nation's youth in the event of a nuclear attack by the Soviet Union.

In 1949, the Soviet Union successfully detonated an atomic weapon, ushering in an era of nuclear brinksmanship with the United States that lasted for much of the remainder of the twentieth century. Subsequently, early atomic-age civil defense efforts were undertaken in the U.S. with the assumption that the nation's largest cities would be among the nation's primary targets. Federal efforts to educate the public about the risks of an atomic attack and strategies to survive took many forms, including the promotion and distribution of short films, radio programs, news articles, posters, and pamphlets. By promoting readiness in the face of atomic war, administrators of the FCDA hoped to alert the public to the dangers of atomic war, alarming them enough to participate in civil defense programs but not enough to panic or become fatalistic.

Duck and Cover was officially released as a film in 1952 by Archer Productions, Inc., a New York advertising firm contracted to produce it for the FCDA. The film's first public viewing came in January, as part of an FCDA-sponsored traveling show called *Alert America*, which toured the country for 9 months in 1952. Beginning in March, with the endorsement of the National Education Association, the film was shown in schools across the United States. The animated main character, Bert the Turtle, provided students with a cheery instructor to guide them in the most up-to-date survival strategy for a nuclear attack. The plan was simple and straightforward. At the first warning of attack, "Like Bert, you duck to avoid the things flying through the air... and cover to keep from getting cut or even badly burned."

"According to the FCDA, 'If *Duck and Cover* is carefully integrated with a study of civil defense, it can help your pupils acquire a quick and easy technique for self-protection from an atomic explosion as well as help them understand the need for civil defense.' Unfortunately, the advent of hydrogen-bomb technology in 1952 made Bert the Turtle's advice worthless, allowing for the development of weapons hundreds of times more powerful than those dropped on Hiroshima and Nagasaki, Japan, during World War II. Nuclear weapons developed throughout the remainder of the 20th century were even more powerful, convincing many Americans that the only way to

Continued

survive a nuclear attack would be to prevent one from happening in the first place."

Written by Joshua Binus, © Oregon Historical Society, 2004."

Source: The Oregon History Project (2002). http://www.ohs.org/education/oregonhistory/ historical_ records/dspDocument.cfm?doc_ID=CBD9A0CB-9020–5BBE-6AD0AB659BBE0E1F

Disaster Response and Recovery

For many years, radio and television were the singular media communicating messages to the public before, during, and after a major disaster event (see Fig. 2.2). In hurricane-prone states the preparedness mantra is to store water and canned food, board up the windows, and have fresh batteries on hand for your transistor radio. Often times radio stations with exceptionally strong signals are the sole source of information in the immediate aftermath of a large hurricane. This has been the case with WWL Radio in New Orleans, a 50,000 Watt AM radio station whose signal can be heard across the Gulf Coast states. Several times in the past, WWL became the

FIGURE 2.2 Rochester, MN, August 30, 2007—FEMA Public Affairs Officer Brad Caine and SBA PIO Richard Daigle are interviewed at a local radio station about FEMA and SBA's programs designed to assist flood victims. Photo by Patsy Lynch/FEMA.

sole source of information for hurricane survivors as far away as Florida. In the aftermath of Hurricane Katrina, WWL was virtually alone in providing information to those people who rode out the storm in their homes and had no access to television because the electricity was out.

□ □ □

Radio Disaster Report

Radio Iowa News

Three Counties Declared Disaster Areas Due to Flooding

Tuesday, April 29, 2008, 10:42 a.m.

By Darwin Danielson

"The governor has declared Bremer, Blackhawk, and Louisa Counties in eastern Iowa state disaster areas due to flooding. Emergency Management Division director, David Miller, says the designation allowed the state to give them help.

Miller says those counties were getting pumps and sandbags from the Corps of Engineers and the D-O-T was used to transfer the equipment. He says there are other counties that are fighting flood waters, but haven't yet asked for state help.

Miller says the flood fight is starting to ease in some areas, such as Denver in Black Hawk County, where they returned pumps to the Corps of Engineers today. But, Miller says it's an ongoing problem. He says they're concerned a little about rain later this week and the impact that could have. Miller says the crests are moving downstream from Denver and Black Hawk County down to Vinton and Anamosa. He says the flow will continue down to Davenport and Burlington as it flows on into the Mississippi.

Miller says his agency is keeping close contact with the National Weather Service to try and gauge the impact as the water moves downstream. Miller says each morning they do a conference call with the weather service and the counties and to look at stream and river projections. He says the good news is that water flows have been a little lower than projected—although there's still flooding.

Miller says several homes and businesses have already been hit by flooding. He says a number of families have been impacted and people hit by flooding should work with their county emergency management coordinators. Miller says the state has the individual assistance program for low-income residents hit by the flooding, and he says you should work with human services on that program.

Miller says it's too early to tell a dollar amount of damage yet. Miller says they'll work with county coordinators as the flood waters go down to assess the damage and determine where they go from here. The governor was already scheduled to be in eastern Iowa today, and will be touring flood damage in Davenport."

Source: Radio Iowa (2008). http://www.radioiowa.com/gestalt/go.cfm?objectid=9ADA24A0-A312-A14D-FBCBB89ADDDE7653.

□ □ □

Television has fully embraced disasters, especially the cable news outlets with their 24/7 news cycles. Disaster programming has become a staple of these cable networks and in recent years these media outlets have provided intensive coverage of even the smallest disaster event. Large events such as September 11, Hurricane Katrina, the Asian Tsunami, and the Okalahoma City bombing have received around-the-clock television coverage from the broadcast networks and the cable news outlets. The broadcast networks (CBS, NBC, and ABC) with their large news staff and national reach have historically been the primary source of information on disaster events for the public (see Fig. 2.3). Several veteran reporters and news anchors including Dan Rather, John Chancellor, and Tom Brokaw made their reputations and advanced their careers by first reporting on hurricanes and other disasters.

In recent years it is the cable news outlets that are leading the disaster coverage. More and more Americans are turning to the 24/7 coverage of disaster events provided by CNN, MSNBC, Fox News, and others. The broadcast networks continue to cover major disaster events but the cable news outlets are grabbing larger and larger audience share with each new event. Major disaster events mean increased ratings for the cable news outlets and they are investing their resources accordingly. It is no accident that during Hurricane Katrina, CNN's Anderson Cooper, following

FIGURE 2.3 Vanderbergh County, IN, November 7, 2005—Indiana Lt. Gov. Becky Skillman speaks to the press about the tornado that destroyed part of a mobile home park during the early morning hours of Sunday, November 6. Photo by Gay Ruby/FEMA.

in the foot steps of Rather and Brokaw, became the most recent example of a reporter significantly advancing his career through his work in a major disaster.

Beginning in the mid 1990s, the Internet started to become an information backstop for media coverage of disaster events.

□ □ □ ▬▬▬▬▬▬▬▬▬▬▬▬▬▬▬

Another Voice: Bob Mellinger

Bob Mellinger is the founder and president of Attainium Corp, which he launched to deliver business continuity, emergency preparedness, and crisis management services. www.attainium.net

In the summer of 2002, I was seeking a way to communicate on a regular basis with my Attainium clients and other professionals involved in disaster response and business continuity. After talking to a large number of business continuity professionals, I discovered that most of them did not have access to a regular source of information on this rather complex subject. I wanted, therefore, a vehicle that would provide—and be perceived as providing—real value, keeping business continuity professionals and other interested parties up to date on issues of concern to them. The result was a weekly newsletter that would provide links to Internet articles on a variety of business continuity and disaster response topics.

Although we were advised that a weekly newsletter probably would not work (because people wouldn't bother to read it that often), I felt it was worth trying. We devised a very simple format for an e-mail newsletter—we chose a topic, researched articles on that topic, wrote a brief introduction, and started with an initial contact list of approximately 200 people. Recipients were given the opportunity to opt out, because we did not want to be considered as spammers.

The response was quite surprising ... many complimentary e-mails were received after the first issue landed, thanking Attainium for providing valuable information in an extremely usable format. Bit by bit, the subscription list grew as folks signed up on Attainium's Web site and the original subscribers passed it along to their colleagues. Subscribers to the *Business Continuity NewsBriefs* have increased fivefold since it was launched and there are very few opt outs. In addition, several issues have been published on topics that were requested by subscribers; reader input is always welcome.

As I said, the format is simple. We begin with a two- or three-sentence opening to introduce the topic (i.e., Testing, Training, & Evaluation; Business Continuity Planning; Negligent Failure to Plan, etc.). Then we briefly describe what each article is about. Here's a sample of the descriptions from a recent newsletter:

"We're told that, in an emergency, we need supplies for 3 days; what's the real story? (Item #1). Here's a general guide for preparing a shelter-in-place plan in the workplace (Item #2). You'll probably need to educate tenants if you expect them to shelter-in-place (Item #3)."

Continued

"This white paper weighs the risks of evacuation against the difficulty of sheltering in place (Item #4). This article answers many of the questions you may have about sheltering in place (Item #5). Finally, we provide a list of sites that offer shelter-in-place supplies (Item #6)."

Six articles per week is standard. For each, we use a headline, a very brief synopsis of the article, and a live link. We provide a quote of the week, which is related to the week's topic. The whole thing is a quick read so nobody has to spend a lot of time reading unless they are interested in particular articles.

As I travel around the country with my "Disaster Experience" tabletop exercise simulation program, I add topics to our list based on my conversations with BC professionals covering a wide variety of industries. The response to the newsletter continues to be exceptional and can be attributed to the timeliness of the material, the short, simple format, and the flexibility to include topics when events warrant (the Virginia Tech shootings, for example).

Interested parties can view archived issues of or sign up for the NewsBriefs at http://www.attainium.net

Another Voice: Greg Licamele

Greg Licamele works in the Fairfax County (Virginia) Office of Public Affairs. Before his time there, he worked for The George Washington University's public relations office and the emergency management office.

I've walked the flooded streets of despair. I've walked the tenuous Florida Gulf Coast beaches of potential damage. I've walked east and west coast cities, each with their own risk of hazards.

In all this walking, it's always been clear to me how important communicators are to emergency management. Communicators are the bridge between the emergency manager's technical world and the public's plain language needs.

During my time with the Fairfax County (Virginia) Office of Public Affairs, I have served as part of a team that has built this critical bridge. In 2006, a small area of the county flooded after an historical rainstorm. When the flooding began, I reported to the county's emergency operations center at 11 p.m. and started writing messages; served as a liaison between departments; and published information quickly to the county's Web site. Through these—and other—tasks, I completely understood how important it was to communicate response information that night and the recovery steps in the following days. Walking the flooded streets a few days later further confirmed how critical it is for skilled communicators to be actively involved so we can offer real solutions, provide advice, and reduce rumors.

Continued

I'm reminded of the importance of communicators wherever I am—whether it's in New York City wondering what happened that day; at a beach town lying in the path of a potential hurricane; or in San Francisco wondering what will happen one day in the future. Communicators make a difference.

But we know that people's personal preparedness levels in the United States are generally low. It's up to communicators to be creative and inclusive to tell people about the importance of preparedness. As such, I led the communications efforts for an innovative preparedness campaign for faith communities in Fairfax County. A partnership was formed among the county government, the American Red Cross, and the local Citizen Corps Council to educate hundreds of faith community members of all beliefs. All of these faith communities shared our core message: be prepared as an individual or family so you can then help others in need. We held training sessions for faith community members, who would then train their communities. Each training session I attended was followed with big thank yous from the attendees because our messages and materials helped make a difference.

As communications evolves into new media outlets like YouTube, social networking sites, and microblogging, how are we, as communicators, evolving, too? Are we embracing new technologies? It should be our solemn responsibility to find multiple ways to deliver our common messages through many voices and outlets. If certain demographics are using technology more, then that's where they seek their information. Fairfax County has taken the leap, and now has a YouTube channel, and we are using it to share preparedness messages.

And as our communities evolve and become thicker melting pots of culture, are we being inclusive enough of people who speak other languages and who have very specific cultural needs? For example, the word "once" has radically different meanings in two languages. ("1" in English, "11" in Spanish.) Are we aware of what communities live in our own backyards, especially those in communities the U.S. Census Bureau identifies as "linguistically isolated?" How do we tell a Korean community to prepare and respond to a disaster? Do we know what kind of meals to provide to Vietnamese communities during traditional "hot" and "cold" periods? Are there new media sites for these communities, too?

As communicators, we can deliver hope during tough times. We can be that critical bridge. But we must also evolve as communications and communities change, too.

New Media and Disaster Communications

On May 2nd, 2008, Cyclone Nargis struck the Irrawaddy Delta region of Myanmar (Burma). The cyclone with winds of 120 mph made landfall at the mouth of the Irrawaddy River—a low-lying, densely-populated region—and pushed a 12-foot wall of water 25 miles inland, killing at least 80,000 people, leaving as many as 2.5 million homeless.

Ten days later, on May 12, 2008, a 7.9 earthquake devastated China's Sichuan province, toppling buildings, collapsing schools, killing more than 69,000, injuring over 367,000, and displacing between 5 and 11 million people.

Two disasters. One common link. They demonstrated that new technologies—the Internet, text messaging systems, camera phones, Google Map mash-ups—and citizen journalists, especially bloggers, have irrevocably altered the nature of disaster reporting and replaced the top–down flow of information from the government and the traditional media in times of crisis with a dynamic and democratic two-way exchange.

"Burmese Blog the Cyclone"—BBC News Headline

In Myanmar, where internet and cell phone access are limited, the military government refused to allow aid workers or journalists to reach disaster areas and moved fast to restrict communications. Ironically, it was a local online news source, *Burma News*, that reported on the "guidelines" the junta had set for journalists' coverage specifically prohibiting showing dead bodies or reporting about insufficient aid for victims.[3]

In spite of these restrictions, Burmese blogs and news sites were quick to react by posting eyewitness accounts of the disaster and mobilizing fundraising efforts.

According to BBC News, "People inside Burma have been giving their updates from the disaster zone. Burmese blogger Nyi Lynn Seck has a section of his blog devoted to daily updates from the Delta region. 'They are seeing dead bodies,' he writes. 'Nobody has cremated or buried these dead bodies.' He also carries a report of how one private donor in Bogalay was forced to give his donation to the local authorities rather than people in need."[4]

The BBC also noted that the Mizzima news site, based in India and run by Burmese exiles, used long-standing personal networks to gather compelling accounts of loss and survival. Other exile Burmese news sites such as Yoma3 reported on the spread of disease among the cyclone victims in Bogalay. Stories of monks and local residents pulling together and co-coordinating local clean-ups and sharing water could be found on the Democratic Voice of Burma and other sites such as The Irrawaddy. The Rule of Lords blog reported that people were being turned away from hospitals because of the lack of electricity and water.

In addition to the news gathering done by citizen journalists online (bloggers), other new media technologies helped tell the story of the Burmese disaster and recovery.

Twitter—a short messaging service (SMS)—that uses cell phones and 140 character messages that are also posted online—emerged quickly as an important medium for coverage of the crisis. Aid agencies working in Burma including AmeriCares and the Salvation Army also used Twitter to disseminate information and coordinate activities.[5]

---

[3] Burma News (2008, May 13). *Burmese Journals Face Restriction on Cyclone Coverage.* http://myamarnews. blogspot.com/2008/05/burmese-journals-face-restrictions-on.html

[4] BBC News (2008, May 8). "Burmese Blog the Cyclone." Retrieved May 8, 2008 from http://news.bbc.co.uk/2/hi/asia-pacific/7387313.stm

[5] Washkuch, Frank (2008, May 20). Relief Groups Turn to Twitter Amid Crises. *PR Week*, http://www.prweekus.com/Relief-groups-turn-to-Twitter-amid-crises/article/110368/May 20

YouTube hosted scores of videos recording the devastation and feeble response. User AfterNargisYgn uploaded a multi-part series of videos featuring images of the effects of the cyclone in Yangon, Myanmar's largest city, previously known as Rangoon. His series also documented the growing anger and desperation of the storm victims. Burma4u uploaded a video of the aftermath in Latbutta, with Cyclone Nargis' victims crowded in refugee shelters, trying to sleep (see Fig. 2.4). Videos depicting dozens of people who died in the cyclone, which were banned by the junta, were also posted on YouTube.[6,7]

Flickr and Picasa—two photo sharing sites featured pictures of destruction posted by individuals and relief organizations including "disasteremergencycommittee" and "cyclonerelief."[8]

Google Earth and the Associated Press produced interactive maps that tracked the cyclone's passage through the county and illustrated the extent of the storm damage—especially the dramatic erosion of shoreline and degree of inundation.

FIGURE 2.4 Burma Story on YouTube.

[6] Rincon, Juliana (2008). Myanmar: Citizen Videos in Cyclone Nargis Aftermath. *Reuters Global News Blog*, http://blogs.reuters.com/global/tag/burma/.

[7] YouTube (2008). http://www.youtube.com/user/AfterNargisYgn.

[8] Global Voices Online (2008). Myanmar Cyclone 2008. http://www.globalvoicesonline.org/specialcoverage/myanmar-cyclone-2008/

Global Voices Online and traditional media like *The New York Times*, BBC, and CNN featured, linked to, or aggregated coverage by bloggers and linked to videos and photos recorded by eye witnesses.

In China, New Media Helps Speed Recovery

Twitter broke the news of the Sichuan earthquake, according to several news accounts, before the U.S. Geological Survey was able to perform its official role and report it.[5]

A fast-moving network of text messages, instant messages, and blogs became a powerful source of firsthand accounts of the earthquake—testament to the fact that in the wake of disaster, the Chinese government gave reporters and bloggers unprecedented freedom.

According to the Associate Press, "China is now home to the world's largest number of Internet and mobile phone users, and their hunger for quake news [forced] the government to let information flow in ways it [had not] before."[10]

Almost instantly and nonstop since the earthquake, the uncensored opinions of Chinese citizens popped up online, sent by text and instant message—either through Twitter or FanFou:[9]

"CCP if you can't save people then hurry up and get the hell out of the way.
I strongly demand for foreign assistance."—Ameko

"You can phone Sichuan mobile phones and get through now."—Tokyoegg

"Urgent notice: Sichuan's AB blood at emergency levels!!!" winning

"The road to Wenchuan is cut off again"[9]

And the AP noted that even critical postings were not restricted:

"Why were most of those killed in the earthquake children?"

"How many donations will really reach the disaster area? This is doubtful," read another.[10]

In another measure of how much the reins on the information flow had been loosened, Mashable, an online site that covers social networking news, reported that in the regions hardest hit by the quake, generators were brought to special buildings to allow people to recharge their mobile phones and crews made repairing cell towers affected by the quake and subsequent aftershocks a priority so "information could flow with as few complications as possible."[11]

[9] Global Voices Online (2008). Sichuan Earthquake 2008. http://www.globalvoicesonline.org/specialcoverage/sichuan-earthquake-2008/

[10] Anna, Cara 2008. China Allows Bloggers, Others to Spread Quake News. Associated Press http://ap.google.com/article/ALeqM5g96Dwm9sQnJkXfZN9xxDlNLBveawD90O62RG1, May 18.

[11] Aune, Sean (2008). China Allows Bloggers Freedom in Earthquake Aftermath. *Mashable* http://mashable.com/2008/05/18/china-bloggers-earthquake/, May 18.

In addition, the Chinese language "Wikipedia" site on the 2008 Sichuan earthquake was set up more quickly than its English-language counterpart—despite the fact that Wikipedia Chinese had been blocked from within China.[9]

Other online and new media tools included scores of user-shot videos on YouTube that captured the moments the quake struck, bulletin boards to help relatives and friends locate missing people, a channel on QQ Prayer to report fundraising scams and a map mashup on Netease that allowed users in Wenchuan to report in live time what was happening in their area.[9]

In addition to using online technology to report on the earthquake damage, Chinese citizens also used the same tools to expedite the recovery. According to *The Washington Post*, the nation's "wary rulers" allowed grassroots groups and informal networks, "aided by the proliferation of online bulletin boards, blogs, and on-the ground-coordination centers" to function as legitimate relief organizations.[12]

Volunteers used e-mail, text messages, and cell phones to gather information on where help or supplies were needed and to direct relief. "No one from the government told us what to do. In this urgent situation, we decided to share some of the responsibility," one of the volunteer coordinators told *The Washington Post*.

Guo Hong, a Chengdu-based sociology professor and relief volunteer, explained "From this disaster, the government has come to realize the power of the grassroots. This power will be helpful in establishing and managing a real civil society. But the problem is how to allow the grass-roots groups to take part in an orderly way. Taxi drivers used to be considered the least-civilized group, but they were the first to respond to the disaster, organizing themselves to drive to the hospitals."[12]

New Media: New World

When disasters happened in the past, we learned about them after the fact. No more. New technologies—laptops, cell phones, text messaging systems, digital cameras, the Internet have changed the way news is gathered and distributed. These technologies have also profoundly altered the flow of information, undermining the traditional gatekeepers and replacing the centralized, top-down model used by the government and professional media with a more dynamic flow of information that empowers citizens and creates ad hoc distributive information networks.

"These technologies create new ways for citizens to be heard, governments to be held accountable and the State to answer to failures of governance. Ordinary citizens ... are increasingly using technology, through devices such as mobile phones, to support powerful frameworks of transparency and accountability that citizens can use to hold decision makers responsible for the action, and indeed, inaction," Dan

---

[12] Fan, Maureen (2008). Citizen Groups Step Up in China. *The Washington Post*, May 29.

Gillmor and Sanjana Hattotuwa explained in their essay, "Citizen Journalism and Humanitarian Aid: Boon or Bust?"[13]

According to Gillmor, the days of news as a "lecture"—when traditional media told the audience what was news—are done. Now news is more of a conversation and the lines have blurred between producers and consumers: "The communications network itself will be a medium for everyone's voice, not just the few who can buy multimillion–dollar printing presses, launch satellites, or win the government's permission to squat on the public's airwaves...."[14]

According to a seminal study on participatory journalism, "The venerable profession of journalism finds itself at a rare moment in history where, for the first time, its hegemony as gatekeeper of the news is threatened by not just new technology and competitors but, potentially, by the audience it serves."[15]

The once passive audience has become an active participant in the creation and dissemination of news, and the flow of information is no longer controlled by journalists and government agencies.

"The participatory nature of news coverage ... erases the line between those affected by the news and those who cover the news," according to Tim Poster, who writes the blog First Draft. "In a world of digital and reflexive communication, we are all reporters."

The increasing participation and power of ordinary citizens in emergency communications is starting to have more observable consequences. The Aspen Institute report, *"First Informers in the Disaster Zone: The Lessons of Katrina"*, noted in its conclusion: "...There was a difference in how the online environment changed the media mix and altered the flow of information during and after the disaster.... At times the traditional flow of information from government to media to public reversed course... As one pair of new media experts put it, Katrina 'revealed extraordinary changes taking place within a society increasingly connected by digital networks, a society at the cusp of a new era in human history in which individuals possess an unprecedented capacity to access, share, create, and apply information.'"[16]

One participant in the Aspen Institute's assessment of lessons learned from Katrina was Jon Donley the editor of NOLA.com—*The New Orleans Times-Picayune's* online companion and the primary source of news when the daily could not print in the weeks following the hurricane (see Fig. 2.5). He explained that the new media had fostered a two-way flow of information, in contrast to the old paradigm in which information flows down from government and media to a passive

---

[13] Gillmor, Dan and Sanjana Hattotuwa (2007). Citizen Journalism and Humanitarian Aid: Boon or Bust? *ICT for Peacebuilding,* http://ict4peace.wordpress.com/2007/07/30/citizen-journalism-and-humanitarian-aid-bane-or-boon/.

[14] Gillmor, Dan (2006). *We the Media: Grassroots Journalism By the People, For the People.* O'Reilly Media Inc.

[15] Bowman, Shayne and Chris Willis (2003). *We Media: How Audiences are Shaping the Future of News and Information.* The Media Center at the American Press Institute.

[16] May, Albert L. (2006). *"First Informers in the Disaster Zone: The Lessons of Katrina,"* The Aspen Institute, 2006.

FIGURE 2.5 Photographs of Hurricane Katrina on the nola.com Web site.

audience. "I would really encourage everybody to think about this new media age that we're in, where the audience isn't playing that game anymore. We have had a revolution."[16]

In addition to forcing the traditional media to reconsider and redefine its role in disaster communications, the new participatory media enhanced the amount of information and number of sources and added to the problems endemic in disaster—the need to sort truth from rumor and the tension between media demanding transparency and accessibility and government officials changed with managing information during a disaster.

The information available to citizens at times of crises is often inadequate, incorrect, or dated. According to Gillmor and Hattotuwa, "Studies show that the problem lies not with the technologies (or lack thereof) but with the culture of information sharing. The access, dissemination, and archiving of information is often controlled by government's agencies, institutions who have a parochial interest in controlling its flow—what gets out where, to whom, how, and when."[13]

"If we waited for the government to release information during a disaster, it would be days before the public would know anything," complained to one participant in the Aspen Katrina assessment. Another participant, Chet Lunner, acting director of state and local government coordination in DHS and a former national reporter for the Gannett News Service spoke from the government's perspective.

He disagreed with a comment from CNN's David Borhman that the government instinct in a crisis was to hide. "They are not hiding. They are sort of defensive, in a crouch . . . because [they] don't trust the media."[16]

Katrina, the Aspen report concludes, exacerbated the already burgeoning distrust between media and government. "As rival proxies for the public, the two institutions clashed openly during and after the storm. . . . The first failure was caused by lack of good situational awareness by federal officials themselves, who painted a rosy scenario that clashed with the pictures and reports from the scene from journalists. 'Don't you guys watch television? Don't you guys listen to the radio,' ABC's Ted Koppel famously asked Michael Brown, then FEMA director. 'Federal, state, and local officials gave contradictory messages to the public, creating confusion and feeding the perception that government sources lacked credibility,' the White House report concluded."[16]

The emergence and proliferation of citizen media complicated the information mix and increased the tension between the government and traditional media.

"Information in the hands of citizens continues to instill fear and loathing in the minds of those who wish to manufacture public opinion to their benefit by the careful selection and publication of information. . . . ," explained Sanjana Hattotuwa, in "Who is Afraid of Citizen Journalists?"[17]

Government official Chet Lunner explained his unease in the Aspen report: "I get concerned when I see the term "citizen journalists" and "blogs" lumped in with everything else as if that were journalism in the way that it is practiced by professionals. That is often the problem we have, which is that something that starts out as a blog does not necessarily meet the standards of most source-tested journalism that has been in practice for all these years. . . We have enough trouble with things that do go through the [mainstream media] filter. The amount of time and energy and social unrest by readers and/or the people trying to practice in the field dealing with these things that are exaggerated rumors, etc., is a problem, particularly in the framework of these disaster times when people are depending upon or relying on that."[16]

"On the other hand," the editor of NOLA.com explained, "the very first reports [that] we had of life threatening flooding in New Orleans came from citizens typing it into cell phones. The very first news we had of clear levee breaks, of looting, of a shooting death, or a suicide in the Superdome—every one of those things we heard first from citizens who we were encouraging to have a two-way dialogue with us."[16]

Participatory journalism and the generation of news and information from "first informers"—citizens on the scene when disaster happens, are not trends that are going to go away. In fact, the 2008 disasters in Burma and China may mark the coming of age of text-messaging, blogging, and video sharing as tools that can bring faster coverage of a news event than traditional media.

---

[17] Hattotuwa, Sanjana (2007). *Who is Afraid of Citizen Journalists? Communicating Disasters*, TVA Asia Pacific and UNDP Regional Centre in Bangkok.

The challenge now for traditional news sources and cautious governmental hierarchies is to plan for and maximize the use of an increased and accelerated flow of information, to seize the opportunity to share information and help build and engage the community that online media creates.

User-generated content is here to stay, according the Lou Ferrara of the Associated Press. "The landscape has changed, but we're all about getting this information. What's the best way to do it? Do we outsource, partner, do it ourselves?"[18]

"We are living in the middle of a remarkable increase in our ability to share, to cooperate with one another, and to take collective action, all outside the framework of traditional institutions and organizations," observed Clay Shirky, a longtime Internet expert.[19]

Yahoo's Bill Gannon, reflected on the Katrina communications experience. "What we realized is that users wanted not just to read information, but they wanted to be empowered," he said. "What they wanted to do was get personally involved either through a message board or simply by making a donation." How to channel and sustain that empowerment is the challenge of the next crisis.[16]

The Evolution of New Media Use in Disasters

The magnitude and frequency of natural disasters are increasing. According to the Center for Research on the Epidemiology of Disasters, there were four times as many weather-related disasters in the last 20 years then in the previous 75 years. With this new "Age of Extreme Weather,"[20] has come the evolution and maturation of new media tools and technologies, a dramatic rise in the number of citizen journalists, and an almost annual increase in their contribution to the flow of new information during disasters. "Disasters have provided a unique trigger that have consolidated technological advances in concert with democratizing influences operating outside the traditional brokers of information and aid."[21]

Even though the 1990s was a time of transformation in communications technology with the emergence of the World Wide Web, 24/7 cable television, and array of digital tools—from affordable and widely available wireless mobile devices and high-resolution satellite maps—new media was not a factor in natural disaster coverage or recovery until 2001.

In the aftermath of the September 11, 2001 terrorist attacks, citizen-shot videos of the attacks on Twin Towers dominated news coverage and Americans turned to the Internet for information. But the sharp spike in traffic froze and crashed Web sites. In many ways, 9/11 was the last disaster covered under the old model of crisis

---

[18] Ferrara, Lou (2007). AP's "NowPublic" Initiative. Remarks at the Associated Press Managing Editors' Conference, "*Fast Forward to the Future*," http://www.j-lab.org/apme07notesp5.shtml, October 2.

[19] Shirky, Clay (2008). *Here Comes Everybody: The Power of Organizing Without Organizations*. The Penguin Press.

[20] Blow, Charles M. (2008). Farewell, Fair Weather, *New York Times,* May 31.

[21] Laituri, Melinda and Kris Kodrich (2008). *On Line Disaster Response Community: People as Sensors of High Magnitude Disasters Using Internet GIS*. Colorado State University.

communications: newspapers printed "extra" editions, people turned to television for news and "the familiar anchors of the broadcast networks—Tom Brokaw, Peter Jennings, and Dan Rather—took on their avuncular roles of the past for a nation looking for comfort and reassurance."[16]

Every disaster since September 11 has involved more citizen journalists and expanded the use and utility of the new media tools and technologies.

In 2003, during China's SARs epidemic, people used text messaging to exchange information the government tried to suppress.[17]

Three major disasters within 9 months—the Asian tsunami (2004), the London transit bombings (2005), and Hurricane Katrina (2005)—marked the coming of age of participatory media.

The December 26, 2004 Asian tsunami has been defined by Dan Gillmor as "the turning point—a before-and-after moment for citizen journalism."[22] Blogs, Web sites, and message boards provided news and aid—and in real time. One blog, "waveofdestruction.org" logged 682,366 unique visitors in 4 days.[22] Wikipedia—a group-created Web site that is editable by any user—became the site for basic information, particularly for hotlines that allowed people to search for missing loved ones and find housing, medical, and other assistance.

Minutes after four bombs rocked London's transportation system, a definitive Web page "July 7, 2005 London Bombings" was started with five sentences on Wikipedia. The page "received more than a thousand edits in its first 4 hours of existence as additional news came in." Users added links to traditional news sources, and information was posted about what public transportation was shut down, listing contacts to help track a missing person and offering directions to commuters trying to get home. "What was conceived as an open encyclopedia in 2001 [became] a general purpose tool for gathering and distributing information quickly...."[19] (See Fig. 2.6.)

A cell phone photo taken by a commuter in a smoked-clogged tunnel in the Tube became the iconic image of the disaster. Londoners pooled their digital photos on Flickr—a photo-sharing site and service that allows people to tag pictures with comments and labels. "The photos that showed up after the bombings weren't just amateur replacements for traditional photojournalism: people did more than provide evidence of the destruction and its aftermath. They photographed official notices ("All Underground services are suspended"), notes posted in schools ("Please do not inform children of the explosions"), messages of support from the rest of the world ("We love you London") and within a day of the bombings, expressions of defiance addressed to the terrorists ("We are not afraid" and "You will fail.") Not only did Flickr host all of these images, they made them available for reuse, and bloggers writing about the bombings were able to use the Flickr images almost immediately, creating a kind of symbiotic relationship among various social tools." Police

---

[22] Cooper, Glenda (2007). Burma's Bloggers Show Power of Citizen Journalism in a Crises. *Reuters Alert Net*, http://www.alertnet.org/db/blogs/30708/2007/09/3-134022-1.htm, October 3.

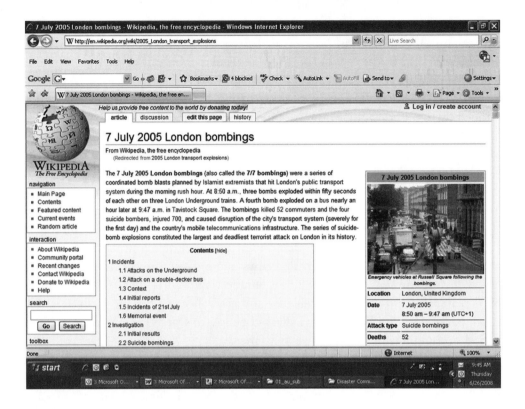

FIGURE 2.6 Wikipedia London bombing page.

asked people to supply them with cell phone pictures or videos because they might contain clues about the terrorists.[19]

In August 2005, Hurricane Katrina, a category three hurricane tore through New Orleans, LA; Mobile, AL; and Gulfport, MS. Over 1500 people were killed and tens of thousands left homeless. Blogs became the primary information-providing tool used by both traditional media and citizen journalists. Staff reporters for New Orleans' daily newspaper, *The Times-Picayune*, created a blog that for a time became the front page of their news operation. It enabled members of the community isolated by flood waters and debris to show and tell each other what they were seeing.[14]

Message boards provided critical information about shelter locations, family tracing, and missing persons. Internet expert Barbara Palser counted 60 separate online bulletin boards that were created to locate missing people within 2 weeks of the storm. "These sites included major portals such as Yahoo and Craigslist, an array of newspaper and television sites, Web sites hosted by government and relief organizations, and individual technologists, including a group of programmers who enlisted about 2000 volunteers to create a database called the Katrina PeopleFinder Project." PeopleFinder was established "to create a consolidated database of missing people built outside the traditional, centralized institutions (i.e., FEMA, Red Cross)."[16]

Google Earth and Google Map, which provide and use online satellite imagery were used to illustrate damage assessments—particularly to the Gulf coast and barrier islands.[21]

After the Java earthquake in 2006, mobile phones became mobile news services. Internews, an international media support group, worked with 180 Indonesian journalists to set up a text messaging service that helped local radio stations to report on the recovery.[17]

In October 2007, wildfires in Southern California resulted in the loss of nearly 2200 homes and over $1 billion in damages and marked a major step forward in the integration of mainstream media and citizen journalists. "Local media has been highlighting user-submitted photos and videos, and embedding new technology in their prime coverage. San Diego's public television station, KPBS, used Twitter to give its audience updates when its Web site went down, and the Twitter updates now have a prominent place on their home page."[23]

San Diego TV station News 8 responded to the crisis by taking down its entire regular Web site and replacing it with a rolling news blog, linking to YouTube videos

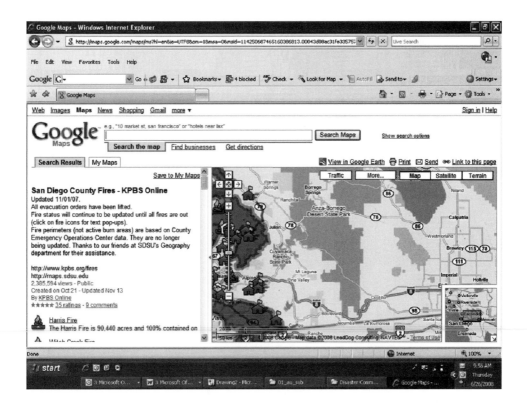

FIGURE 2.7 Google map for 2007 San Diego fires.

[23] Glaser, Mark (2007). California Wildfire Coverage by Local Media, Blogs, Twitter, Maps and More. *MediaShift*, http://www.pbs.org/mediashift/2007/10/the_listcalifornia_wildfire_co_1.html October 25.

of its key reports, plus Google Maps showing the location of the fire.[24] Also on the site were links to practical information that viewers needed, including how to contact insurance companies, how to volunteer or donate to the relief efforts, evacuation information, and shelter locations. "It's an exemplary case study in how a local news operation can respond to a major rolling disaster story by using all the reporting tools available on the Internet."[25]

Local and national television stations asked for submissions from wildfire witnesses and victims. The NBC-affiliate in San Diego received over 2000 submissions of pictures and video related to the wildfires. CNN's I-Reports section reportedly received about the same number of fire-related submissions.[23]

The Google Map (Internet GIS) tool was used to develop maps of shelter locations and fire updates, as Figure 2.7 shows.[26]

Clearly a symbiotic relationship is emerging between citizen journalists and the mainstream news media. With every new major disaster, the mainstream media's use of internet-facilitated reporting has increased. Government, however, has been slow to appreciate the power or exploit the potential of the new media tools and internet culture.

[24] Stabe, Martin (2007). California Wildfires: A Round Up. *OJB Online Journalism Blog*, http://onlinejournalism blog.com/2007/10/25/california-wildfires-a-roundup/October 25.

[25] Catone, Josh (2007). Online Citizen Journalism Now Undeniably Mainstream, *ReadWriteWeb*, http://www. readwriteweb.com/archives/online_citizen_journalism_mainstream.php October, 26.

[26] Wagner, Mitch (2007). Google Maps and Twitter Are Essential Resources for California Fires. *Information Week*, http://www.informationweek.com/blog/main/archives/2007/10/google_maps_and.html October 24.

Principles of a Successful Communications Strategy

A successful disaster communications strategy is built on a set of basic principles that ensure that emergency managers effectively communicate with their customers and partners in all four phases of emergency management—mitigation, preparedness, response, and recovery. These principles provide guidance to emergency managers and other officials involved in emergency operations and programs on how to talk to their customers, how to ensure that they can talk to their customers, what to say and what not to say, how to be accurate and timely, when to talk, and how to connect to their customers when you talk.

These principles combine basic directions on communicating effectively (i.e., be available, ensure there are adequate resources for communications, invest in media training) with a set of values (i.e., don't lie, be informed, don't make promises you can't keep) that taken together should effectively guide emergency managers and others in communicating emergency management messages. These principles fall into the following nine general categories:

- Focus on the needs of your customers
- Make a commitment to effective communications
- Make communications an integral part of all planning and operations
- Be transparent in your communications
- Ensure that your information is accurate
- Release information in a timely manner
- Make yourself, your staff, and others, where appropriate, available and accessible
- Create an emotional connection with your audience
- Build a partnership with the media and the "first informer" community

Several of the principles discussed in this chapter were noted in Chapter 1 of this book. The following sections present detailed discussions of each these principles.

Focus on the Needs of Your Customers

Principle: Customer Focus

- Drives all actions
- Provide needed information
- Work on customer's schedule
- Use language customers understand
- Recognize language and cultural differences
- Work with trusted community leaders
- Respect special needs populations
- Use appropriate media to reach your customers
- Drives all actions

Meeting the needs of your customers should be the primary focus of all emergency managers. All emergency operations, including communications, must be focused on the needs of the customers. The principle customer the emergency managers serve is the public, whether they are victims of a disaster or seeking to prepare for or mitigate against the next disaster. Additional emergency management customers include elected and appointed government officials, community officials, business leaders, partners, the media, and anyone with a stake in the community. An effective communications strategy is built around understanding and meeting the needs of these customers.

- **Understanding what information customers need**—In a response scenario, important information includes how and where to get assistance, what are the responders doing, where is it safe and where is it unsafe, how long before people can return to their communities and their homes, how to locate missing relatives, etc. Critical information before an event occurs may include evacuation or shelter-in-place orders, locations of shelters, etc. Preparedness messages may include how to protect your home or business, how to create a family plan, how to work with others in your community such as Citizen Corps Councils, etc. Mitigation messages may include how to assess your vulnerability, what can be done to reduce your vulnerability, how to access resources in order to take action, etc. Survey research and data are available from the Federal Emergency Management Agency (FEMA), the American Red Cross, and academic studies that have charted the emergency management information needs in all four phases of emergency management. (See Preparedness Messages Appendix in the Resources section in the back of this book.)

- **Work on your customer's schedule and not your own**—This seems simple and just plain common sense but often emergency managers allow the requirements of their work to determine when assistance is made available or when preparedness workshops or mitigation forums are scheduled. As an example, small business owners have a difficult time attending off site workshops and training sessions even if the sessions are free and conducted in their neighborhood. They just do not or cannot leave their business for even an hour to attend these events. The best way to reach them may be going directly to their place of business and working one-on-one with each business owner. This may not be the most time or cost effective means of reaching this audience, but you will reach this audience.

- **Use language that most people can understand**—In talking to the public directly or through the media, don't use jargon or acronyms that most people would never understand. Don't use pronouns extensively. Clearly identify individuals and organizations that you are talking about. In preparing preparedness and mitigation materials, use easily accessible language that makes it clear what actions you want individuals to take. There is academic and scientific research available to help in developing these materials so that your customers will understand them. (See Preparedness Messages Appendix in the Resources section in the back of this book.)

- **Recognize language and cultural differences among your customers**—English is not the first language of a vast number of Americans. Plan to have translations of messages made and translators available to effectively communicate with non-English-speaking populations. The Tulsa, OK Citizen Corps Council sponsors, "The Language/Culture Bank, coordinated by the Tulsa Volunteer Center and the local Retired Senior Volunteer Program (RSVP), provides volunteers with foreign language skills, such as Spanish or Vietnamese, or multicultural experience on an "on-call" basis to assist community agencies with public health and safety issues. These volunteers also make themselves available for speaking engagements to schools and civic organizations."[1]

- **Identify trusted community leaders who can facilitate communications in disadvantaged neighborhoods**—Your messages may be ignored in some neighborhoods where the residents are suspicious of government authorities. Identify and recruit trusted community leaders in these neighborhoods to carry your messages to the residents and to provide you with information from the neighborhood before, during, and after a disaster. These trusted leaders could serve not only as communications hubs but also as allies in establishing Community Emergency Response Team (CERT) programs, Citizen Corps Councils, and preparedness and mitigation programs in their neighborhoods.

- **Respect special needs populations and take action to meet their specific communications needs**—Individuals with disabilities (hearing, learning, cognitive, etc.) reside in every community and emergency managers must include specific steps in their communications plans for all emergency phases to ensure that these individuals are informed.

- **Use the appropriate media to reach your customers**—Television remains the most effective and efficient means for reaching the largest segment of a community's population. However, some people get their information from the radio and a growing number from the Internet. Older citizens are more likely to read newspapers than students who are getting their information from My Space and Facebook. Understand the media preferences of your customers and plan your communications programs accordingly.

---

[1] Tulsa Citizen Corps (2008). http://www.citizencorps.gov/councils/cc_councils/tulsa.shtm

Make a Commitment to Effective Communications

Principle: Leadership Commitment

- Be an active participant in communications
- Include communications director on senior management team
- Hire and maintain professional staff
- Invest in ongoing training for staff
- Invest resources in communications

Be an Active Participant in Communications

A good measure of leadership commitment to communications is the active participation of the leadership planning and executing the communications strategy including being the principal agency spokesperson during disaster response and recovery, being directly involved in designing and implementing preparedness and mitigation awareness campaigns, and working with elected officials in communicating with the public.

Include Communications Director on Senior Management Team

The communications director should be involved in all planning and operational meetings and decisions. Membership on the senior management team ensures that communications issues are raised and considered by senior management and that the communications aspects of any plan, operation, or action are developed and agreed on by the senior management team. This makes it clear to all staff that communications is a leadership priority.

Hire and Maintain Professional Staff

At minimum have at least one communications specialist on staff who can work with the media during response and recovery and assist in the design and implementation of a preparedness and mitigation awareness campaign. If resources are available, consider adding communications staff during response and recovery and to work on Internet and new media activities to support preparedness and mitigation campaigns.

Invest in Ongoing Training for Staff

At minimum the communications director should receive media training which will make that person more effective in communicating with the public through the media. Additional training for communications staff might include media relations (how to work with the media), marketing (how to pitch story ideas to the media), and Web-related training.

Invest Resources in Communications

In addition to investing resources for staff and staff training, invest in the creation and maintenance of an information collection, analysis, and dissemination program. Also consider investing additional resources in new online media, Internet, and print production costs and, for special projects, animation. Also consider using resources to acquire consulting help in all areas—media relations, Internet, new media as well as customer research and message development.

Make Communications an Integral Part of All Planning and Operations

Principle: Integrate Communications into Planning and Operations

- Bring communications professionals to the table
- Run all decisions through the communications filter
- Develop communications strategies to support operations
- Create communications strategies to promote plans

Bring Communications Professionals to the Table

Include communications professionals on planning and operations teams that traditionally include logistics, legal, support, and first responder staff.

Run All Decisions Through the Communications Filter

Decisions in all four phases of emergency management should always be run through the communications filter in order to identify potential communications problems and to design communications solutions to support and enhance operational performance.

Develop Communication Strategies to Support Operations

In anticipation of the communications demands in a response and recovery scenario, develop a strategy to deliver timely and accurate information to the public that includes creating mechanisms to provide regular media updates, collect and disseminate facts and stories, respond to media inquiries, provide access to the disaster site for the media, make response and recovery officials available to the media and, when appropriate, deliver preparedness and mitigation messages concerning future disasters. This strategy should also identify how to use the Internet and new media to support response and recovery communications.

Create Communications Strategies to Promote Plans

Identify opportunities for communications staff to work with the traditional and new media to promote preparedness and mitigation awareness and education campaigns.

Be Transparent in Your Communications

Principle: Transparency

- Don't lie
- Don't talk about what you don't know
- Don't talk about actions of other organizations
- Don't make promises you can't keep

FIGURE 3.1 Purvis, MS December 16, 2005—Mark Ackerman, a FEMA specialist for housing, talks to the press after hosting a meeting with members of various Mississippi disability rights groups. Photo by Patsy Lynch/FEMA.

- Be informed
- Acknowledge the conversation
- Focus on performance (Fig. 3.1)

Don't Lie

This is a no brainer but critically important. Nothing will destroy your credibility and the credibility of your organization quicker. There really should never be a need to lie and if you do you will be caught. Equally important, don't get caught in an unintentional lie by not confirming the information you are communicating.

FEMA Meets the Press, Which Happens to Be...FEMA

"FEMA has truly learned the lessons of Katrina. Even its handling of the media has improved dramatically. For example, as the California wildfires raged Tuesday, Vice Adm. Harvey E. Johnson, the deputy administrator, had a 1.00 p.m. news briefing.

Reporters were given only 15 minutes' notice of the briefing, making it unlikely many could show up at FEMA's Southwest D.C. offices.

They were given an 800 number to call in, though it was a "listen only" line, the notice said—no questions. Parts of the briefing were carried live on

Continued

Fox News (see the Fox News video of the news conference carried on the Think Progress Web site), MSNBC, and other outlets.

Johnson stood behind a lectern and began with an overview before saying he would take a few questions. The first questions were about the "commodities" being shipped to Southern California and how officials are dealing with people who refuse to evacuate. He responded eloquently.

He was apparently quite familiar with the reporters—in one case, he appears to say "Mike" and points to a reporter—and was asked an oddly in-house question about "what it means to have an emergency declaration as opposed to a major disaster declaration" signed by the President. He once again explained smoothly.

FEMA press secretary *Aaron Walker* interrupted at one point to caution he'd allow just "two more questions." Later, he called for a "last question."

"Are you happy with FEMA's response so far?" a reporter asked. Another asked about "lessons learned from Katrina."

"I'm very happy with FEMA's response so far," Johnson said, hailing "a very smoothly, very efficiently performing team."

"And so I think what you're really seeing here is the benefit of experience, the benefit of good leadership and the benefit of good partnership," Johnson said, "none of which were present in Katrina." (Wasn't *Michael Chertoff* Department of Homeland Security (DHS) chief then?) Very smooth, very professional. But something didn't seem right. The reporters were lobbing too many softballs. No one asked about trailers with formaldehyde for those made homeless by the fires. And the media seemed to be giving Johnson all day to wax on and on about FEMA's greatness.

Of course, that could be because the questions were asked by FEMA staffers playing reporters. We're told the questions were asked by *Cindy Taylor*, FEMA's deputy director of external affairs, and by *"Mike" Widomski*, the deputy director of public affairs. Director of External Affairs *John "Pat" Philbin* asked a question, and another came, we understand, from someone who sounds like press aide *Ali Kirin*.

When asked about this, Widomski said: "We had been getting mobbed with phone calls from reporters, and this was thrown together at the last minute."

But the staff did not make up the questions, he said, and Johnson did not know what was going to be asked. "We pulled questions from those we had been getting from reporters earlier in the day." Despite the very short notice, "we were expecting the press to come," he said, but they didn't. So the staff played reporters for what on TV looked just like the real thing.

"If the worst thing that happens to me in this disaster is that we had staff in the chairs to ask questions that reporters had been asking all day," Widomski said, "trust me, I'll be happy."

Heck of a job, Harvey."

Source: Al Kamen, *The Washington Post*, October 26, 2007, http://www.washingtonpost.com/wp-dyn/content/article/2007/10/25/AR2007102502488_pf.html

Don't Talk About What You Don't Know

Next to lying this is the quickest and surest way to destroy your credibility (see J. R. Thomas's "Another Voice" below.). If you do not know the answer to a question don't make up an answer. Instead say you don't know the answer and that your staff will investigate and get the answer to the media as quickly as possible. (See Jane Bullock's "Another Voice" for more on this point.)

□ □ □ ▬▬▬▬▬▬▬▬▬▬▬▬▬▬▬▬▬▬▬

Another Voice: J.R. Thomas

After 20 years of local emergency management experience, J. R. Thomas is now Save the Children's associate vice president overseeing emergency responses within the United States.

The Day the Levee Didn't Break

Former President Ronald Reagan used to say "Trust But Verify." I wish I would have subscribed to that phrase in 1992 when the word was passed the Emergency Operations Center that a levee had broken and flooding was imminent.

Columbus, Ohio experienced a devastating flood in 1913 which was immortalized by the James Thurber story "The Day the Dam Broke." In this story, the rumor spread that a dam broke causing the Scioto River, which runs along the western edge of downtown, to overflow its banks motivating the residents on the east side of the river to run further east to save themselves. This fictional story was what the humorist Thurber envisioned could have happened. By the way, in the story the dam did not really break but the rumors caused the spontaneous evacuation.

What actually occurred was a devastating flood that engulfed the west side of the Scioto River commonly referred to at the time as "The Bottoms." Imagine yourself standing in the middle of the river looking north. To your right is downtown Columbus on very high ground. Look to your left and it is obvious that the area has been a flood plain for decades. In fact it resembles a bowl with slightly higher banks sloping into what is the bottom or low point.

In 1913, the Scioto River actually did overflow its banks and devastate The Bottoms. The pictures (see www.photolib.noaa.gov/brs/nwind27.htm Photos 1307–1334) show how deep the water was a day or two after the occurrence. A small tributary of the Scioto River, the Dry Run, was the point where water poured into The Bottoms. A levee was built on the Dry Run after the flood to prevent another occurrence.

In 1992, I became the Director of the Franklin County Emergency Management Agency after serving as operations officer and then deputy director. During the previous eight years, the agency was building relationships with

Continued

emergency responders, health officials, and other groups to lay the ground work to grow the agency thereby providing the community with information on local hazards and how to prepare. Columbus Division's of Police and Fire were becoming very good working partners and we worked closely together to begin to sort out response issues.

One night in July 1992, a weather system was moving into the Columbus area from the west. The storms had extensive lightning and heavy rains. There was a Severe Storm Watch issued by the National Weather Service so the Emergency Operations Center was opened with minimal staffing just in case the storms intensified.

The system moved through Columbus and stalled dropping an immense amount of water over, and north of, the area that flooded in 1913, now known as Franklinton. The Scioto River was already high so any tributaries would be backing up and possibly flooding. As it happens, the storm stopped right over the Dry Run which, remember, caused a lot of the damage in 1913. The stalled system continued to dump rain all night so at about 5:00 a.m. we asked the Columbus Police about the Dry Run levee. "How high is the water? Is it rising quickly? Is the levee holding?" The community had been concerned about a repeat of the 1913 flood so the agency staff was highly tuned that.

A patrol car was dispatched and provided a message back to the dispatch center that the Dry Run levee had broken and water was streaming through.

My first reaction was to notify the residents. It is now about 6:00 a.m with the local morning news just coming on the air. I call the three local television stations to alert the public that the levee had broken and flood water would be imminent.

The story aired reporting that the Franklin County Emergency Management Agency was warning the residents of Franklinton to evacuate due to a breech in the Dry Run levee.

You know the rest of the story. The dispatcher called back to say the officer was mistaken. The levee did not break.

So, now I had to call each of the news directors to say I was wrong. That the information I received was incorrect. They were not too happy but put a retraction on the air highlighting several times that the Franklin County Emergency Management Agency was in error.

Luckily, this turned out well but it could have resulted in a spontaneous evacuation, potential injuries, and/or even the death of people trying to climb up to the elevated railroad track.

This incident, in the long run, did not affect the working relationship built up over the years; including the media.

So, lesson learned. Be sure you know and trust someone that provides you with emergency information and verify it before having it broadcast to 1 million people.

□ □ □

Another Voice: Jane Bullock

Jane Bullock is the former chief of staff to FEMA Director James L. Witt and a principal in Bullock & Haddow LLC, a Washington, DC-based disaster management consulting firm.

Interview 101: Practical Experience for Being Interviewed (Part One)

The first major media interview I was asked to do was for the CBS television investigative news show *60 Minutes*. I had just been appointed temporary director of the office of public affairs for the FEMA after the elections of 1992. *60 Minutes* was looking into allegations that FEMA was operating a classified program that would take over certain local governmental activities under a continuity of government issue in the event of a domestic event. They were also looking into the "black helicopters" theory that FEMA was doing domestic spying. You really don't want to start your interview career in this way but I had no choice.

As it turned out, the interview became a critical learning experience that provided lessons that carried me through my years as an interviewee. Jim Stewart, the *60 Minutes* correspondent, met me before the interview and asked my background, I told him I had no public affairs background and little experience in being interviewed. He kindly, gave me one of the best pieces of advice I ever got. He said "whatever you do don't lie, because the camera can tell and the audience will know." He also said that if you don't know the answer to a question; don't be afraid to say so. He did the interview and, apparently, it went OK from the FEMA perspective because the story was never aired on *60 Minutes*.

I wanted to tell that story because Jim Stewart provided fundamental truths about doing media interviews, in television, radio or the written press; don't lie and if you don't know the answer to a question, it's okay to say so. I would hope that the first premise is something we would all embrace but the second, admitting that you may not know the answer, is sometimes hard to remember and adhere to because when we are being interviewed, we are supposedly experts on the subject matter and, under those circumstances, it's sometimes hard to admit we don't know everything. Jim Stewart's advice has served me well especially when being interviewed under controversial or adversarial circumstances.

□ □ □

Don't Talk About Actions of Other Organizations

It is always best to let representatives from other organizations speak for their organization and what their organization is doing. Talking about others can very possibly lead to misunderstandings and it is much simpler to include representatives of other organizations available to speak about their organization than it is to correct a misstatement about another organization.

Don't Make Promises You Can't Keep

If you are not 100% sure that you or your organization can deliver on a promise do not make it. You will be held accountable for any promises and coming close to meeting your promise is not enough. If you say assistance will be available in 2 days you must be very sure this assistance will be there in 2 days because if it takes 3 days, you will be in trouble with the public and the media.

Be Informed

The very best way to avoid making false or misleading statements to the media and the public is to be well informed. This involves a commitment by leadership to pay attention when briefed and have an effective process for collecting, analyzing, and disseminating information.

Acknowledge the Conversation

Old and new media are aggregations of information and images, acknowledge—affirm or rebut—but be aware and learn from this public exchange.

Focus on Performance

When talking to the media and the public, focus on what your organization is doing, what it has done, and what it hopes to do in the future to meet the needs of its customers.

Ensure that Your Information is Accurate

Principle: Accuracy

- Make information a priority
- Invest in information collection
- Invest in information management
- Use only confirmed information
- Make decisions based on good information

Make Information a Priority

Having a clear understanding of the situation on the ground in a disaster response or understanding what people need to know to take action to prepare for the next disaster are examples of how important good information is to effective communications. Make collecting, analyzing, and disseminating information a top priority of your organization.

Invest in Information Collection

Invest in building the infrastructure needed to collect information in a timely manner. This investment can take many forms including financial resources, staffing, training, and time in creating partnerships with other government, private, and voluntary organizations to collect and share information. Any funds and efforts to collect information will be well spent.

Invest in Information Management

The analysis and dissemination of information collected, especially in disaster response, is as important as collecting the information in the first place. Invest in an information management system that ensures that all collected information is analyzed based on criteria set by your senior management team and shared in a timely manner with both internal and external audiences. This investment would include staff, training, and possibly technology.

Use Only Confirmed Information

Develop protocols to confirm all data collected. You do not want to spread information that is based on rumors. Well trained staff and cooperating partners should follow protocols that clearly indicate the types of information to be collected, potential information sources, and criteria by which information collected can be judged to be credible. This information could come from the public—do not automatically reject data from an army of people who are using cameras, cell phones, Short Message Service (SMS), and the Internet to collect and share information.

Make Decisions Based on Good Information

Use the information you collect and analyze. Don't make decisions without the benefit of information that has been confirmed. You may not have complete information, especially in a disaster response scenario, but you should at least have some information before you make a decision to allocate resources in the field.

Release Information in a Timely Manner

Principle: Timeliness

- Don't hold onto information—share it
- Conduct regular updates
- Make special updates when new information emerges
- Reach out to as many media outlets as possible

Don't Hold Onto Information—Share It

The most powerful person in the room in a disaster response is the person who shares information. Don't let the information age and thus become useless. There are examples of the successful use of information sharing in recent disasters such as September 11, the Northridge Earthquake, Hurricane Floyd, and the Okalahoma City bombing. Develop mechanisms to share information with all internal and external partners and audiences in a timely manner.

Conduct Regular Updates

Establish a schedule of updates with all audiences that allow you to share information. This will make you a consistent presence in the eyes of the media and the public and ensure that all parties remain informed. Conduct these regular updates even if you have no new information. Use the time to promote preparedness and mitigation messages as well as to assure all parties that you and your organization remain on top of the situation.

Make Special Updates When New Information Emerges

Call a media briefing or request time on television or radio or send out an emergency e-mail or Internet notice when you get new information that should be shared immediately. There is no reason to hold this type of information back until the next regular update, especially if the information is critical to your operations and the health and welfare of your customers.

Reach Out to As Many Media Outlets As Possible

Inventory all media outlets in your area of operations and reach out to get all of them involved. No media operation is too small to help you get your message to the public. Many communities now have online news sites, bloggers who collect and comment on local news and they are increasingly becoming reliable sources used by the public and should be included in your outreach. Collect e-mail addresses, phone numbers, and fax numbers for all media outlets and be prepared to meet requests for information from all.

Make Yourself, Your Staff, and Others, Where Appropriate, Available and Accessible

Principle: Availability

- Be available and accessible to media
- Make the incident commander available to media
- Work with elected and appointed officials
- Support your public information officer (PIO)
- Make technical staff available to media
- Include officials from other emergency agencies
- Secure media training for yourself and staff

Be Available and Accessible to Media

As the leader of the emergency management organization, you are the ultimate decision maker and it is important that the media and the public see that you are engaged and active in all operations. One way to portray this engagement is to work directly with the media to communicate with the public.

Make the Incident Commander Available to Media

The incident commander is another commanding presence in a disaster response and you should be comfortable with that person's communications skills to make him or her available to the media. This person should be well briefed and should be perceived as a credible source of information on response activities.

Work with Elected and Appointed Officials

Elected and appointed officials will talk to the media during a disaster. The key is to ensure that these people are communicating critical messages and that whatever information they are sharing is accurate and timely. Coordinating with these officials and providing them with a platform to talk to the media and the public will help them to support what you are trying to accomplish (see Fig. 3.2).

Support Your Public Information Officer

Empower your PIO to manage all communications efforts. This individual will be the person on your staff who spends the most time working with the media and it is important that the media understands that the PIO is a full member of the management team, privy to all decisions, and that you have ultimate confidence in his or her capabilities.

FIGURE 3.2 Lady Lake, Fla., February 3, 2007—FEMA Director David Paulison speaks at a press conference as (l to r) Florida Governor Charlie Crist and U.S. Senators Bill Nelson (D-FL) and Mel Martinez (R-FL) look on. The director described how FEMA is responding to tornadoes that struck central Florida last night. Photo by Mark Wolfe/FEMA.

Make Technical Staff Available to Media

In every disaster and with every preparedness or mitigation campaign it will be necessary to bring your technical staff to the stage to discuss specific aspects of your operations or campaign. It is important that these individuals be fully prepared and understand what role they will play in the overall communications strategy. Let your PIO make the decision when and where to use technical staff and to prepare them to meet the media (see Fig. 3.3).

Include Officials from Other Emergency Agencies

Allow representatives from partner agencies to participate in your media events and to get their messages out to the public. This ensures that the media and the public are getting the full picture and keeps you from taking on the frustrating and possibly treacherous task of speaking on behalf of other agencies, which you should never do (see Fig. 3.4).

Secure Media Training for Yourself and Staff

If you and your staff will be talking to the media on a regular basis, then get media training for all. Such training is widely available and will go a long way to making

FIGURE 3.3 Enterprise, AL, March 3, 2007—FEMA Public Information Officer (PIO) Marvin Davis (right) is interviewed by CBS Radio News concerning FEMA's response to the recent Alabama tornadoes. PIOs disseminate important information about FEMA programs to the public and the press. Photo by Mark Wolfe/FEMA.

FIGURE 3.4 Waterloo, IA, June 4, 2004—State and FEMA officials held a joint press conference to remind residents who suffered losses from the May 25 tornado and other recent storms to register for assistance. Susann Cowie, FEMA Operations Section Chief and Bill Vogel, FEMA Federal Coordinating Officer, were joined by Pat Hall, Iowa Emergency Services Coordinating Officer, and SBA Communications Specialist Bill Koontz. Photo by Greg Henshall/FEMA.

you more comfortable in talking to the media and will ensure that your message is clear and consistent and reaches the public intact.

Create an Emotional Connection with Your Audience

Principle: Connect to the Audience

- Give your organization a human face
- Assure audience who is in charge
- Be the source of information for media and public
- Share information
- Speak in plain and direct language
- Ensure that all parties are served
- Be emphatic
- Be accountable
- Be consistent

Give Your Organization a Human Face

People need to place a human face on the organization that is helping them (see Fig. 3.5). A familiar, recognizable, go-to spokesperson is an asset in establishing trust and credibility. Think of Rudy Giuliani after the September 11 attacks.

Assure Audience Who is in Charge

A continued presence in the media and in front of the public assures your customers that someone is in charge and that someone is accessible and a constant presence in the operation.

Be the Source of Information for Media and Public

Establish your organization as the principle source of accurate and timely information. This will ensure that you are heard by the media and the public and will also allow you to effectively respond to the inevitable rumors and inaccurate information that will surface during your operation or campaign.

FIGURE 3.5 Eureka, MO, March 22, 2008—Lieutenant Governor Peter Kinder speaks at a news conference with local and state officials to discuss the current operations in place to prepare for the cresting of rivers in the area. Photo by Jocelyn Augustino/FEMA.

Share Information

Always, always share information and resist the temptation to hold on to information for any reason. The information only has value if it is shared with the public and your partners so that it can be acted on to help people.

Speak in Plain and Direct Language

Be yourself and talk plainly and directly to your customers. Don't use acronyms and avoid using overly technical terms whenever possible. When using new terms, define them clearly and repeat these definitions until you feel they are understood by all.

Ensure that All Parties are Served

Seek to ensure that the information needs of all parties are met. This is especially important for communicating with special needs populations.

Be Emphatic

People are or will be hurting and you and your organization are helping to ease this pain. Show that you understand the pain and articulate how you are going to relieve it.

Be Accountable

You are in charge and you are responsible for the actions of your organization and your partners. Embrace this responsibility but make it clear to the media and the public that you hold your self and your organization and partners accountable for your decisions and actions. Don't blame others.

Be Consistent

Always have prepared remarks, always have facts and statistics available, always take questions, and always treat the media and the public with respect. Set a standard of conduct and information sharing and stick to it.

Build a Partnership with the Media

Principle: Media Partnership

- Maintain a trained media relations staff
- Be consistently accessible to the media
- Be the central information source
- Provide safe access to disaster site
- Respond to media inquiries
- Understand media deadlines and information needs

- Work with all media—traditional and new
- Monitor media stories
- Thank media for their help

(See Ann Patton's "Another Voice" on this point.)

□ □ □

Another Voice: Ann Patton

Ann Patton is a Tulsa-based writer and consultant. She was founding director of Tulsa Project Impact, Citizen Corps, and Tulsa Partners, Inc.

Tulsa News Media

A field worker in the business of emergency and disaster management needs partners from many groups to help create a safe and sustainable community. You need support from and effective communication with elected officials, business leaders, civic groups, first responders, grassroots citizens—the list goes on and on.

But if you told me I had to choose one—and only one—group to help create a resilient community, for me it would be an easy choice: the news media. Why? Because the news media, in my experience, do more to shape public opinion than any other community sector. The media can best inform and lead opinions of all those other groups. Give me a good relationship with the news media, and I will pretty much forecast success, whatever the community-building mission.

Of course, it is not really so simple. Reporters and editors can be great partners, but in a unique way. As hometown residents, we all share the same stake in building a good community. But the news media must maintain a little distance. If you respect their independence, proceed with openness and honesty, and help them do their jobs of informing the community, there's a pretty good chance you can work together well.

In my town, the news media have made all the difference. Here are a couple of stories from the many Tulsa examples of news media support.

In 1984, after the latest in a series of terrible floods, the mayor proposed buying out some houses that had flooded up to the ceilings time and again. Political and public opposition was swift and overwhelming, and it appeared we were doomed to continue an endless cycle of flood-rebuild-flood. But lucky for Tulsa, we had a crop of reporters and editors who had schooled themselves in smart floodplain policy, and they launched public-education campaigns that turned the tide. Tulsa ultimately relocated hundreds of flood victims to safe sites and turned the most dangerous floodplain into a park. One editor even raised $90,000 to build a walking trail along the creek.

Tulsa is in the heart of Tornado Alley. When we launched an initiative in 1998 to encourage people to build tornado SafeRooms, the news media jumped

Continued

on the issue. The *Tulsa World* wrote 30 SafeRoom stories in 1999. When we ran a contest to collect storm-survival stories; the *World* and a TV station ran very elaborate public-education ads and programs to help and announced the winners—all of that without charge, of course.

Before that media campaign, no one in Oklahoma knew what a SafeRoom is. Very quickly, thanks to the media, virtually everyone in Oklahoma knew, and we all wanted one.

Such is the power of the media, which is simply the power of communication. It is worth our while to learn to work together well, to build stronger and safer communities.

Maintain a Trained Media Relations Staff

Your PIO is your direct link to the media and to the public. Maintain this single capability at all costs and expand on it whenever possible, even if it is only temporary.

Be Consistently Accessible to the Media

Don't talk to media one day and not another. Don't take questions one day and not the next. Don't share information one day and not the next. Strive to become a reliable and consistent source of information for the media.

Be the Central Information Source

Establish your organization as the source of information on the disaster response or awareness campaign. Have the facts, statistics, and story lines available that the media need to communicate your messages to the public.

Provide Safe Access to Disaster Site

Safe access to a disaster site is critical for media reporting. Unlimited access to the site is often not doable but limited access can be accomplished. For example, provide seats on a helicopter tour of the site to a pool reporter and camera person who will share the information and footage they collect with all reporters on the scene.

Respond to Media Inquiries

This should a priority for your PIO and media relations staff. Media inquiries should be responded to promptly and consistently and help should be provided wherever possible. These inquiries should not be treated as nuisances but as opportunities. Not responding to a media inquiry allows someone else to tell your story and often results in a bad story.

Understand Media Deadlines and Information Needs

All reporters have deadlines. Learn the deadlines and work to help reporters to meet their deadline whenever possible. Information comes in a variety of forms and is used

FIGURE 3.6 Washington, DC, September 4, 2005—A FEMA media monitor keeps an eye on the reporting coming out of New Orleans after Hurricane Katrina. Federal aid and supplies are being rushed to the area. Photo by Bill Koplitz/FEMA.

differently depending on the media. Your organization must strive to make information available in all of its forms to effectively meet the needs of the media.

Work with All Media—Traditional and New

The media remains the most effective and cost efficient means for communicating emergency management information and messages to the public. Do not exclude one form of media in favor of another for any reason. Work with all media, traditional and new, in order to maximize your reach to the public. Increasingly, traditional and new media are setting up their own partnerships in recognition of the value of the information and images new media adds to the narrative. Don't be left out of that information exchange.

Monitor Media Stories

Regularly monitor media reports to ensure that the media is accurately communicating to the public the information you are sharing with them (see Fig. 3.6). Don't hesitate to contact media outlets that are not reporting information in accurately. Monitoring the media can also help you understand how your information is being received by the media and communicated to the public.

Thank Media for Their Help

Acknowledge that the media is your partner in communicating with the public and thank them on a regular basis for the critical role they play in keeping the public informed.

4

Application of Communications Principles to All Four Phases of Emergency Management

Emergency management is comprised of four phases—mitigation, preparedness, response, and recovery. These phases are best seen as a continuum where actions taken in any single phase are appropriate to carry over to and have implications for the next phase and beyond. Each phase feeds the next and they are all interdependent. (See Fig. 4.1.)

Effective communications, based on the principles discussed in Chapter 3, are a critical element in all four phases of emergency management. While the types of information to be communicated and the means for collecting, analyzing, and sharing this information may vary to some degree from one phase to the other, the basic principles of focusing on customer needs, leadership commitment to communications, and including communications in all planning and operations cross all phases. The timing and the delivery of the information may vary between mitigation and response but the need for the delivery of timely and accurate information that individuals and communities can act on is constant. Many of the mechanisms used to deliver these messages including television, radio, print and the Internet, and "new media" have also become constant.

The purpose of this chapter is to provide guidance on how emergency managers can develop and implement effective communications plans in all four phases of

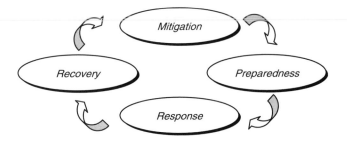

FIGURE 4.1 Four phases of emergency management. Source: FEMA, http://training.fema.gov/emiweb/downloads/is10_unit3.doc

emergency management based on the principles discussed in Chapter 3. The chapter contains four sections—mitigation, preparedness, response, and recovery.

□ □ □

Communications Principles

- Focus on the needs of your customers
- Make a commitment to effective communications
- Make communications an integral part of all planning and operations
- Be transparent in your communications
- Ensure that your information is accurate
- Release information in a timely manner
- Make yourself, your staff, and others, where appropriate, available and accessible
- Create an emotional connection with your audience
- Build a partnership with the media and the "first informer" community

□ □ □

Mitigation

It is generally accepted that hazard mitigation planning and actions take place prior to the next disaster. Certainly this is the goal of all hazard mitigation programs—to reduce the impacts in terms of loss of life, injuries, and damage to property, infrastructure, the economy, and environmental resources caused by future disasters. However, many mitigation programs are planned and implemented after a disaster strikes. FEMA's largest hazard mitigation program, The Hazard Mitigation Grant program (HMGP), is funded by FEMA's Disaster Relief Fund that can only be spent after a disaster strikes. In fact, FEMA did not have authority to spend funds on pre-disaster mitigation until the passage of the Disaster Mitigation Act of 2000. Bottom line, communicating mitigation messages can occur both pre- and post-disaster and mitigation communications plans must be able to function in both scenarios.

□ □ □

Another Voice: John Copenhaver

John Copenhaver is currently the president and CEO of DRI International, a business continuity planner certification organization, and served as FEMA Region IV director from 1997–2001.

Talking Hazard Mitigation

As the regional director of FEMA's eight-state Southeast Region, my experiences with the media were primarily with local radio and television stations.

Continued

These experiences could typically be divided into two main categories: first, carefully planned encounters during which I conveyed one or two messages previously agreed upon by FEMA's public affairs group and our executive team, and second, disaster-related appearances. The first category included radio and television interviews that had typically been set up through my regional Public Affairs Office, and in which I was asked questions pertaining to a central "theme."

Examples of these "theme" interviews included those done at the start of a new hurricane season (e.g., the National Hurricane Center's (NHC) "Hurricane Hunter Media Tour" with the NHC's director), interviews about grants FEMA was authorizing to address specific threat categories (such as those helping to purchase weather-alert radios for schools and senior-care facilities), and interviews about programs administered by FEMA like flood insurance or Project Impact, a trailblazing program designed to help communities lessen the potential impacts of future disasters. In these interviews, the questions were typically structured to give me opportunities to highlight positive actions being taken by FEMA and its local, state, and federal partners to strengthen American communities against catastrophes; as a result, these pieces tended to be broadcast in the "local news" segments of local media outlets. The interviewers were upbeat, rarely asked "hard" questions, and used "live-to-tape" formats for television spots (actual "live" interviews for this sort of piece were mostly conducted on radio shows).

Disaster-related appearances were different, both in tone and in message. While I, as the head of Region IV, was usually given the go-ahead by our Washington Public Affairs office to do interviews, the implicit understanding was that interviews with the media after high-profile events were riskier to the Agency and were to be done with care. In situations where lives had been disrupted or lost and property damaged or destroyed, the interviews given by senior FEMA officials had to be more precise, conveying both information about the current situation and the actions being taken by government responders to quickly address the needs of the disaster victims. Emotions often ran high in these interviews, and at times it was difficult to strike a balance between being a "FEMA official" and a human being seeing devastation and suffering first-hand. In these situations, anticipating questions from the media was much harder, and at times the media representatives would ask insensible questions that sounded more like blanket condemnations than requests for information or opinion. Fortunately, even in these trying times, trying to be as honest as possible seemed to help defuse potentially explosive encounters.

After leaving FEMA in 2001, I have been interviewed almost exclusively by national media instead of local outlets, and usually in conjunction with "opinion" pieces where I am asked about a government (usually federal) response to a major event such as Hurricane Katrina. These interviews are almost always much different than those I gave as a senior FEMA representative. For starters, it is a common practice for major networks to conduct a "pre-interview" with potential guests

Continued

before a network appearance, especially before "live" interviews. In these "pre-interviews," someone from the network (often a producer of the show on which the interview will be aired, but occasionally the on-air interviewer himself/herself) asks the questions that will be asked during the interview itself.

These "dry runs" seem to serve two purposes: first, to make sure the person being interviewed has relevant, well-thought-out (but succinct) answers to the questions, and second, to make sure the interviewer isn't surprised by the answers. Cynics may say that this process is designed to ensure that the on-air piece represents exactly the news that the network *wants* to report, and this may be true on occasion, but the process also makes certain that the quality of the interview is maintained at a high level—network airtime is coveted and very expensive, and thus it is understandable that networks want to air the best "product" possible. This is particularly true in the ultimate media interviews, a "live" interview on a major network prime-time broadcast where the interviewers are well-known personalities and highly skilled in the interview process. For those of us who don't have opportunities like these every day, these interviews are somewhat nerve-wracking (but fun, particularly when they are finished!). In all of these national media interviews, the challenge I faced was to say what I wanted to say in such a way that I made the points I thought were important while giving the interviewers the "sound bites" they wanted (but not ones that might later come back to haunt me!).

The focus of hazard mitigation programs is to prompt action by decision makers—homeowners, small business owners, community leaders—to take action to reduce future disaster impacts. Developing a hazard mitigation program involves four steps:

- Establish a community partnership that involves all members of the community in developing a community-based hazard mitigation plan
- Identify the community risks (i.e., floods, hurricanes, earthquakes, etc.)
- Identify potential mitigation actions to address these risks and develop a prioritized plan
- Generate the funding, political, and public support needed to implement the plan

Building support for the community mitigation plan will require a form of communications commonly referred to as marketing. This requires approaching the media to educate them about mitigation and the community mitigation plan and to provide information that the media can transmit to the public. In the 1990s, FEMA created Project Impact: Building Disaster Resistant Communities, a nationwide community-based mitigation initiative. The goal of the initiative was to provide communities with seed money and technical assistance to develop and implement local hazard mitigation programs. FEMA designed and implemented an aggressive public affairs effort to promote Project Impact among the public; the media; and local, state, and federal elected officials.

☐ ☐ ☐

Project Impact Case Study

FEMA's promotion of Project Impact provides an excellent example of how to sell disaster mitigation programs to the public (see Fig. 4.2). The FEMA public affairs team engaged and involved the public and explained the program in terms they could understand and value, partnered with the media to get its message out, and made effective use of policy windows.

Project Impact is a community-based mitigation initiative, facilitated and partially funded by FEMA. It includes getting local businesses to partner with the local government and community organizations to prepare for and reduce the effects of future disasters. Preliminary surveys had indicated that communities were interested in reducing risk, so Project Impact was born.

The communications team's first challenge was to frame the program in terms that the public could understand. Although the program is a mitigation initiative, the team wanted to move away from emergency management jargon and describe the program in a manner with which the public would be more familiar. The slogan "put FEMA out of business" was developed. The term *mitigation* was replaced with *disaster-resistant*, and then *prevention*, and finally

FIGURE 4.2 Washington, DC, June 3, 1998—National Press Club newsmaker announces disaster resistant communities. FEMA News Photo.

Continued

risk reduction. The slogans "prevention pays" and "prevention power" were used to reinforce the message.

A public affairs campaign was launched, both at the grassroots levels within target communities and through the print and television media when possible. The communications model employed was based on the following guidelines:

- **Keep the message simple and understandable.** Literature was developed at the fourth-grade level. A "three little pig's analogy" was used to explain the difference between preparedness and prevention.
- **Stick to the message or point.** Spokespeople used a "remember three things" tactic, whereby three main points are repeatedly mentioned in straight, clear language. Also, the Project Impact pamphlet was reduced to one page, containing five simple prevention tips.
- **Explain what's in it for the public.** The selling point to the public was that Project Impact would result in fewer losses from future disasters.
- **Educate the media on mitigation.** A media partner guide was developed to help Project Impact proponents explain to the media why mitigation is a story, why it's important, and how the media could help spread the message.
- **Involve partners.** The Salvation Army and Red Cross were solicited as partners in promoting Project Impact.
- **You are the message.** Project Impact hats and T-shirts were provided to team members.

From a media standpoint, articles were placed in the *USA Today* Op/Ed section and *Parade* magazine, and Al Roker of the *Today Show* did a spot on Project Impact. The team also took advantage of policy windows by sneaking prevention messages into interviews during major disaster operations. Spokespeople such as FEMA's Kim Fuller promoted Project Impact in interviews during Hurricanes Irene and Floyd. An animated video on mitigation steps was provided to the networks and displayed during the interviews. Also, pre-prepared press releases on how people could rebuild better for the future were provided to the media.

Source: Interview with Kim Fuller, October 2001.

Another good example of marketing mitigation is the Living Rivers Project in Napa, CA. The community of Napa spent two years hammering out a 20-year plan to reduce flooding from the Napa River. The final step before implementation of the plan was to create a local funding source that could be used to match federal and state government and private sector funds to finance the plan. Community leaders working with business, environmental, and other community groups, decided on a ½ cent sales tax increase as the best means for providing that local funding source. Increasing the sales tax required a referendum be passed by 2/3 of all voters casting a ballot. A marketing and communications plan was developed that included providing the public with easily understandable information on what mitigation projects would be funded, what the results would be in terms of reduced flood impacts in the future, and what this would mean to the economy and environment in the Napa River Valley. A variety of printed materials were developed and distributed, media interviews were conducted with elected and appointed officials, and news articles were generated analyzing the plan and its project benefits. The voters passed the referendum and the plan was implemented. Today, 10 years later, flooding impacts have been significantly reduced, sensitive environmental areas have been enhanced and preserved, and the local economy has seen a boom in investments in tourism-related projects.

In the aftermath of the 1997 Grand Forks Floods, officials from government, the business community, and the non-profit sector from Minnesota, North Dakota, and the Province of Manitoba, Canada came together to create the International Flood Mitigation Initiative (IFMI). The Vision of the IFMI participants was: "By the Year 2010, the community of the Red River Basin has addressed flooding through mitigation that achieves significant flood damage reduction goals while enhancing economic, social, and ecological opportunities." The Mission of IFMI was, "To promote and develop achievable and action-oriented flood mitigation goals and implementation strategies by engaging citizens, their communities, and governments." One of the implementing strategies advocated by IFMI was "establishing a broadcast media partnership on water issues." This was accomplished by the creation of River Watch, a public-private partnership with Prairie Public Broadcasting that provided residents in the Red River Basin information concerning flood mitigation and the Red River through programming on television, radio, the Internet, and a documentary film.

□ □ □ ▬▬▬▬▬▬▬▬▬▬▬▬▬▬▬▬▬▬

International Flood Mitigation Initiative (IFMI) Media Partnership

In the aftermath of the 1997 Flood, the IFMI established its goal to *provide comprehensive, continuous, consistent, complete, current, and accurate flood forecasting, flood mitigation, flood preparedness, flood response, and when necessary, flood recovery information to the people of the Red River Basin.*

To fulfill this goal, Prairie Public Broadcasting has established and maintained *RiverWatch*—using cross-border and cross-media partnerships—to provide flood preparation, recovery, and mitigation news, as well as news about other drought and water quality issues facing the Red River. These informational resources are provided through television, radio, Internet, and public outreach. RiverWatch is viable and respected because, together with its research, content, and relationships, Prairie Public Broadcasting has also contributed its technical capacity to gather and distribute information along the entire length

Continued

and breadth of the Red River Valley. Over the past 5 years, project elements have included:

- **Television:** Weeknight news updates air every night on Prairie Public Television during peak flood months (March–May), with features on flood preparation, recovery, and mitigation efforts by individuals and communities. In addition, year-round television segments cover a wide variety of relevant topics, such as ice rescue diving, emergency levee construction, fishing, invasive aquatic plants, and chemical contaminants in the Red River.
- **Radio:** News reports and features are integrated into *Morning Edition* and *All Things Considered* on North Dakota Public Radio. In addition, *Hear It Now*, North Dakota Public Radio's daily public affairs show, airs interview and discussion segments together with RiverWatch features.
- **Web:** Year round river and flood related news updates are posted daily to the River Watch Web site at www.riverwatchonline.org. In addition, RiverWatch online provides comprehensive links to authoritative flood/water management and educational resources, together with flood preparation and recovery resources, information, and links. Updates and information on the Greenway on the Red and other educational opportunities along the Red River are also posted on RiverWatchonline.org. During times of flooding, the people of the region consistently visit www. riverwatchonline.org to get the latest weather, river levels, news, and flood recovery information and resources, with an average annual visitation of over 350,000. RiverWatchonline site features more than one thousand pages of public information.

RiverWatch continues to gather and share information, news and resources with more than 40 partnerships of Red River Valley media outlets, communities, municipalities, and federal, state and provincial agencies. The RiverWatch team continues to pursue additional partnerships with agencies, organizations, and municipalities in the United States and Canada. In addition, a documentary entitled *Red River Divide* has been produced and disseminated throughout the Basin. *Red River Divide* investigates the Red River Valley's geology and land-scape, the history of flooding and flood mitigation, and the tremendous benefits the Red River provides. The documentary also explores what preparations are underway for drought relief and protection of the river's water quality. This 60-minute documentary will be rebroadcast multiple times on Prairie Public Television, with an audience across North Dakota, northwestern Minnesota, Manitoba, and eastern Montana. Through these collective efforts, RiverWatch will continue to provide a significant service to the thousands of residents living in the Red River Valley—before, during, and after flooding events.

Source: Dick Gross, The Consensus Council Inc., http://www.agree.org

Components of a Communications Strategy for Mitigation include:

- Include communications staff in the design of the mitigation program and inform how the program will be promoted
- Archive all information concerning the mitigation program and make it accessible to the public, the media and decision-makers through a variety of mechanisms including reports, brochures, and the Internet
- Identify audiences and collect data to help shape messages promoting the mitigation program including measuring their current level of understanding of their risks and what the mitigation program can do to reduce their risks, what the benefits of the mitigation program mean to them, and how best to communicate mitigation messages to them
- Craft messages that will connect with the target audiences using the program information and audience data collected
- Employ an array of communications mechanisms in a coordinated way to deliver your messages to your targeted audiences including:
  - Town hall meetings and workshops—work with community-based organizations (CBOs) to schedule special meetings or to be included in the agenda for a regular meeting to present your program
  - Television, radio, and print interviews—reach out to these traditional media to schedule interviews with program leaders and experts to discuss your mitigation program and to refer your targeted audience to additional information and activities listed on your Web site and printed materials
  - Internet and printed materials—develop a full set of materials concerning your mitigation program and how individuals and groups can become involved—search engines and promotional activities in other media will drive your audience to these materials
  - Paid advertising—if you have funds available, produce and place television, radio, or print ads (may also consider pop-up ads on the Internet) with local media outlets promoting the program and referring the audience to Internet and printed materials—recent public service campaigns have been successful in requesting that media outlets match your media buy so that you are able to double your media buy
  - Public Service Announcements (PSAs)—request that local media outlets run your ads as a public service with no charge—one problem with this approach is that your PSAs often run at 3 a.m. in the morning when most of your audience is asleep
  - Grass roots communications—work with community-based organizations to create neighborhood communications networks that involve local trusted leaders in developing two-way communications networks with these leaders, delivering mitigation and preparedness messages to neighborhood residents prior to the next disaster and working with local emergency officials during and after a disaster to deliver messages from emergency

officials on response and recovery activities and programs and to collect and communicate information on conditions and activities in the neighborhood to emergency officials

  ○ Social networking—engage in those social networking Web sites that appeal to your target audience to communicate your mitigation program messages and to generate action among individuals

• Monitor all media-related activities, track the types of media coverage you receive, and update your communications strategy and tactics accordingly

Preparedness Programs and Actions

There are two general types of preparedness programs—preparing for the next disaster and providing warning information designed to advise the population whether to evacuate or shelter-in-place as the next disaster approaches. Both of these programs are heavily reliant on communicating messages to the general public and to targeted audiences to be successful.

□ □ □ ▬▬▬▬▬▬▬▬▬▬▬▬▬▬▬▬▬▬▬▬▬

Another Voice: Rocky Lopes

Rocky Lopes is the former manager of Community Disaster Education at the American Red Cross and currently serves as manager, Homeland Security at the National Association of Counties.

Promoting Disaster Preparedness Through the American Red Cross

Many people nationwide looked to the Red Cross as a trusted source of safety information. However, in the mid-80s, while there was eagerness from local Red Cross representatives to share disaster preparedness advice, there wasn't much reliable or consistent information available for them to use. Many Red Cross chapters developed their own educational materials in the form of flyers, brochures, and even coloring books.

That was all well and good, except when you compared them side-by-side. One brochure would advise to stand in a doorway during an earthquake, with an illustration that was factually inaccurate. Another would say never to use a doorway, but then didn't say what to do instead. The lists of "dont's" far exceeded the lists of "do's." Photos of disaster damage prevailed, with no illustrations of the appropriate action to take—so there was a lot of "don't let this happen to you" messaging. The situation was that most preparedness education in the '80s was based on folklore—that is, information that was believed to be correct, but not scientifically tested or based on research. There was no recognition of the field of "Risk Communication" and the effects of human perception of risk on learning and behavior.

Continued

To exacerbate the problem, federal agencies were doing the same thing. The National Weather Service, FEMA, and the USGS all published lots of stuff, yet when compared with each other, they reflected the folklore of the times, and not necessarily the science or research depicting appropriate behaviors or practices. I'll never forget the arguments I had with colleagues at the National Weather Service over a film about flooding that showed a dramatic rescue of a man from his submerging car during the rescue to retrieve a book. Or an internal argument about the cover of a Red Cross annual report, showing a man standing in waist-deep flood waters holding a baby wrapped in a plastic bag. What kinds of messages are given here?

That's when it became most inspiring to be working with the Red Cross in this field. We gathered colleagues from federal agencies and national non-profits to challenge the question, "what are we saying, and how do we know it's right?" Thus was born the concept of the National Disaster Education Coalition and ultimately its *Talking About Disasters: Guide for Standard Messages*.

Using that compendium of reviewed, vetted, and grounded disaster advice, the Red Cross began anew its dissemination of nationally-produced but localizable disaster education approaches. More than brochures or videos, a culture of "educating the educators" grew into an internationally-recognized program of activities.

At its heyday in the '90s and early 2000s, the Red Cross, together with many other organizations and agencies, jointly produced educational materials and disseminated them to audiences each organization could reach effectively. And, with the Internet becoming so accessible by the public, electronic delivery became commonplace. Best of all, the messages in jointly produced materials were consistent, accurate, and appropriately worded for risk-based communications.

As is typical with large organizations, initiatives tend to work on broad cycles. I have seen historical documents co-branded with the Red Cross and the Weather Bureau dated in the 1940s. I also have seen co-branded materials dated in the late 60s and early 70s between Red Cross and the then Office of Civil Defense (predecessor to FEMA).

Since 2004, the effort to co-brand and jointly disseminate information seems to have declined. There appears to be more variability and inconsistency of disaster preparedness information available via the Internet. As people shop around for information, they are more inclined to accept disaster preparedness advice from what their search engine produces, regardless of the source—especially if the advice is simple and doesn't impose a burden in time or cost on recommended action—even if the advice is incorrect. That's because most people still don't want to think anything bad can happen, and if it does, there isn't much they can do.

But take heart. The *Talking Guide* remains available. Research on accurate messaging is still being done. The field of Risk Communication is growing

Continued

in interest and support. We need to strive to "get it right" and make sure that what we're saying is appropriate for the audience, accurate (regarding the research), and delivered using methods that reach those who are most vulnerable to disaster (which isn't necessarily using the Internet, e-mail, or texting). And while the Red Cross is no longer leading the way nationally, the core of energetic volunteers at the local level remains in place. And they're creative and crafty in finding ways to help those in greatest need.

Promoting preparedness programs is very similar to promoting hazard mitigation programs. The purpose is to provide targeted audiences with information that they can use to be better prepared to deal with the next disaster. These programs include public awareness and evacuation, training, and exercise elements. They are best implemented at the local level but will involve support and participation from state and federal emergency management operations. See Fig. 4.3.

Designing and implementing a communications strategy to support these types of preparedness programs involves many of the tasks used in promoting a hazard mitigation program, including full participation of communications staff in program design and implementation, collection and presentation of all information, identification of

FIGURE 4.3 Washington, DC, June 1, 2007—FEMA administrator holds a press conference to urge everyone to get ready for hurricane season which begins today. He also demonstrated FEMA's video teleconference ability at FEMA headquarters. Photo by FEMA/Bill Koplitz.

target audiences, message development, use of a broad range of communications mechanisms, and monitoring and updating communications strategies and tactics.

One factor emergency managers should strongly consider in designing exercises as part of a preparedness program is full inclusion of reporters, news producers, bloggers and other media representatives in exercises. Having professional reporters, et al. participate in the exercise (as opposed to actors or volunteers playing reporters, et al.) will allow for a more accurate and effective test of the emergency operations communications plan and activities. Additionally, media participants can make recommendations on how to improve information flow and communications with the media during a real disaster.

Communicating warning and evacuation messages is also part of disaster preparedness and leads directly into the response phase of a disaster. Informing the public of a pending disaster event such as a tornado, hurricane, flood, or wildfire involves matching information about a specific disaster event with easily understood and familiar terms that are related to how individuals should act and delivering those messages to the public in a comprehensive manner. (See text box on severe weather watches and warnings.) Trusted messengers are essential to providing effective disaster warning and evacuation information.

□ □ □ ▬▬▬▬▬▬▬▬▬▬▬▬▬▬▬▬▬▬▬▬▬▬▬▬▬▬▬▬▬▬▬▬

Severe Weather Watches and Warnings Definitions

Flood Watch: High flow or overflow of water from a river is possible in the given time period. It can also apply to heavy runoff or drainage of water into low-lying areas. These watches generally are issued for flooding that is expected to occur at least six hours after heavy rains have ended.

Flood Warning: Flooding conditions are actually occurring or are imminent in the warning area.

Flash Flood Watch: Flash flooding is possible in or close to the watch area. Flash Flood Watches generally are issued for flooding that is expected to occur within six hours after heavy rains have ended.

Flash Flood Warning: Flash flooding is actually occurring or is imminent in the warning area. It can be issued as a result of torrential rains, a dam failure, or an ice jam.

Tornado Watch: Conditions are conducive to the development of tornadoes in and close to the watch area.

Tornado Warning: A tornado has actually been sighted by spotters or indicated on radar and is occurring or imminent in the warning area.

Severe Thunderstorm Watch: Conditions are conducive to the development of severe thunderstorms in and close to the watch area.

Severe Thunderstorm Warning: A severe thunderstorm has actually been observed by spotters or indicated on radar and is occurring or imminent in the warning area.

Continued

Tropical Storm Watch: Tropical storm conditions with sustained winds from 39 to 73 mph are possible in the watch area within the next 36 hours.

Tropical Storm Warning: Tropical storm conditions are expected in the warning area within the next 24 hours.

Hurricane Watch: Hurricane conditions (sustained winds greater than 73 mph) are possible in the watch area within 36 hours.

Hurricane Warning: Hurricane conditions are expected in the warning area in 24 hours or less.

Source: FEMA, www.fema.gov

Elements of effective disaster warning and evacuation communications include:

- Information Collection—timely and accurate information is the basis for effective disaster warning and evacuation communications. The National Incident Management System (NIMS) and the Incident Command System (ICS) promoted by FEMA both recognize the importance of collecting information about an upcoming disaster event. Emergency management operations must dedicate staff and resources to collecting information about a disaster event. This information can come from a variety of both traditional and new sources. The traditional sources include first responders, weather forecasters working at NOAA or the National Hurricane Center, the media, and field staff. New sources include individuals who are witnessing an event unfold and have the means through their cell phone or other device to communicate information in multiple forms including voice, text, photographic, and video. Emergency management operations must both solicit such information gathering and be capable to receive and process this information. Verifying information from the field from any information source can be difficult and in many cases time consuming. Recruiting and training individuals in your community to become first informers is one way to build trust into the process and more easily verify the information being received.

- Information Dissemination—once warning and evacuation information has been received it must be analyzed to determine a course of action to be taken to protect people from the pending disaster. There are two primary courses of action to be considered—evacuation and shelter-in-place. For tornadoes, the best course of action is often shelter-in-place. For approaching hurricanes and wildfires, evacuation is likely to be the best option. For a chemical, biological, or dirty bomb attack both options might be on the table. Once a course of action has been determined, the priority becomes communicating this course of action to the public. As with communicating information concerning pre-disaster preparedness programs, communicating evacuation or shelter-in-place information uses a variety of traditional and new communications mechanisms including:

○ Traditional media (television, radio, and print)—television reaches the largest audience and both network and cable channels are willing partners in getting evacuation or shelter-in-place messages out to the public. Radio is also effective especially in areas that have already lost their electricity and battery and crank-operated radios remain functional. Both television and radio are capable of getting information immediately to the public. Newspapers are best equipped to provide more detailed information but are not as timely as television and radio.

○ New media (Internet, online news services, bulletin boards, cell phones, PDAs)—the Internet is capable of proving both immediate communications as well as more detailed information much the way a newspaper does. Bulletin boards established by individuals or community groups can get information out to their audience very quickly as well as drive their audience to other information sources. Cell phones and PDAs are becoming popular vehicles for relaying warning, alert, and evacuation/shelter-in-place information to subscribers. A number of communities around the country have established these types of programs. (See text box on one such alert system in Arlington, VA.) The federal government is exploring such a program as well (see text box on federal alerts).

☐ ☐ ☐

Arlington (VA) Alert

Arlington Alert is an alert system that allows the county to contact you during an emergency by sending text messages to your:

- e-mail account (work, home, other)
- cell phone
- text pager, BlackBerry

When an emergency occurs, the county will instantly notify you with updates, instructions on where to go, what to do, or what not to do, who to contact, and other important information.

Arlington Alert is a free county service. However, your carrier may charge you a *fee* to receive messages on wireless device(s). Please read the *FAQs* for more information. This service does not replace existing public safety warning methods also used by the county.

Arlington Alert is open to all county **residents, commuters,** and **visitors.**

What is Arlington County's Community Alert System?

Arlington County is one of the first counties to deploy an emergency notification system for its residents and people working for businesses located in the county.

Continued

The Community Alert System will be used to broadcast emergency notifications, updates and other important information to you during a major incident.

What Types of Alerts Will Be Sent?

Alert types may include life safety, fire, weather, accidents involving utilities or roadways, team activation notifications, or disaster notification such as a terrorist attack. A few examples of the types of messages that can be sent through Roam Secure Alert Network (RSAN) are:

Emergency Situations:

- Notify citizens of the location of the nearest emergency shelter, available bed space, and hours of operation during a crisis;
- Notify citizens of available evacuation routes during an emergency;
- Activate special teams within the community, based upon an event.

Precautionary Warnings:

- Severe weather warnings;
- Activate a citizen watch group if mischievous activity is reported by the police;
- Precautionary evacuation order if on high alert.

How Are Alerts Sent and How Do I Receive Them?

Alerts are sent across the RSAN. You will need to sign up for an RSAN account to receive the alerts.

What is the Roam Secure Alert Network?

RSAN is an emergency communication system used by governments, emergency management agencies, and first responders to send emergency alerts, notifications, and updates to your cell phone, pager, Blackberry, PDA, and/or e-mail account. All you have to do is sign up for an RSAN account to receive emergency alerts.

What is the Cost of This Service?

Arlington County is offering the Community Alert System service free to residents of Arlington County and people working for businesses located in Arlington County. You may sign up for an RSAN account free of charge. Your cell phone carrier may charge you a few pennies per text message received. Arlington County does not assume any responsibility for costs charged to you by your carrier.

What is a Roam Secure Alert Network Account?

Each resident of Arlington County, or people working for businesses located in Arlington County may sign up for an RSAN account. You can add multiple devices (cell phones, pagers, PDAs) to an RSAN account. An alert will be sent to each e-mail account, cell phone and other mobile device listed in your Roam Secure Alert Network account.

Continued

How Does the Community Alert System Work?

In an emergency situation an alert will be sent by Arlington County authorized personnel and you will receive e-mail notifications, and several text messages on your cell phone or mobile device. Read these messages promptly and follow the instructions.

Additional instructions may follow throughout the emergency situation so keep your phone near you. Even if the cell phones are busy, the messages should still come through to your phone.

When you do receive an alert message, please follow the instructions on that message. Please do NOT call 911 or Arlington's Emergency Communications Center as they are already aware of the emergency—and your call will tie up precious resources, further endangering the emergency situation.

We will make every effort to update the county's Web site www.co.arlington.va.us in real time with more information about the emergency. In addition, you should tune to local TV and radio.

Will My Cell Phone Work in a Major Emergency?

Alerts are delivered using the text messaging (Short Message Servive [SMS] network) feature of your cell phone. The alerts come across like a page on a pager. ALL cell phone carriers, and paging companies, offer text messaging. Nearly all phones purchased within the past few years are text messaging capable. If you are unsure, contact your carrier to ask about your phone and text messaging.

What is Text-Messaging and How Do I Sign Up for It?

Text messages are short messages sent to your phone, similar to receiving a page. Each message contains between 100 and 160 characters, or about 15 words, depending upon your carrier. An example of a text message is the notification you receive on your phone when you have new voicemail.

Most carriers activate the service automatically. You should check with your carrier to make sure your text messaging is active. See the carrier matrix for a list of carriers and contact information.

If you are unfamiliar with reading text messages on your phone, try these links to learn more about your particular phone:

Nokia http://www.nokiahowto.com

Motorola http://commerce.motorola.com/consumer/QWhtml/manual.html

Ericsson http://www.ericsson.com/consumers/

How Many Devices/E-mail Addresses Can I Add to My Account?

You may have two devices and two e-mail addresses for your RSAN account.

How Do I Prevent Arlington Alert Messages from Going to My Bulk/Junk Folder?

We are currently working with e-mail providers to ensure that our messages are delivered to your Inbox and are not seen as bulk or junk mail and filtered to

Continued

other folders. You may also be able to take a few simple steps to help ensure messages arrive at your Inbox by configuring your bulk/junk mail settings to recognize our messages and place them in your Inbox.

MSN/Hotmail Safe List

One way for users with MSN/Hotmail accounts to ensure that messages are delivered to their Inboxes is to add our domain to their Safe List. Follow the steps below to add a Safe List entry:

1. Login to your MSN mail account
2. Click on the Options link on the upper right part of the page (next to Help)
3. Select Mail from the menu on the left
4. Click on the Junk E-mail Protection link
5. Click on the Safe List link
6. Enter **arlingtonalert.com** in the "Type an address or domain" box
7. Click Add

   Your Arlington Alert messages should now be delivered to your Inbox.

How Do I Register My BlackBerry?

You can register your BlackBerry in two ways:

1. Enter the 10-digit mobile number and select the carrier (Nextel 1-way, AT&T, etc.). Alerts will be cut into 150 character blocks.
2. RSAN can also deliver full text alerts directly to BlackBerry devices without going through a corporate BlackBerry Enterprise Server (BES), thus ensuring redundancy (in case of power outages, congestion, DOS attacks, etc. at your BES). To register this way, pick "BlackBerry WebClient" as your carrier and enter your full WebClient e-mail address (e.g.: jsmith@nextel.blackberry.net) as the device identifier. For more information about this service go to http://www.blackberry.com/support/client/index.shtml

How Do I Receive Arlington Alerts on XM Satellite Radio?

Sign up for Arlington Alerts at www.arlingtonalert.com and visit www.xmradio.com to learn about subscribing to the XM Satellite Radio service. In addition to e-mail and text messages on cell phones, pagers, and PDAs, important Arlington Alerts will be broadcast over the Metro Washington, DC Weather, Traffic, and Emergency Channel 214 on XM Radio.

Source: Arlington, Virginia. https://www.arlingtonalert.com/index.php?CCheck=1

□ □ □

Federal Government Explores Cell Phone Alert and Warning System

Nationwide Cell Phone Alert System in the Works

"Federal regulators as early as today are expected to take a major step toward development of a nationwide emergency alert system that would send text messages to cell phones and other mobile devices wherever a crisis occurs. Lack of a simple way to deliver vital warnings to residents has hindered emergency response in disasters such as Hurricane Katrina, recent college-campus shootings, and a spate of devastating tornadoes in the Southeast in February. The Federal Communications Commission (FCC) is slated to establish technical standards and other requirements that for the first time would make such communication possible, two FCC officials say. The officials requested anonymity because commissioners have not yet voted on the plan. Although wireless carriers would not be required to upgrade their networks to accommodate the alerts, those that agree to participate would have to implement the FCC's standards. All four national cell phone providers—AT&T, Verizon, Sprint Nextel, and T-Mobile—said they almost certainly will take part if the FCC adopts an advisory committee's recommendations on how the system would work. The agency is expected to approve those proposals, which, among other things, would initially limit warnings to the English language and 90 characters in length, officials say. 'We look forward to offering mobile emergency alerts to our customers,' says Jim Bugel, assistant vice president of federal affairs for AT&T. The network is expected to be up and running by 2010."

Source: USA Today (2008, September 8). http://www.usatoday.com/tech/wireless/2008–04–08-fcc-emergency_N.htm

□ □ □

□ □ □

Disaster Communication from a Trusted Source

When it comes to disaster communications, what you say is as important as how you say it. Researchers at Temple University's Center for Preparedness, Research, Education and Practice (C-PREP), speaking today at the American Public Health Association meeting, argue in favor of points that we've made here before: transparency is key to successful disaster communication; and people are as likely or more likely to get information from non-traditional sources, so official communications can't rely solely on official outlets.

[Public Health Professor Sarah] Bass defines effective risk communications as timely, relevant and true.]

Continued

"Effective communication during a disaster provides for people's doubts," she explained. "It can also reduce the mental stress and anguish that comes with anticipating and coping with disasters." [...] As the researchers expected, people universally rely on television and radio for information during an emergency. But surprisingly, they say, half of respondents would go to their clergy for information, highlighting the important role that non-traditional communicators play in emergency response.

Source: Jamais Cascio (2005, December 14). Disaster Communication. http://www.world changing.com/archives/003859.html

When issuing alerts, warnings, and evacuation/shelter-in-place information, emergency officials must consider a number of additional factors:

- **Messengers**—Individuals are more likely to act on alert, warning, and evacuation/shelter-in-place information if it comes from a trusted elected official and emergency management director. Don't always have a public information officer (PIO) deliver these messages. Knowledgeable officials with the appropriate credentials and authority are the best messengers to deliver this type of information.

- **Special need populations**—Consider the difficulties in communicating with special needs populations and plan accordingly. These populations include hearing impaired, cognitive impaired, elderly, children, and the disabled. (See Holly Harrington's "Another Voice" section on communicating with children.)

- **Community-based communications networks**—some members of your community do not get their information from traditional or new media and if they do they may not trust the information they receive and therefore may not take action to protect themselves from an approaching disaster. Access to traditional and new media may be limited in some neighborhoods and among selected populations. These people are more likely to listen to and trust someone they know to deliver this type of information and to take action. Emergency management operations must work with community-based organizations to establish neighborhood-based communications networks that recruit and train trusted community leaders to deliver alerts, warnings, and evacuation/shelter-in-place information to neighborhood residents. It is important that trusted community leaders are involved as they can validate the information and the information source. For example, many elderly people, especially those elderly people living alone, will not respond to a knock at their door unless they know who is knocking. (See text box on trusted sources.) This is true even for police or firefighters going door-to-door to alert people to impending danger. However, this same group will respond to a knock on their door from someone they know and trust. This is true for other groups including new immigrants and non-English-speaking populations.

- **Non-English speakers**—acknowledge that there are non-English speakers residing in your community and ensure that information is translated and communicated in their native language.

□ □ □ ▬▬▬▬▬▬▬▬▬▬▬▬▬▬▬▬▬▬▬▬▬▬▬

Another Voice: Holly Harrington

Holly Harrington is the special assistant to the director in the Office of Public Affairs at the U.S. Nuclear Regulatory Commission and an adjunct professor of communication at Trinity University, in Washington, DC.

Federal Emergency Management Agency for Kids

In 1996, the FEMA's credibility was soaring under Director James Lee Witt, who, among other accomplishments, was trying new ways to communicate preparedness and mitigation information to the public. The agency's Web site had already been revamped and visits were climbing. In fall, 1996, FEMA decided to reach out specifically to children via the Web. The reasons were two-fold:

- Children were victims of disasters and information could help them protect themselves; and
- Children were great conduits of information to parents who often are uninterested in preparedness or mitigation.

I was new to FEMA's Office of Public Affairs and given this creative opportunity. Even better—I was given near full autonomy to create the site as I wished. Eventually, FEMA for Kids became one of the first federal government sites aimed at—and speaking directly to—school-age children.

   We began with a few basics:

- We were targeting third through sixth graders, although we would later find our demographics included much younger children, teens, and adults.
- The site would be as "cool" as possible.
- It would be a safe place where parents would let their children surf without supervision.
- There would be much interaction and learning disguised as fun to keep children on the site.
- A Teachers/Parents section would be secondary so children saw the site as their own.
- A "What's Happening Now?" section would link to current disasters and FEMA's actions.

I developed a mock-up of the site, and a Web contractor created the edgy graphics and bright colors that remain the mainstay of the site more than a decade later. The initial games were basic and included a coloring book and an activities list

Continued

for those wanting to become a "Disaster Action Kid." Over time, we were able to create more sophisticated games—all with a disaster-related theme or message.

The site was tested with students who wandered through the sections while we watched and asked questions. They were very positive. A small informal team of teachers also reviewed the site before its debut. FEMA for Kids was immediately successful and the number of hits climbed rapidly, due both to word-of-mouth and FEMA public relations efforts. See Fig. 4.4.

As a new way to present the material, I eventually wrote two storybooks. The first, *Julia and Robbie: The Disaster Twins*, included chapters on various natural disasters the twins encountered, with preparedness and mitigation messages subtly—or not so subtly—included. The book was aimed at third/fourth graders and could be downloaded; print versions were also available. Some 250,000 copies were eventually disseminated. Teachers then asked for material suitable for younger children, and I wrote *Herman, PIC, and the Disaster Proof Shell*. For kindergarten through first graders, this book was also available online and in hardcopy. Herman, the hermit crab whose shell kept getting damaged by natural disasters, later became the site's mascot.

The site always had an e-mail function, which visitors didn't hesitate to use. E-mails often led to new content. In one case, an e-mail prompted specific guidance during a media conference. A young girl had written that she was

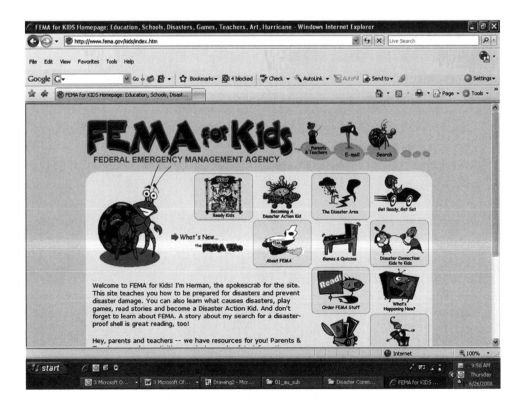

FIGURE 4.4 FEMA for Kids Web page. Source: http://fema.gov/kids/index.htm

Continued

frightened about the four hurricanes churning in the Atlantic at that time. Her parents, she wrote, wouldn't talk about them and she feared for her life. FEMA was tracking the precedent-setting number of brewing hurricanes and I crafted material for Director Witt to discuss with the media about how parents should talk to their children about disasters. It was a good example of a "feedback loop" often missing in public communication.

Over time, we added pop-up facts, audio, new games and photographs, a section for those around kindergarten age and online safety rules. After 9/11, teachers told me they needed help talking to their students about the attacks. Writing the "National Security Emergencies" section for FEMA for Kids was difficult, as I tried to balance sensitivity with information suitable for the age group. I also wrote a chapter for the disaster twins book about an emergency drill at the school, which included ways to respond to various terrorism scenarios. In addition, we added a heroes of 9/11 section highlighting the work of FEMA search and rescue teams.

The site has stood the test of time and still does its job educating elementary-age children about disaster preparedness, response, and mitigation—with the help of Herman the hermit crab, flashy colors, and those still-edgy graphics.

Response

The primary purpose of communications activities in a disaster response to provide accurate and timely information to the public. This information is comprised chiefly of situation reports describing what has happened and is happening in the aftermath of a disaster event; what impact the disaster event has had on individuals, the community, and the physical landscape and what is being done by the various organizations responding to the disaster to help individuals and communities to get back on their feet. There are many ways to communicate in a disaster response and the list of communications options continues to get longer with advances in technology and the growing involvement of individual citizens in reporting on disasters.

In a disaster response, the traditional media come to the emergency management officials for information and access to the disaster area. Unlike the marketing and promotions activities that characterize communications concerning hazard mitigation and preparedness programs, communications work in disaster response is about working in partnership with a very interested media to get accurate and timely information to the public.

In recent years, beginning primarily with the 2004 Asian Tsunami, individual citizens have been playing a larger role in providing first person accounts of disaster events coupled with photographs and video shot by them using their cell phones or digital cameras. In addition, community-based neighborhood communications networks, established through partnerships with community-based organizations to promote hazard mitigation and preparedness programming and activities, can be very useful in communicating information through trusted community leaders to their neighbors but also in collecting valuable information about conditions on the ground in neighborhoods struck by the disaster. Working with the traditional media outlets, the new media of first informers and neighborhood communications networks should be the focus of PIOs during a disaster response.

In order to maximize your communications in a disaster response, emergency management operations should:

- Develop an emergency communications plan—(See text box on emergency communications.)

☐ ☐ ☐ ▬▬▬▬▬▬▬▬▬▬▬▬▬▬▬▬▬▬▬

Communicating During Emergencies

Communicating with the public is one of the critical tasks facing emergency management agencies (EMAs). Reaching the widest possible audience with the most up-to-date, credible information can save lives and property, reduce public fears and anxiety, and maintain the public's trust in the integrity of government officials.

We recently conducted a survey of how EMA communicators had fared during a number of national disasters and terrorist attacks. Our concern about the adequacy of EMA communications planning has been heightened by a striking change in the intensity of media coverage. In describing their work with the press, our respondents used imagery very much like that they applied to the emergency event itself. They found themselves swamped by a veritable "tidal wave" of reporters almost literally beating down their doors.

In this article we review the findings of our survey and interviews, and lay out the principal suggestions we received from a cross-section of EMAs on putting the personnel and infrastructure in place to execute robust, flexible communications plans.

Methodology

This article is based on responses to a questionnaire which we received from communicators involved in the following recent natural disasters or terrorist attack, including interviews in most cases with the principal spokesperson involved:

- Tropical Storm Allison, Harris County Texas, Office of Emergency Management, Mayor's Office, June 5–10, 2001
- The Hayman forest fire, Colorado, Public Affairs, U.S. Forest Service, Rocky Mountain Region, summer 2000
- Attack on the Pentagon, northern Virginia, Office of the Assistant Secretary of Public Affairs and Media Relations, U.S. Department of Defense, September 11, 2001
- Attack on the Pentagon, northern Virginia, Capitol Police, September 11, 2001

Continued

- Sniper attacks, Washington, D.C. metro area, Media Services, Montgomery County Police Department, fall 2002
- Anthrax attack on Hart Senate Office Building, Washington, DC, October, 2001
- Anthrax attacks, Office of Communications, Division of Media Relations, Centers for Disease Control and Prevention, fall 2001
- F4 level tornado, La Plata, Maryland, Maryland Emergency Management Agency, April 28, 2002

Planning

Creating a communications plan on the fly during a crisis is an extremely daunting task. The absence of a plan virtually guarantees that communicators will not be able to reach the public as effectively as they would if they had a plan in place.

Producing a workable written plan is inherently an agency-by-agency process, contingent on available personnel, budget limitations, etc. By soliciting critical review of the plan from all the affected participants—the public, the press, other government agencies—EMAs have the opportunity to produce the best possible plan under the circumstances.

Some of the EMAs we talked with had highly elaborate communications plans. But regardless of length, they all agreed that their plans made them more effective during emergencies. And the EMAs who had been through a trial by fire without a written communications plan were equally adamant about putting such a plan in place as soon as possible.

Source: *The Australian Journal of Emergency Management*, 19(2). May 2004, http://www. ema.gov.au/agd/ema/rwpattach.nsf/viewasattachmentPersonal/ D2E92526C776295CCA256EB6001B5A87/$file/AJEM%2003–07%20May04web-2.pdf

- Collect and analyze information—this is the first and most important aspect of your communications efforts during a disaster response. Timeliness and accuracy are the keys. Emergency management organizations should have protocols and trained staff in place prior to a disaster striking for collecting damage assessment and other information in the immediate aftermath of a disaster event. This information should be analyzed to identify and prioritize needs and then forwarded to decision-makers to apply appropriate resources to address the identified needs. In a major disaster event involving all three levels of government, voluntary organizations active in disasters (VOADs), nongovernmental organizations (NGOs), the private sector, and other groups, there will be numerous potential sources of information. For example, the American Red Cross traditionally has conducted preliminary damage assessments to homes and businesses and is the primary source for data on individuals in shelters and their needs. A system must be put in place to collect information and data from all potential sources including from first informers and neighborhood communications networks.

- Disseminate the information—sharing timely and accurate information with the public, media, partners, and stakeholders is the goal of disaster response communications. There are numerous means for doing so, including:

  ○ Regular media briefings—quickly establish a schedule of regular briefings as soon as possible in the aftermath of a disaster event. This is one of the best ways to ensure that information is presented to the widest media audience and through the media to the public (see Fig. 4.5). These briefings could occur 1–3 times a day depending on the size of the event and flow of information coming into the information collection unit. In scheduling these regular briefings, public affairs officers should be cognizant of the deadlines of the traditional media and plan accordingly.

  ○ Involve leadership in media briefings—the leaders of the emergency management agency responding to a disaster should serve as the primary source of information for the media and the public. This person must be the

FIGURE 4.5 Jackson, Miss., October 18, 2005—FEMA Deputy FCO James N. Russo answers press questions at Governor Haley R. Barbour's weekly press conference, while MEMA Deputy SCO Mike Womack, Col. Don Taylor of the Miss. Dept Human Services, and Governor Barbour look on. The weekly joint press conferences are a direct source of information about state and federal progress in providing services to those impacted by Hurricane Katrina. Photo by George Armstrong/FEMA.

lead briefer during the regular media briefings and in effect become the human face of the disaster response efforts. On occasion, this role may be shared among leaders of responding agencies in a major disaster. In the aftermath of the Northridge earthquake, California Office of Emergency Services Director Dick Andrews and FEMA Director James Lee Witt held two briefings each day for several weeks. The recurring themes of these briefings were: this is what we did yesterday, this is what we are doing today, and this is what we hope to do tomorrow. The constant flow of information coming from high ranking, credentialed officials served not only to establish the scope and size of the disaster and what was being done to address the needs of the individual and community victims but also to provide assurance to the public that the government and its partners were fully engaged in the response and that everything that could be done was being done to help. Elected officials may also assume this role as was the case with Mayor Rudy Giuliani during the response to the September 11 attacks, Governor Frank Keating after the Oklahoma City Bombing in 2005, and Florida Governor Jeb Bush during the spate of four major hurricanes striking Florida in 2004. Officials from agencies other than emergency management may assume this role as Montgomery County (MD) Chief of Police Charles Moose did during the 2002 Washington, DC sniper crisis. There are times these briefings could be handled by a high ranking public affairs officer but the primary spokesperson at these briefings, especially in the beginning of the disaster response, should be the leaders who are in charge of the response efforts.

○ Make your response staff available to the media—leadership and public affairs officer are the primary spokespersons for a response effort but on occasion it will be necessary for you to make available to the media members of your staff involved in specific aspects of the disaster response. Their role should be to provide information about the activities they and their staff are engaged in as part of the response. They should not talk about the work of other parts of your organization or the work of other government, non-governmental, and private sector groups involved in the response. Your staff should receive media training and should be comfortable talking with the media. Public affairs officers should work with designated staff to prepare for and conduct media interviews and briefings.

○ Provide media with images and words they need to communicate your information—television is a visual media and radio is dependent on sound bytes and actualities, newspapers require photos and words, and the Internet uses all of these features. Help these various media outlets to secure the images, words, and sound bites they need to get your information out to the public (see Fig. 4.6). Provide access to the disaster site for photographers and video cameras. If access to the disaster site must be limited for security or other reasons, use your own staff to shoot photos and video to provide to the

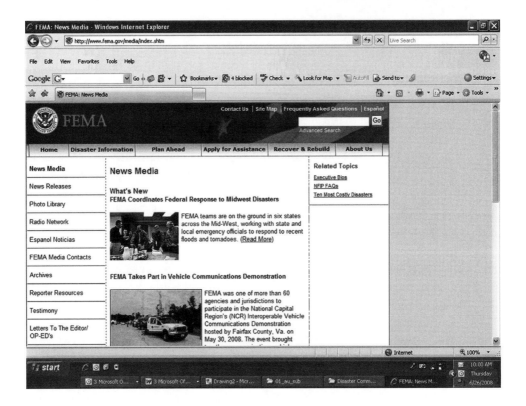

FIGURE 4.6 FEMA media Web page. (Source: http://www.fema.gov/media/index.shtm).

media. The first photos and video from Ground Zero in New York City after the September 11 attacks were shot by camera operators working for FEMA. Provide concise and up-to-date situation reports to the media. Provide leaders and staff to be interviewed in briefings or one-on-one. Become the source for accurate facts and statistics concerning the impact of the disaster (i.e., deaths, injuries, property damage, destruction of infrastructure, etc.) and what is being done to help people (i.e., provision of food, water, and shelter; resumption of utilities; provision of emergency child care; emergency health care; etc.).

○ Respond to media inquiries—rumors and misinformation abound in a disaster response. Responding quickly with accurate information to counter rumors and misinformation is critical to maintaining the credibility of the response effort. Often it is the media that brings rumors and misinformation to the attention of the response team. PIOs must be trained to treat these inquiries seriously and to take action immediately to respond. The basic communications principles apply here—don't lie and don't talk about what you don't know about. Work with the response staff to determine the truth and relay that information to the media. (See Jane Bullock's "Another Voice" comment for advice on being interviewed.)

☐ ☐ ☐ ▬▬▬▬▬▬▬▬▬▬▬▬▬▬▬▬▬

Another Voice: Jane Bullock

Jane Bullock is the former chief of staff to FEMA Director James Lee Witt and a principal in Bullock & Haddow LLC, a Washington, DC-based disaster management consulting firm.

Interview 101: Practical Experience for Being Interviewed (Part Two)

The process of being interviewed by a member or members of the media is never dull. It can be very important and beneficial to getting your message out, it can be informative and even fun, but it is always stressful and the only way to reduce the stress is to make sure that you take the time to prepare for any interview. What follows are some thoughts and ideas on how to approach a media interview based on the hundreds of interviews I have given over the past 20 plus years. My goal is to share with you what helps me get ready for an interview, to feel more confident and to reduce the nervousness.

Building on my experience, I have learned the following lessons:

1. Always, always, prepare for any interview, even if you already know the subject matter
2. Decide on three or four points that you want to make in the interview no matter what the person(s) who are interviewing ask you and
3. Use different approaches for interviews with the different media

Preparation for an interview is critical. In most cases, you already know why you are being interviewed or the circumstances of the event that they want to talk with you about. However, before any interview you need to make sure you are current on information about the event, know situational information, what steps are being taken, what the next actions will be, problems that are occurring or could occur, and the process for handling them. Use of language that indicates a proactive approach but recognizes limitations and managing expectations is important in disaster circumstances. Remember to always acknowledge people being impacted by any event or circumstances and voice your concern for their situation. Try to make a personal connection with the event and the people impacted and the activities that are being done to rectify the situation.

Intrinsic to the preparation is deciding on the three or four points/messages you want to make during the interview. This will enable you to get your information out and to get your points across. During the interview, you should keep coming back to these fundamental messages no matter what questions are being asked. This allows you to take some control over the interview. It also allows you to exercise the "I don't know the answer" advice. If you get a question you feel you can't answer, you simply say something to the effect. "That's an excellent

Continued

question and I don't have a complete answer for that but this is what I know"—then you talk about one of your 3–4 major points. This also compliments your questioner and gives you a few minutes to collect your thoughts.

Each different media interview has its own rhythm and time frame. Written press interviews allow you to speak at greater length on any issue, allow you to provide more factual information, and are more lengthy in duration so you have, generally, a greater opportunity to get your points across but also the interview may be longer and more detailed, so preparation is the key.

Radio interviews also provide an opportunity for longer explanations and discussion. However, a good radio interview requires you to articulate your messages and responses to questions clearly, in understandable language, and in small increments so the audience can make sense of what is being said. Knowing your messages and coming back to these messages again and again is a good strategy for radio interviews. Speaking at moderate speed and clearly is important to a good interview as is making a connection with the interviewer by calling them by name, making a connection to the audience by referencing the geographical area, i.e., the city or county names, and recognizing the radio listening audience.

Television interviews are the most stressful and usually occur in 1–4 minute time frames or longer if part of a panel of interviewees. Having a succinct message is absolutely essential for TV interviews as you will probably have less than 30 seconds to answer a question or get your point across. Having facts and figures that support your message are very impressive as long as you have done your homework and know you can stand behind the numbers you give. Feeling comfortable on camera means you wear clothes that you are comfortable in and feel good about. With TV interviews you must always be conscious that you may be on camera at any time and make sure you are always alert, keeping a neutral expression on your face, and not fidgeting. In a panel format, be respectful of fellow panel members but don't hesitate to respond, or interrupt in a courteous way when you want to make a point. Always acknowledge who is interviewing you by name, if possible, as it helps make you seem more comfortable on camera.

The key to a good interview is knowing what you want to say, how you want to say it, and any information, data, etc. that supports what you are saying. That's why preparation is so critical, even if it's only 5 minutes before the interview, when you take a minute to concentrate your thoughts. Practical tips such as taking a few deep breaths before the interview starts, thinking of something that makes you feel confident, and drinking some water all will help.

If you approach interviews as a positive opportunity to get your message out rather than as a defensive exercise, you will feel much more comfortable talking with the media. I think the media is not the enemy as they are often portrayed but people that want to get information out and are usually anxious to help, especially in disaster or risk circumstances. It has been my experience, that very few of the media are out to play "gotcha" and if you approach them as

Continued

people doing their jobs on behalf of their viewers, listeners, or readers, and treat them with respect, they will do the same to you as an interviewee.

Finally, having media experts and friends or co-workers provide constructive criticism on your interview will help you get better and learn personal techniques that will help you in future interviews. It also boosts your confidence.

Hundreds of interviews later, on national and international broadcast networks, NPR, numerous call-in radio, most major newspapers, and even Oprah, I still spend time preparing, getting my messages honed and I still get nervous. But once the interview starts, all of the preparation pays off because I forget about the butterflies, concentrate on my messages and try to be informative and enjoy myself. I just hope I get to be on CNN again sometime soon because the makeup people there always make me look 20 pounds thinner. Good luck and enjoy.

- Work with the new media—first informers, bloggers, bulletin boards and e-mail are becoming credible sources of information during a disaster response and are attracting a growing audience. PIOs should work to build a partnership with the new media and help to meet their information needs. Ultimately, the new media is another mechanism for communicating timely and accurate information to the public.
- Monitor the media—someone should be designated to monitor how the media is reporting on the disaster and the disaster response (see Fig. 4.7). Taping

FIGURE 4.7 New York, NY, September 27, 2001—FEMA workers need to stay current with the news in regards to the terrorist attacks on the World Trade Center and the Pentagon. Photo by Bri Rodriguez/FEMA News Photo.

television and radio programs and reviewing them on a regular basis is one way to monitor these media outlets. Reading newspaper accounts and tracking information on the Internet is another. Staff should regularly check what is being said on blogs and bulletin boards. When problems are identified, PIOs should reach out and work with the media outlet in question to correct the problem.

- Media training—as noted earlier, any official whose job includes talking to the media should receive media training. This training should be done prior to the next disaster and could be conducted by the staff PIO or by outside professional media trainers. The training will help make officials more comfortable in talking to the media and help them to shape their messages so that they are easily understood and consistent.

Recovery

The focus of communications efforts in the recovery phase of a disaster is on providing timely information about the types of relief assistance available to the individuals and communities victimized by the disaster and how they can access this assistance. This assistance comes in a variety of forms including government programs, private sector donations, and help from voluntary and community organizations with roles in the recovery. At this point in the disaster, the attention of the traditional, mainstream media is beginning to wane so communications work in the recovery phase is as much about marketing as it is responding to media inquiries and interest.

The incidence of rumors and misinformation actually increase in the recovery phase as more organizations and groups become involved and accurate information about relief programs can be difficult to obtain. An effective communications strategy for communicating accurate and timely information about what public and private relief assistance is available and how to apply for it is critical to mitigating the rumors and misinformation that surface.

Elements of an effective communications effort in the recovery phase include:

- Information Clearinghouse—there are any number of governmental, non-governmental, volunteer, non-profit, and private sector organizations involved in disaster recovery. The bigger the disaster, the larger the number of these organizations involved. The amount of information individuals and communities impacted by a disaster need to apply and receive disaster relief can be staggering. FEMA and its state and local government partners have tried one-stop shopping in FEMA Disaster Recovery Centers (see Fig. 4.8) with some measure of success. However, with many people getting their information primarily from the Internet, it is important that a Recovery Information Clearinghouse is designated to collect information from all groups offering relief assistance. This type of operation will require extensive pre-disaster planning, but once established should be able to handle information available pre-disaster as well as any new information made available in the recovery

FIGURE 4.8 Queens, NY, September 9, 2007—Marianne Jackson, FEMA Federal Coordinating Officer (FCO) answers questions from the press at the opening of the Disaster Recovery Assistance Center (DRAC) in Queens. Photo by Patsy Lynch/FEMA.

phase. Consideration should be given to establishing a hotline (combination telephone number and e-mail address) individuals can use to get questions answered or to solicit information.

- Communicating recovery information—as with the other phases of emergency management there are numerous mechanisms available to communicate recovery phase information including:
  - ○ Television and radio—used primarily to encourage individuals to apply for assistance, to announce new programs as they come on line and to guide people to more detailed information sources on the Internet, in printed materials, and in newspapers. Regular updates should be conducted by recovery leaders on the progress of the recovery and to reassure disaster victims that they will receive help.
  - ○ Internet and newspapers—source of detailed information concerning relief programs and how to apply.
  - ○ New media—you should make information available to bloggers, bulletin boards, and ListServs on the Internet. These mechanisms are often self started and if kept properly informed can help get information about recovery programs to select audiences.

    ○ Neighborhood Communications Networks—get recovery information to trusted community leaders who will share this information directly with neighbors and can facilitate getting neighbor's questions answered by recovery officials.

    ○ Community Relations Teams—FEMA has been using trained community relations staff to go door-to-door in targeted neighborhoods to talk directly to residents to encourage them to apply for assistance and to explain how recovery programs work and can help them. Even in a small disaster where FEMA is not involved, it may make sense for local emergency management staff to go door-to-door in those neighborhoods where traditional media and new media communications do not reach all residents.

- Monitor media—keep track of what is being said in all forms of media about recovery efforts and be prepared to react quickly when rumors or misinformation are identified.

Conclusion

The time to build an effective communications capability is prior to the next disaster. Promoting hazard mitigation and preparedness programs and activities offer a prime opportunity to create a working partnership with local media; build neighborhood communications networks; and establish protocols for working with first informers, bloggers, and other new media practitioners. These efforts and the relationships that result will serve you well when responding to the next disaster and in helping individuals and the community to recover. At the core of all communications efforts in the four phases of emergency management is collecting, analyzing, and disseminating critical information in a timely and accurate manner to the public, the media, your partners, and other stakeholders. Using all media mechanisms available to you is the key to success.

5

Disaster Communications Audiences

One of the principle purposes of disaster communications is to get individuals and communities to take action. Hazard mitigation and preparedness communications focus on promoting actions that individuals and communities can take to reduce the impacts of future disasters and to be ready when the next disaster strikes. Communications during disaster response provide critical information that individuals and communities can use to take action to survive the disaster and access relief assistance. In the recovery phase of a disaster, communications focus on informing individuals and communities of the types of recovery assistance available from a variety of governmental, non-governmental, and private sector sources to help rebuild their lives and infrastructure.

There are several audiences that must be reached in order to be successful in communicating across the four phases of emergency management—mitigation, preparedness, response, and recovery. (See text box for more details.) First and foremost, there is the public audience which is comprised of a wide array of subsets including special needs populations, children, residents in disadvantaged neighborhoods, tourists and visitors, homeowners, families without cars, etc. The bulk of the disaster communications is focused on reaching the public and helping the public take the correct action during all four emergency management phases. It should be noted that with the advent of the "new media" this critical audience is starting to collect and exchange their own information and act on that information as they see fit.

□ □ □ ▬▬▬▬▬▬▬▬▬▬▬▬▬▬▬▬▬▬▬▬▬▬▬▬

Basic Emergency Management Audiences

Basic emergency management audiences include the following:

- *General public.* The largest audience of which there are many subgroups, such as the elderly, the disabled, minority, low income, youth, and so on, and all are potential customers.
- *Disaster victims.* Those individuals affected by a specific disaster event.
- *Business community.* Often ignored by emergency managers but critical to disaster recovery, preparedness, and mitigation activities.

Continued

- *Media.* An audience and a partner critical to effectively communicating with the public.
- *Elected officials.* Governors, mayors, county executives, state legislators, and members of Congress.
- *Community officials.* City/county managers, public works, department heads.
- *First responders.* Police, fire, and emergency medical services.
- *Volunteer groups.* American Red Cross, Salvation Army, the National Volunteer Organizations Active in Disasters (NVOAD), and so on that are critical to first response to an event.

Source: *Introduction to Emergency Management*, 3rd ed. © Elsevier Inc, 2007.

There are three other primary audiences for disaster communications—elected officials and community leaders, partners and stakeholders, and the media. Elected officials and community leaders serve both as a critical audience for disaster information and also as communicators of disaster-related information to their constituencies. They are positioned to both provide information to emergency officials concerning their constituents and are leaders in their communities who the public trusts and will turn to in a disaster. Partners include first responders, voluntary agencies, community groups, non-governmental organizations, the business community, and others. These groups can also be a valuable source of information and a distributor of information to their customers and the community. Historically, the media has told the disaster story using a variety of sources including the government emergency management agencies. The emergence of the "new media" has created a cadre of ordinary citizens as first informers providing first hand accounts of conditions where they live in real time. The "new media" must also be enlisted in getting information back out from emergency officials to local populations through their networks and contacts.

Communicating with these four primary audiences—public, elected officials and community leaders, partners and stakeholders, and the media—is no longer a one-way street for emergency officials. It is now a cooperative venture that will require new skills, protocols, and technologies to be employed to design, build, and maintain effective disaster communications.

This chapter examines what it takes for emergency officials to communicate and work together with these four primary audiences.

The Public

Traditional communications with the public was done almost exclusively through the media—television, radio, and newspapers. During the disaster response and recovery phases these media outlets relied primarily on the emergency officials for information, access to the disaster site, and progress reports on government and non-government programs. These same media outlets were used by emergency officials to communicate preparedness and hazard mitigation messages and to urge the public to act on warning and alert notices. These traditional media outlets were the principle dispensers of government disaster-related information because they reached the largest percentage of the population and could be trusted to get the information right if they worked in partnership with emergency officials.

In the 1990s, the Internet arrived and was quickly adapted to provide both timely and detailed information. Recent disasters—the 2004 Asian Tsunami, 2005 Hurricane Katrina, the 2007 London bombings, the 2008 Cyclone Nargis in Myanmar (Burma), and the 2008 Sichuan earthquake in China—have seen the "new media" come to the front and in many ways surpass the traditional media outlets in terms of timely reporting of conditions that provided the public and government agencies with valuable information concerning response operations. The traditional media has taken notice of the "new media" and in many cases have adopted it as part of their regular reporting, especially during disasters. (See text box on CNN's site.)

□ □ □

CNN iReports

CNN provides a space on its Web site (www.cnn.com) for everyday citizens to post written stories, video, audio, and photographs concerning events that they witness (see Fig. 5.1). Many of the postings concern natural disasters.

As of June 9, 2008, CNN had received 102,423 iReports submissions and in May 2008 broadcasted 915 of these submissions on CNN.

The CNN iReports site includes links to the latest submissions, highest rated submissions, most viewed submissions, most commented and most shared submissions, and those submissions that are broadcast on CNN.

CNN also provides a toolkit for iReporters with tips concerning the ingredients of a good story (see below), taking great photos, shooting better video and recording the sound of your story.

There is an Assignment Desk function on the Web site that identifies current topics in the news that CNN would like their iReporters to report on.

The Ingredients of a Good Story

We asked a slew of CNN reporters, producers, and editors what they thought made a good news story and how to craft one, and came up with a few words of advice:

- First things first. Your story needs to include the basics. That is, who, what, where, when, why, and how. It needs to be true, and it needs to be fair.
- It connects. Someone has to care about the story and the people in it, or it's not really worth telling. It's your job as a storyteller to explain why anyone should.

Continued

FIGURE 5.1 CNN iReport Web page. Source: http://www.ireport.com/index.jspa

- It's told in words we all use and understand. If you were going to call your best friend and tell her the story, what would you start with? And how would you describe it? That's probably the best part, and the simplest way to get it across. Start there, and see where it takes you.
- It's got pace. You want your audience to need to know what happens next. Build pace with narrative, quotes, natural sound, or, if you're working with video, creative shot editing.
- It feels real. Emotion is a powerful connector and can go a long way toward helping us understand one another. Think about how you can use images, sound, and words to express the emotional range of a story and its characters.
- Map it out. If you're planning to edit a video, put together a photo gallery or write a text story, it usually helps to put together a plan of action. What are the crucial details? What's the most important part? How are the pieces connected? Draft an outline or sketch a storyboard before you get started with the hard work of writing and editing. You'll be glad you did.

Source: CNN. http://www.ireport.com/index.jspa

In effect, the audience comprising of the public and individual disaster victims have become key players in the collection of disaster information, and emergency officials must design information collection programs and protocols that are equipped to accept this valuable information before, during, and after a disaster strikes. In addition, emergency officials must be ready to share disaster information with these first informers so that the first reporters can distribute this information to their networks via cell phone, e-mail, text messages, and Internet bulletin boards. In working with the public and individual disaster victims, emergency officials must now create and sustain a two-way communications system that maximizes the information collection and distribution capabilities of the new media these audiences employ.

Such a two-way communication system must also be established working with community-based groups that operate primarily in low-to-moderate income neighborhoods and with disadvantaged populations. This subset of the public may not have easy access to the Web-based communications technologies of the new media. These populations may also have trust issues with government officials including first responders such as police and fire officials. Before, during, and after a disaster strikes, these populations may be more inclined to listen to and act on the advice of trusted community leaders. Emergency officials must work with community-based groups to establish neighborhood communications networks that facilitate communications from emergency officials to neighborhood residents via trusted community leaders. These neighborhood communication networks would be designed to collect and transmit real time information from trusted community leaders to emergency officials. This two-way communications system will not only be used in the response and recovery phases of a disaster, but also to spread hazard mitigation and preparedness messages among community members and to prompt action by residents and community groups, take actions designed to reduce the impacts of future disasters, and to be ready when the next disaster strikes.

A significant percentage of the public and individual disaster victims will be members of Special Needs Populations as designated by Federal Emergency Management Agency (FEMA) in the National Response Framework.[1] (See text box for more information on special needs populations.) This population includes individuals:

- with various disabilities,
- who live in institutionalized settings,
- who are elderly,
- who are from diverse cultures,
- with limited English proficiency or who are non-English speaking,
- children, and
- who are transportation disadvantaged.

---

[1] FEMA (2008). National Response Framework: NRF Resource Center. http://www.fema.gov/emergency/nrf/glossary.htm#S

□ □ □

Special Needs Populations as Defined in FEMA's National Response Framework

Special Needs Population: Populations whose members may have additional needs before, during, and after an incident in functional areas, including but not limited to: maintaining independence, communication, transportation, supervision, and medical care. Individuals in need of additional response assistance may include those who have disabilities; who live in institutionalized settings; who are elderly; who are children; who are from diverse cultures; who have limited English proficiency or are non-English speaking; or who are transportation disadvantaged.

Source: National Response Framework (NRF) Resource Center. http://www.fema.gov/emergency/nrf/glossary.htm#S

□ □ □

Communicating with individuals in these groups offers many challenges for emergency officials. Recognizing this challenge and taking steps to meet it are the first steps in designing and implementing a communications strategy that effectively communicates messages to members of these groups before, during, and after a disaster strikes. Attention must be placed on how disaster messages are crafted and delivered to these groups in consideration of the existing communications barriers. Some of these populations are comfortable with the new media (i.e. children) and some have limited, if growing experience, with the Internet, etc. (i.e. elderly, non-English speaking, members of diverse cultures). Emergency officials must appreciate how best to craft their disaster messages to these groups including use of translators and translated materials. Emergency officials must determine the best mechanisms for communicating with these special needs populations using a combination of traditional and new media and neighborhood-based communications networks.

Since Hurricane Katrina there has been growing interest in serving special needs populations and professionals working in government, the non-profit, voluntary, and private sectors have begun to work together to address the basic needs of these populations in disasters. (See Jane Bullock's "Another Voice" on communicating with children about disasters and safety.) The Resources section at the back of this book contains information on Web sites, guides, and research papers concerning communicating disaster messages to special needs populations.

□ □ □

Another Voice: Jane Bullock

Jane Bullock is the former chief of staff to FEMA Director James L. Witt and a principal in Bullock & Haddow LLC, a Washington, DC-based disaster management consulting firm.

Continued

Talking to Children About Hazards: The Sesame Street Get Ready and Fire Safety Projects

In 1969, a new experiment in children's television debuted called Sesame Street. Sesame Street was the product of the Children's Television Workshop (CTW), a group of visionary individuals led by Joan Ganz Cooney who recognized the need for a new approach to children's television. The goal of the program was to focus on the underserved population of children aged 2–5 living in low income to poverty level households. These children needed help to learn cognitive and social skills before entering school and it was felt that education which is accessible to rich and poor alike could play a major role in reducing the gap between low income children and their counterparts in the middle class. To make this program effective, Sesame Street created one of the most rigorous research, message development, product testing, artistic, and evaluative processes to reach their audience. By all accounts, it has been extremely effective.

Which was why, in 1979, the U.S. Fire Administration (USFA) reached out to CTW and Sesame Street in reaction to statistics that indicated a significant increase in fire-related children death and injury rates. The Sesame Street audience was extremely vulnerable to fire threats in their homes; children were prone to play with matches and lighters and often would hide from firefighters entering the home because they looked so foreign in their fire suits. CTW began an aggressive project to identify what messages would work best for the preschool age and primary school-aged children and which medium worked best to communicate them. One classic example of the CTW treatment is "Drop, Stop, and Roll," teaching children what to do if their clothes are on fire. Through songs, skits, and puppet acting, children learned a critical principle of personal fire safety that is now practiced in day care and schools throughout the world. A hallmark of all of the CTW materials are creative songs, coloring books, simple games, and excellent teacher and caregiver aids to help deliver the materials in a non-threatening and educational way.

Building on the success of the Fire Safety Project, in the 1980s, the FEMA, which the USFA became part of in 1979, was extremely interested in reaching out to children to help them understand other natural disasters and how they could be impacted by them, and what they could do to be prepared for hurricanes, earthquakes, and floods. A collateral interest was to see if children could bring the messages home to their parents to influence the adults to take an action, such as make a family plan or an emergency kit, or tie down their water heaters to achieve a greater level of preparedness and mitigation in their homes and communities.

Working with the CTW staff and research process, it became clear that the word "preparedness" wasn't going to work and we needed to find something simpler and more understandable. Out of their exhaustive process came the Big Bird Get Ready Series, which built upon the common childhood idea of "Get Ready, Get Set, and Go."

Continued

Starting with hurricanes, a Big Bird Get Ready Kit and supporting materials were researched, designed, and extensively pilot tested. These kits were geared toward a slightly older audience of 5–12 years of age and could include concepts such as weather and science, watch and warning, etc. as part of the education. Each kit included an informational brochure of three parts: (1) *Get Ready* examples included what does the hazard mean, and how to Get Ready by knowing where to go, knowing what to do in an earthquake, identifying high ground place near a house in a flood, and having an evacuation route and a Family Safety Kit; (2) *Get Set* examples included know what is watch and warning, stay tuned to local radio and television, pick inside and outside safety spots near your home; and (3) *Go to Safety* examples included locating the nearest shelter, dealing with earthquake aftershocks, and staying away from swollen streams.

The brochure was specifically designed to be like a small book and one side was in English and the other in Spanish. It took CTW almost 6 months to research the most widely accepted Spanish dialect to be used for the translation. The other two main components of the kit were a board game and a cassette of songs and stories. At this age level, CTW found that more complex activities such as board games and card games were most effective and an excellent way to reinforce messages and deliver information. A key to these kits was still the cassettes which included stories and creative songs that were written for each hazard.

Hurricane Blues, Beat the Quake, and Get out of the Water were original songs designed in different musical styles popular in the 1980s and designed to be played in classrooms, caregivers operations, day care and after care centers, churches, businesses, and even in family cars. While Big Bird was an anchor to the series, other Sesame Street characters such as Bert and Ernie, Oscar the Grouch, the Cookie Monster, and the Count played starring rolls. In the last kit produced, Get Ready for Floods, a special section was added on how to best talk to children about dealing with a disaster. After the devastation caused by Hurricane Andrew, CTW staff and characters went to the shelters around Homestead and worked with the children using the Get Ready for Hurricanes materials and the songs and stories on the Hurricane Blues cassettes.

A special outgrowth of the Get Ready project was a Sesame Street episode that dealt with Bert and Ernie going through a hurricane disaster on Sesame Street. Originally developed and shown in the early 1990s a newer version of the story was developed as recently as 2004 after the series of four hurricanes swept through Florida.

The kits were a huge success and demand outstripped FEMA's ability to produce them in color and some private sector funding was made available, but FEMA was never able to keep up with the demand. While the program was never officially evaluated, it was recognized by professional teaching organizations, child welfare groups, and the Congress. The key to the success was the CTW process of intensive research and intensive product testing on the audience. The songs Hurricane Blues and Beat the Quake were tested with over 15 different children audiences, as were the board and card games.

Continued

The other key was CTW's knowledge of their audience. Disasters dispro-
portionately impact low income families because of where they must live and
the type of housing they live in, and CTW knew how best to reach them.
They produced well-researched and credible messages, delivered by figures in
Big Bird, Bert & Ernie, Oscar, et al. that children, parents, and caregivers
trusted and made those messages educational, practical, and fun. And they
saved lives. In the aftermath of the Loma Prieta earthquake in 1989, finding
safety spots included in the Get Ready for Earthquake Kit became a standard
school practice.

Elected Officials and Community Leaders

Elected officials and community leaders play significant roles in all phases of emergency management and in both receiving and delivering disaster messages. It is vitally
important that emergency officials keep those elected officials in their jurisdiction
informed before, during, and after a disaster strikes. Elected officials and community
leaders can serve as credible spokespeople in communicating with the public, with
partners and stakeholders, and with the media. This is true with communications
efforts in the response and recovery phases and in promoting hazard mitigation
and preparedness programs and activities.

Local elected officials and community leaders should receive regular briefings and
updates during disaster response on conditions in the disaster site, the status of evacuees, number of dead and injured, and impact of the disaster on community infrastructure and environmental resources. They also need to keep abreast of all response
actions by governmental, non-governmental, voluntary, and private sector responders.
A specific level of detail will be required in these briefings as these leaders will make
decisions on use of community resources and if necessary, appealing for state and
federal disaster assistance.

State officials, particularly the governor, also require detailed information about
disaster impact and response conditions. Only the governor can request a Presidential
disaster declaration that results in provision of federal disaster assistance to individuals and communities. Members of Congress are an important group to keep
informed as they will work with their colleagues to secure federal assistance once a
Presidential declaration has been made, especially in catastrophic disasters such as
Hurricane Katrina and the Northridge earthquake.

At some point in time, any number of local, state, and federal officials will want
to visit the disaster area. This is a valuable communications mechanism as these
political leaders will bring the media with them to the site. Appropriate staff and support resources should be allocated at all level of governments to support keeping
elected officials and community leaders informed.

It should be noted that staff from the offices of elected officials and community
leaders are a valuable source of information on conditions in their jurisdictions and

emergency officials should seek to create a relationship with these staff to facilitate the exchange of information. Additionally, these staff may include communications specialists who could be made available, on request, to assist with communications efforts.

Well informed elected officials and community leaders can make credible and confident spokespersons for communicating information to the public and the media. These officials are often media savvy and well spoken and understand the requirements for delivering a consistent message in a compassionate manner. Involvement in hazard mitigation and preparedness communications programs during non-disaster periods provides opportunities for these officials to learn more about disasters and to become comfortable talking about disaster issues (see Fig. 5.2).

Local community leaders will play major roles in conveying disaster information through neighborhood communications networks. These leaders will also be well acquainted with hazard mitigation and preparedness messages and issues. In disaster response, they should serve a dual purpose of delivering disaster response information to their constituents and collecting disaster impact information in their neighborhoods and communicating this information to emergency officials.

FIGURE 5.2 Bay St. Louis, MS., March 20, 2008—Mississippi Congressman Gene Taylor speaks at a press conference in Bay St. Louis. Governor Haley Barbour, U.S. Senator Roger Wicker, and U.S. Representative Taylor announced $200 million in funding from the U.S. Department of Housing and Urban Development for Hancock County Katrina recovery projects, including the rebuilding of the Hancock County Jail and financing an extensive renovation of downtown Bay St. Louis. Photo by Jennifer Smits/FEMA.

Partners and Stakeholders

There are any number of partners and stakeholders in all phases of emergency management who should be part of an effective communications operation including:

- Other government emergency management organizations
- Voluntary agencies—Voluntary organizations active in disasters (VOAD)
- Non-governmental organizations (NGOs)
- Business sector
- First responders
- Volunteers and service providers

These partners and stakeholders are included in NIMS and ICS and can be sources of information and messengers delivering information to the public and other partners and stakeholders (see Fig. 5.3). Leaders from these organizations should be

FIGURE 5.3 Washington, DC, May 20, 2008—FEMA Administrator Paulison at the podium during a press conference at FEMA headquarters. FEMA is hosting their First Hurricane Awareness Day at FEMA headquarters to highlight the federal government's preparations for the 2008 Hurricane Season. On the dais, Left–Right: Mr. James. J. Madon, Director and Deputy Manager of the National Communications System in the Department of Homeland Security; Major General Guy C. Swan III, Chief of Operations for Headquarters, U.S. Northern Command; Ms. Mary S. Elcano, Acting President and CEO, American Red Cross; Admiral Thad W. Allen, Commandant, U.S. Coast Guard; FEMA Administrator David Paulison (at podium); DHS Secretary, Michael Chertoff; Mr. Paul McHale, Assistant Secretary of Defense for Homeland Defense; Dr. Gerald Parker, Principal Deputy Assistance Secretary for Preparedness and Response, U.S. Department of Health and Human Services; and Major General William H. Etter, Acting Director of the Joint Staff, National Guard Bureau. Photo by FEMA/Bill Koplitz.

routinely briefed and updated on disaster conditions in disaster response and brought in at the beginning of the formulation of hazard mitigation and preparedness programs. Protocols should be developed to ensure that this audience is well informed and that information collected by this audience is secured and processed.

Many of these groups are heavily involved in the recovery phase and should be included in all communications efforts during this period. These groups and their leaders can deliver information on recovery efforts directly to their customers and their workers. They are also the source of updated information on how their recovery efforts are progressing.

As with elected officials and community leaders, some partners and stakeholders employ communications staff who could be made available to work in a Joint Information Center (JIC) and help to collect and disseminate disaster information. These same communications staff could also participate in the design and implementation of hazard mitigation and preparedness communications programs in nondisaster periods. Again, working with these groups in the non-disaster period strengthens relationships that will be very useful when the next disaster strikes.

The Media

In disaster response, the media comes to emergency officials for information, access to the disaster site, and interviews with response officials. Sharing information with the media is a must and does not have to be painful. Regular briefings, access to response officials, and access to the disaster site and disaster victims will meet the needs of nearly all media responding to a disaster. Serving this audience in a disaster is all about scheduling and meeting the media's information needs. Media need not be an adversary; in fact, it does not take much to make the media a partner in the response. Timely and accurate information and a thank you every now and then can help forge a solid partnership with this audience.

However, if you withhold or appear to withhold disaster information and access, then the media is likely to turn on emergency officials and it is Hurricane Katrina all over again. The days of not sharing information or selective sharing of information by emergency officials is over. Not just because the traditional media won't stand for it, but because the new media is becoming a significant new source of information for traditional media.

In recent years, first informers have become trusted sources of disaster information. Emergency officials must engage these first informers in a systematic way—much the way CNN and other traditional news outlets have—and fold these new information sources into the disaster communications efforts.

 6

Building New Disaster Communications Capabilities

Introduction

Communities routinely form online after natural disasters—just as they do in the real world. "Whenever there is a natural or man-made disaster we can observe an emerging community structure. First, people help each other before they are supported or replaced by government entities."[1]

A key difference in the online and offline responses to natural disasters lies in the definition of a "community." In its planning, the government assumes that a "community" refers to people living in the same geographical area. That thinking neglects the underlying shared interests and other connections that constitute social networks.[1]

"Since the World Wide Web gained popularity in the mid-1990s, it has brought people together by creating virtual communities in cyberspace. Virtual communities are where members are not necessarily physically close to each other, have common interests, and receive, create, and exchange information that is not tightly linked to their geographic location. These communities occur when people interact for enough time and with enough feeling and sense of participation to form webs of personal interaction. People form personal relationships and engage in social interactions in virtual space creating networks of communication."[2]

One of the social interactions and primary reasons that people form virtual communities during disasters is to engage in the interactive flow of information. The online community involves "formal networks such as online news reporting, emergency information services, and mechanisms for online donations.... Increasingly, informal social networks of communication have developed that provide first hand accounts of the disaster, posting of pictures and videos, blogs, and chat rooms that assist in locating resources that often link with the formal emergency response network."[2]

---

[1] A. Schellong (2007). *Increasing Social Capital for Disaster Response Through Social Networking Services (SSN) in Japanese Local Governments*. National Center for Digital Government.

[2] M. Laituri and K. Kris (2008). *On Line Disaster Response Community: People as Sensors of High Magnitude Disasters Using Internet GIS*. Colorado State University.

□ □ □

New Media Terms

A *blog* (an abridgment of the term Web log) is a Web site, usually maintained by an individual, with regular entries of commentaries, descriptions of events, or other materials such as graphics or videos. Entries are commonly displayed in reverse chronological order. "Blog" can also be used as a verb, meaning to maintain or add content to a blog.

A *wiki* is a collection of Web pages designed to enable anyone who accesses it to contribute or modify content using a simplified markup language. Wikis are often used to create collaborative Web sites and to power community Web sites. The collaborative encyclopedia Wikipedia is one of the best-known wikis.

Citizen journalism, also known as public or participatory journalism, is the act of citizens "playing an active role in the process of collecting, reporting, analyzing, and disseminating news and information," according to the seminal report "We Media: How Audiences are Shaping the Future of News and Information," by Shayne Bowman and Chris Willis.

Video blogging, sometimes shortened to vlogging, is a form of blogging for which the medium is video. Entries are made regularly and often combine embedded video or a video link with supporting text, images, and other metadata.

YouTube is an enormously popular video sharing Web site where users can upload, view, and share video clips. In January 2008 alone, nearly 79 million users watched over 3 billion videos on YouTube.

Mashup is a Web site or Web application that seamlessly combines content from more than one source into an integrated experience. For example, a Web site for an amusement park that contains a Mapquest page for visitors to get directions.

Short Message Service (SMS) is a communications protocol allowing the interchange of short text messages between mobile telephone devices. SMS text messaging is the most widely used data application on the planet, with already 2.4 billion active users, or 74% of all mobile phone subscribers sending and receiving text messages on their phones. The SMS technology has facilitated the development and growth of text messaging.

Twitter is a free social networking, short message service + micro-blogging service that allows users to send "updates" (or "tweets," text-based posts, up to 140 characters long) to the Twitter Web site, as an instant message, or to a third-party application such as Twitterrific or Facebook (see Fig. 6.1).

Flickr is an online photo management and sharing application designed to help people make their content available to the people who matter to them and to enable new ways of organizing photos and videos. Flickr gets photos and videos from the Web, from mobile devices, from the users' home computers, and from whatever software they are using to manage their content and pushes them out on the Flickr Web site, in RSS feeds, by e-mail, or by posting to outside blogs.

Source: Wikipedia.com, 2008.

Continued

FIGURE 6.1 Twitter Web page. Source: http://twitter.com/

Using online technologies (see text box on new media) during disasters changes and improves communications, by:

- Speeding Up the Flow of Information
  The Internet accelerates the distribution of information (and misinformation) to an unlimited audience.

  Online media facilitates communication among families, friends, and others, both inside and outside the country in which the disaster occurs, during a disaster.[2]

- Increasing the Means and Odds that People Can Access and Share Information
  Mobile technology allows people to access this information anywhere, anytime through cell phones, PDAs, and laptops.

  "Web sites, wikis (see Fig. 6.2), and blogs can offer immediate assistance and assurance to a community, such as information on relief efforts, locations of impacted areas, potential dangers, shelter locations, donations, and ways to assist."[2]

- Decentralizing and Democratizing the Flow of Information
  The Internet makes it possible for crisis communication to become multidirectional (not just top–down) and interactive—meaning information can be acquired, shared, aggregated, and archived quickly and efficiently, provided people have the

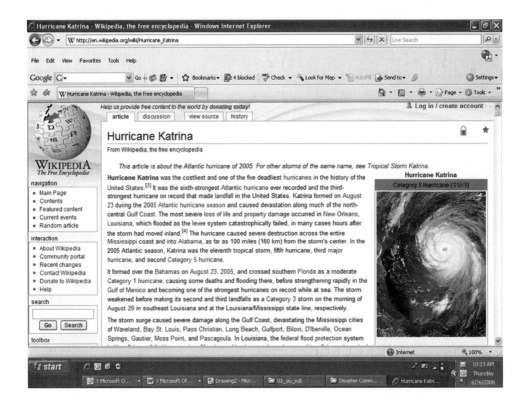

FIGURE 6.2 Wikipedia Hurricane Katrina Web page. Source: http://en.wikipedia.org/wiki/Hurricane_Katrina

means to access the technology. "This multidirectional form of crisis communication allow[s] the audience to compare and evaluate different sources and to understand better the biases of official information."[3]

• Humanizing the Crisis
Online crisis communications involves the use of personal technologies in public events. Unlike traditional media it allows people to express their emotions, to share "their story" in their own time and words, and to seek and provide information on a micro, intimate level about the intensely local.

    The stories and images contributed by citizen journalists, often in real time, faster, and unfiltered by traditional media, allows personalized coverage of an event once only prized if it were reported objectively.

• Expanding the Community
The whole world can and does watch. People living around the world have the opportunity to learn about the human tragedy that results from a disaster (provided they have Internet access) and this fosters a sense of global community. The messages and images carried about a disaster convey a sense of urgency to the world.[2]

---

[3] H.J. Bucher (2006, October 2). Crisis Communications and the Internet: Risk and Trust in a Global Media. http://www.firstmonday.org/issues/issue7_4/bucher/October 2, 2006.

- Enlarging the Perspective
  Not only do online technologies dramatically increase the number of people involved in the exchange of information, but new media provides new ways of looking at disasters. Tools like Google Earth make it possible to look at wide scale disasters like cyclone Nargis in Burma or the flooding of New Orleans. These tools provide rapidly available data that depict "the geographic extent of the event and satellite images provide a bird's eye view of the location."[2]

- Altering the Narrative
  "Different forms of media interact to fuel news stories and information dissemination. The Internet, online media, and blogs work in concert, remixing, and reamplifying information."[2]

  The media becomes the message. "The September 11 events demonstrated very clearly that media communication is inextricably interwoven in the crisis itself. Media reporting about crisis shapes the picture of the crisis, and is itself a factor in the dynamic of the crisis. Much has changed since the earliest newspapers of centuries ago, where months would lapse between events and their reporting in the media. Thanks to real-time coverage, the event and its image fall together today. That means no one can deal with a crisis without taking into account its images."[3]

- Enriching, Expanding, and Enhancing the Coverage
  The ability to capture and share events as they happen increases the numbers of "reporters;" removes time, distance, and institutional filters from the coverage of a crisis; and makes for better journalism. "In any disaster," explained *Toronto Globe and Mail* reporter Matthew Ingram, "One of the first things people look for is the eyewitness account, the first person description, and the man on the scene."

  Today, instead of sending one TV crew to an event after it occurs, "we now have a thousand, all of them recording, bearing witness, and publishing".[4]

Citizen Journalists and the Traditional Media

Key to this flow of information are the citizen journalists—the "first responders of the wired world." Citizen journalism (see Fig. 6.3) is the act of citizens "playing an active role in the process of collecting, reporting, analyzing, and disseminating news and information."[5] Citizen journalists are made up of the "former audience" armed with online information and photo and video-sharing technologies. "….These techniques are irrevocably changing the nature of journalism, because they're giving enormous new power to what had been a mostly passive audience in the past."[5]

---

[4] Gillmor, Dan (2006). *We the Media: Grassroots Journalism By the People, For the People,* O'Reilly Media Inc.
[5] S. Bowman and W. Chris (2003). *We Media: How Audiences are Shaping the Future of News and Information.* The Media Center at the American Press Institute.

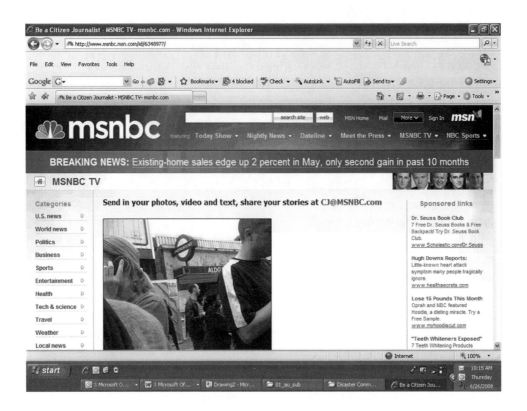

FIGURE 6.3 MSNBC Citizen Journalist Web page. Source: http://www.msnbc.msn.com/id/6348977/

"This is all about decentralization. Traditionally centralized news-gathering and distribution is being augmented (and some cases will be replaced) by what's happening at the edges of increasingly ubiquitous networks. People are combining powerful technological tools and innovative ideas, fundamentally altering the nature of journalism in this new century."[5]

And the news-gathering industry—unlike the government—has decided that the participation of citizens in disaster coverage is an asset for the community and the traditional media uses the information and images generated online to complement, expand, deepen, and, in some cases, substitute for their own coverage. The traditional media has begun to appreciate, incorporate, and rely on citizen journalism.

The willingness of traditional media to experiment is undoubtedly affected by the fact that their world is unraveling—newspaper readership has declined dramatically in the past two decades and with the advent of cable, TIVO, and online video streaming, the old line television networks have lost their monopoly as news providers and their command on the public's attention. Economically, new media and citizen journalists offer value to the newsroom at no cost.

Three models for incorporating and accommodating new media have emerged as follows:

- Calls for contribution
- Formal partnerships
- Replacement of traditional media altogether

Calls for Contribution

Mainstream media are now asking the "former audience" for help and actively encouraging citizens to submit content through dedicated portals. CNN, BBC, CBS, Reuters, Associated Press (AP), Al-Jazeera, *The Washington Post, The New York Times* and local papers, television, and radio stations now routinely ask for and feature the work of citizen journalists. The Web sites for these outlets feature both the invitation to contribute and directions for uploading or e-mailing content.

Jan Schaffer, the executive director of J-Lab at the University of Maryland explains that, "A huge architecture is being built, creating a new culture of citizen participation in the news." She provided examples of how people are powering newsrooms around the country:

"New media techniques include crowd sourcing—inviting readers or listeners or viewers to contribute pieces to a larger story. A newsroom in Fort Myers, FL has even recruited citizens, including a former FBI agent, to join Team Watchdog to assist in investigations.

"Google mashups are becoming a very cool way to map news in communities. For example, ChicagoCrime.org creates mashups to document where crimes take place, but other cit-media sites have used the software to invite citizen posts that track everything from potholes, to closed roads, to tear-downs and construction of McMansions.

"Real people are contributing audio and video to bring obituary announcements to life. For example, humorist Art Buchwald got the last word (and the last laugh) by recording his parting thoughts as part of his own obit in *The New York Times*.

"Mainstream print media is now getting the message that "the medium is the message" and they are using compelling citizen video to help tell their stories. *The Washington Post*'s series on "Being a Black Man" is a good example.

"Wikis are growing in popularity as gathering places for shared knowledge and information. Niche blogs are taking off, such as The Indianapolis Star's IndyMoms.com and aggregators are bringing it all together: BlogHer.com now links 10,000 blogs by, for, and about women. A local example, PhillyFuture.org snags blogs about Philadelphia.

"Mainstream media are also harnessing resources for greater community participation in sports coverage. *The Orlando Sentinel* set up Varsity MyTeam, which is a site featuring individual pages for every high school sports team and player who feed into databases tracking scores, rankings, and other statistics.

"Interactive clickable maps enabled citizens of Everett, WA to let public officials know what kind of development they wanted and didn't want on their waterfront."[6]

---

[6] J. Schaffer (2007, October 2). *Twenty in Thirty: Twenty Good Ideas for Citizen Participation.* Remarks at the Associated Press. Managing Editors' Conference. Fast Forward to the Future. http://www.j-lab.org/apme07notesp3.shtml

Formal Partnerships

Online news operations and traditional media are also entering into formal ventures in shared news gathering.

Global Voices Online (see Fig. 6.4), a nonprofit global citizens' media project founded at the Harvard Law School's Berkman Center for Internet and Society, was designed to fill the void left by economically-driven declines in international reporting by traditional news operations and to expand the "conversation" about world events by diversifying the numbers and sorts of voices engaged in coverage.

The Global Voices Online site asks: "The world is talking. Are you listening?" And explains:

"At a time when the international English-language media ignores many things that are important to large numbers of the world's citizens, Global Voices Online aims to redress some of the inequities in media attention by leveraging the power of citizen's media. We're using a wide variety of technologies, blogs, podcasts, photos, videos, wikis, tags, aggregators, and online chats—to call attention to conversations and points of view that we hope will shine a new light on the nature of our interconnected world."[7]

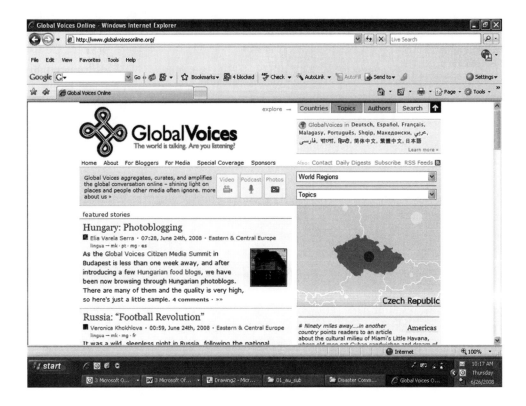

FIGURE 6.4 Global Voices Online Web page. Source: http://www.globalvoicesonline.org/

---

[7] Global Voices Online, *About on Home Page,* http://www.globalvoicesonline.org/about/

Global Voices Online invites citizen journalists to contribute or hires them as editors, "because they understand the context and relevance of information, views, and analysis being posted everyday from their countries and regions.... They are helping us make sense of it all."[7]

In the online world, where the rule is to publish, then filter, Global Voices Online has made itself a filter—and assigned itself a job that was once the domain of traditional media—determining what news was worth. "With tens of millions of people blogging all over the planet, how do you avoid being overwhelmed by information overload? How do you figure out who are the most influential or respected or credible bloggers or podcasters in any given country? Our international team of volunteer authors, regional blogger-editors, and translators are your guides to the global blogosphere."[7]

The value of Global Voices Online content and scope of coverage was recognized by Reuters International which entered into a formal alliance with the project on April 14, 2006. Reuters now uses Global Voices Online content as part of its reporting and to expand its coverage. And the editors of Global Voices seized the opportunity to join forces with Reuters as a way "to help Reuters—and the global media community as a whole—to understand blogging better and the impact of citizen's media on the world of journalism. We believe that the information, opinions and perspective that bloggers share complement conventional journalism and that bloggers and journalists can work together to give us a more accurate and representative picture of events and opinions around the world."[8] The AP has also entered into a formal partnership with NowPublic, an international site for crowd sourced news. Lou Ferrara, deputy managing editor, Multimedia and Sports for AP, explained "The AP is everywhere, but we can not be everywhere all the time. These folks have citizens all over."[9]

All AP bureaus now reach out to NowPublic, primarily for images and videos. Ferrara said the arrangement has transformed the culture of the AP newsroom. He cites the example of a cyclone in Oman—explaining it would have taken AP a day to get there, but they had photos the same day because of NowPublic.

AP is also using their collaboration with NowPublic to raise the quality of citizen photojournalism. Ferrara explained, "We've set up a page on NowPublic on how to take great photos, along with images showing why we used them. The photos need to be images that include people, illustrate the scale, the human emotion, and the context of a story."[9]

Replacing Traditional Media with Online News Sites

As more newspapers close their doors, communities are using the Internet and online technologies to fill the void. In other communities where traditional media has a

[8] E. Zuckerman (2006, April 14). Announcing our Alliance with Reuters. Global Voices Online, http://www.globalvoices online.org/2006/04/14/announcing-our-alliance-with-reuters/April 14, 2006

[9] L. Ferrara (2007, October 2). AP's "NowPublic" Initiative. *Remarks at the Associated Press. Managing Editors' Conference*, Fast Forward to the Future. http://www.j-lab.org/apme07notesp5.shtml

monopoly on the type and tone of coverage, online news sites are being created to provide opposing views and diversified coverage.

iBrattleboro.com was a pioneering online news site, established in 2003 in Brattleboro, Vermont. It offers much of the same content as a traditional newspaper, but it is written by the people of Brattleboro. In the site's welcome, participants in Brattleboro's original, locally owned citizen journalism site, are invited to "Read and write your own news, interviews, and more. Pick a local Brattleboro story and cover it yourself. Home of the Job Market, the Brattleboro Community Brain Trust, plus Brattleboro weather, stocks and finances, BrattleBarter, BrattleRide, mazes, links to comic, and more."

Greensboro101, created in North Carolina in 2005, is an online news site built around existing bloggers. The site aggregates blog contents to "deliver a more personal and sometimes probing view of Greensboro news and events." Founder Roch Smith, Jr. explained, "I was frustrated there was little opportunity beyond the 200-word, once-a-month letter to the editor to present an opposing view and no way to correct or counter the reporting of TV. It was simply incredible."

Jan Schaffer, executive director of J-Labs at the University of Maryland explained that "Some smart news organizations are concluding it's time for a new core mission, one that repositions the newspaper in the community and revisits knee-jerk practices."[10]

She recommended that news organizations construct the hubs that will enable ordinary people with passions and expertise submit content. And she recommended that new organizations "be on a constant lookout for the best of these efforts, trawling the blogosphere, hyperlocal news sites, nonprofits, advocacy groups, journalism schools, and neighborhood ListServs. Your goal is to give a megaphone to those with responsible momentum, recruit them to be a part of your network..."

"Ultimately, your goal is to rethink who are really the experts in that community. Is it just the heads of organizations, or people with titles, or elected officials, Or is it the people who live there day after day? What is the ethic that has ignored those voices or relegated them to the color quotes? A more responsible journalism would mine that expertise and amplify it. But first you have to find it and nurture it. This new mission is requiring journalists to embrace new partners, validate supplemental news channels, and support—without always controlling—a vibrant local newscape."[10]

New Media and Government

New media technologies and the participatory culture are changing the form and function of traditional media (see Fig. 6.5). But governments have been slow to use the new technology or exploit its capacity to gather and share news and information.

---

[10] J. Schaffer (2008, May 8). *Participatory Media: Challenges to the Conventions of Journalism.* Ruhl Lecture, University of Oregon. http://www.j-lab.org/ruhl_lecture_08.shtml

FIGURE 6.5 Florida Division of Emergency Management Media Web page. Source: http://www.fdem-mediacenter.org/

The technology that governments worldwide are starting to embrace is text messaging or SMS. As the survivors of disasters from 2005 Hurricane Katrina to the 2008 Sichuan earthquake have learned, this technology works when others do not. "Since SMS is more resilient to mass scale destruction of the telecommunications infrastructure, it can be the foundation for early warning systems."[11] And that is how governments from the Netherlands to India are using texting technology.

The Dutch government uses a mobile alert system based on cell broadcast technology—which does not require the sender to know the mobile phone number of the recipient. A cell broadcast message is more like a radio message—it's broadcast to a specific area (the government with the cooperation of the country's wireless industry divided the Netherlands into 5,000 cells [areas])—and anyone with a mobile phone will receive it. Finland uses a similar alert system.[12]

In India, their National Disaster Information System pushes out the warning simultaneously in 14 languages "through SMS and dynamically-generated voice messages to wireless public address systems and phones. The entire process is expected to take 33 seconds."[13]

---

[11] Hattotuwa, Sanjana (2007). *Who is Afraid of Citizen Journalists? Communicating Disasters*, TVA Asia Pacific and UNDP Regional Centre in Bangkok.

[12] J. Clothier (2005, November 10). *Dutch Trial SMS Disaster Alert System*. CNN.com, http://www.cnn.com/2005/TECH/11/09/dutch.disaster.warning/index.html

[13] J. Cascio (2006, February 16) "*National Disaster Information System in India*," WorldChanging.Com, http://www.worldchanging.com/archives//004113.html

In the United States, more government agencies are also using SMS, specifically "Twitter," which uses cell phones to send and post messages no longer than 140 characters online ("tweets").

The "Hey there!" text box presents an example of the use of Twitter (and tweets) by the Los Angeles Fire Department.[14]

Hey there! LAFD is using Twitter.

Twitter is a free service that lets you keep in touch with people using the Web, phone, or IM. **Join today** to start receiving **LAFD's** updates.

UPDATE: 3946 S. Bledsoe Ave. Firefighters were able to rescue 2 dogs, alive, from inside house... Read more at http://tinyurl.com/4z7wy6 about 8 hours ago from TwitterMail

UPDATE: 3946 S. Bledsoe Ave. Knockdown 13 minutes, 20 firefighters, no injuries—Ron Myers### about 9 hours ago from TwitterMail

Structure Fire 3946 S. Bledsoe Ave.; TG 672-D3; FS 62, Single family home with fire showing. no reported injuries.; Ch:7,12 @9:04 PM— ... about 9 hours ago from TwitterMail

LAFD

UPDATE: 15535 W. Devonshire St. Knockdown @ 2232. No reports of injury.—d'Lisa Davies### 10:39 PM May 29, 2008 from TwitterMail

Structure Fire 15535 W. Devonshire St.; TG 501-G4; FS 75, 1 story restaurant w/fire showing.... Read more at http://tinyurl.com/4jl6b7 10:13 PM May 29, 2008 from TwitterMail

UPDATE: 2449 N. Beachwood Dr. Correction: 3 story apt bldg w/1 unit on 1st floor well involv.... Read more at http://tinyurl.com/4akr7w 08:54 PM May 29, 2008 from TwitterMail

---

[14] Los Angeles Fire Department, Twitter Sign-Up Page, http://twitter.com/LAFD

It is of no surprise that the government has made the most and best use of the technology that can be used to make the old "top-down" model more efficient. The government is still in the business—albeit using new tools—of disseminating information using the command and control approach. For the most part, governments have yet to figure out how to partner with or exploit the tools that generate a two-way exchange of information.

Working with the News Media

Introduction

Working with the media—old and new—is core to effective disaster and emergency management communications. And working with the media has become increasingly important in these times of 24/7 news gathering and dissemination. The news hole will be filled—if not by official information channels, then by others. The information provided by citizen journalists and "first informers" on the scene has often proven to be accurate and occasionally inaccurate—but it is broadly accessible and not controlled by the government agency in charge of managing an event or the mainstream media charged with covering it.

New media technologies and citizen journalists now produce a glut of information and images—more than can be managed. And what was once a tense relationship between the two powers in a crisis—government and media—now involves three parties. The genie of online-generated and shared news cannot be put back into the bottle, it is a force to be reckoned with.

The Aspen Institute report, "*First Informers in the Disaster Zone: The Lessons of Katrina,*" noted in its conclusion: "...there was a difference in how the online environment changed the media mix and altered the flow of information during and after the disaster.... At times the traditional flow of information from government to media to public reversed course."[1]

Specifically, the Aspen Report listed as communications lessons learned from Katrina:

"• The digital communication revolution exposed novel channels and networks for information flow that require reexamination of the relationships between media, government, and citizens. The traditional top-down paradigm was replaced by a more dynamic flow of information that empowered citizens and created ad hoc distributive information networks.

• The disaster environment created a new cadre of "first informers" that introduced fledgling players in crisis communication who enhanced the amount of information and number of sources, challenged the old gatekeepers of government and the traditional media, and exacerbated the pre-existing problem of sorting out truth amid chaos.

---

[1] A. L. May (2006). *First Informers in the Disaster Zone: The Lessons of Katrina.* Berlin: The Aspen Institute.

- Journalists sought greater access to operational leaders and experts and more transparency by government. Government officials promised more of both but expressed concerns about exposing classified information, disseminating misinformation, and overtaxing personnel and resources that are already stretched thin.[1]"

The traditional media, in an "if you can't beat them, join them" approach that recognizes the value (and low-to-no financial costs) of using news, video, and photos produced by the public, is forming partnerships with online news sites and sources (bloggers). They recognize this content can augment, enrich, deepen, and even replace their own coverage. They understand the top-down flow of information has changed with the online culture and been transformed by the "world is flat" notion of peer-to-peer information exchanges. The idea of news as a lecture no longer holds. We have entered a world where news is more a conversation—where the audience is an active participant. And where the mantra for traditional media was once filter, then publish—it is now publish, then filter.[2]

The government—still uncomfortable with the old command and control model that required sharing information with the media and trusting television, radio, and print reporters to deliver it accurately—has yet to recognize or embrace the role of new media.

As government official Chet Lunner explained in the Aspen Institute forum on Katrina, *"We have enough trouble with things that do go through the [mainstream media] filter.* The amount of time and energy and social unrest by readers and/or the people trying to practice in the field dealing with these things that are exaggerated rumors, etc., is a problem. . . ."[1]

Yet online technologies and citizen news gatherers and disseminators have had an ever-expanding and increasingly influential role to play in the coverage of events and development of the disaster narrative since the December, 2004 South Asian Tsunami. But examples are starting to emerge of government agencies in the U.S. and abroad recognizing the power and reach of citizen journalists and online social networks. During Hurricane Katrina, the St. Tammany Parish Sheriff's office was persuaded to give out information through the Slidell Hurricane Damage Blog. Distressed by a dearth of information about his hometown, Slidell, a New Orleans suburb, evacuee Brian Oberkirch posted the blog from Dallas. "He started by aggregating anything he could find about Slidell on mainstream news sites and citizen sites such as Flickr.com, which features pictures posted by the site's users. As his posts built, Oberkirch increasingly made contact with friends and neighbors, who in turn became contributors. He persuaded the local sheriff's office to start feeding him information. Almost overnight, the suburb of about 26,000 people had a new media outlet, the Slidell Hurricane Damage Blog, which Oberkirch said drew 80,000 unique visitors in the first week."[1]

---

[2] C. Shirky (2003, January). The Music Business and the Big Flip. Clay Shirky's Writings About the Internet. http://www.shirky.com/writings/music_flip.html

And because, "researchers have argued that social networks within a community have positive effects on people's behavior in the four stages of disaster," Japan officials are experimenting with ways to use social networking sites akin to FaceBook and MySpace "with the intention to improve community building, the democratic process, and disaster management."[3]

It remains unclear how well the government will adapt to the new media environment that accelerates and reverses the information flow. But clearly, it will be "a challenge for cautious governmental hierarchies and an opportunity in which the new media can be used to improve situational awareness."[1]

A first step in breaking down silos, to build trust, and form partnerships with the media is to understand how newsrooms and operations work.

News Operations

Here are some basic facts of life about news gathering operations now:

The Never-Ending News Cycle: It's Never Too Late for News

Before the Internet became broadly available, a "news cycle" was generally 8–24 hours. The response to a charge leveled in the morning news was aired on the evening news or the afternoon edition, or the next morning's paper. No more.

The *Austin American-Statesman's* Health and Human Services Reporter, Corrie MacLaggan, says the news cycle "is never over. It's never too late. It used to be if public meetings went beyond time you had to file to make the press deadline, you left before the meeting was over. Now you stay, even if the meeting goes to four in the morning. Even after you've filed, you blog at home in the evenings, on weekends."[4]

The Internet has made the news cycle instantaneous and the newsroom a continuous 24/7 operation.

The public's "tapeworm" hunger for information and their ability to access it anytime has forced news operations and reporters to accelerate and multi-purpose their news gathering efforts.

According to Jinah Kim, a Los Angeles-based reporter for NBC and its local affiliate, "Everyone is in a race to get it out there first, and in a 24 hour news cycle there is more 'report now—retract later' type of news."[5]

Reporters Now Write Their Story, Do a Web Version, Blog, and Post Audio and Video

Driven by the ceaseless demand for information and financial downsizing, a fewer reporters are being asked to do more work. Kim explained that most local station's

---

[3] A. Schellong (2007). *Increasing Social Capital for Disaster Response through Social Networking Services (SSN) in Japanese Local Governments*. Amherst. National Center for Digital Government.

[4] C. MacLaggan Austin, Health and Human Services Reporter (2008, June 4). Interview with Kim Haddow. *American-Statesman.*

[5] J. Kim, NBC reporter (2008, May 12). Interview with Orli Cotel.

reporters are expected to file a Web story as well as a regular story. Network reporters are expected to blog everyday. The *Statesman's* MacLaggan now carries a digital audio recorder and video camera with her to news events—and posts what she records online on the newspaper's Web site before she writes her story.

Respect What's Being Generated Online by the Public: The Media Does

Viewer and reader submissions are an increasingly important and regular part of the news. Most stations—network and local—and newspapers feature requests and portals for citizen information and images.

iReport (www.cnn.com/ireport) is CNN's public journalism initiative that allows people from around the globe to contribute pictures and video of breaking news stories from their own towns and neighborhood. The site, with its headline "See it first. Your Stories. No Boundaries." includes an "Assignment Desk" which encourages citizen journalists to cover stories CNN is interested in telling on air—in effect "enlisting" an army of reporters to share their stories about living with $4 a gallon gas, their commute, or living in today's job market. The site also features tutorials on storytelling ("Tell your story like a pro" and "Shoot better video,") aimed at upping the quality of the submissions. CNN also weekly aggregates the best viewer submitted content to make up a weekend show, "News to Me" that airs on *Headline News.*

CNN's success with "iReport" has spawned a variety of similar initiatives, including ABC "i-caught" (http://ugv.abcnews.go.com), Fox Network's "U-Report" (www.foxnews.com/us/ureport) and MSNBC's "FirstPerson."

Radio stations are also encouraging participatory journalism. NPR's Washington, DC affiliate WAMU has launched a social network for its listeners called "The Conversation." "The Conversation," according to WAMU's Web site (http://conversation.wamu.org), "is an online meeting place for WAMU 88.5 listeners, producers, hosts, and reporters. On The Conversation, they can start forums on news topics—preferably something they heard on the radio—engage with other public radio listeners, give story ideas and news tips to WAMU 88.5 reporters and producers, and generally continue the on-air conversation online. . .

"The social network attempts to meet two needs: the ever-increasing desire by consumers of all media to communicate directly with not just news professionals, but with each other; and the need for a citizen journalism outlet that helps reporters and producers build networks of sources and ideas."

Reporters Mine Online Content for Story Ideas and Sources

Reporters pay attention to the Web. Online content is integrated into their reporting. "There is still some skepticism" about the quality and credibility of viewer-generated content in traditional newsrooms, according the NBC's Kim. "We verify viewer submissions on a case-by-case basis."

But reporters do recognize the contribution made by citizen journalists. "We can't be everywhere at once. Odds are we are not going to be driving in the neighborhood where a tree has fallen on a house. But the neighbors can capture the shot and get it to us," MacLaggan explained. And she said she had been given and used story ideas from survivors of Hurricane Rita, from comments on the paper's political blog and even used FaceBook to look for sources who might be willing to be interviewed for a story about the youth vote in the 2008 elections. Bottom line: online sites are a good way to pitch and promote your stories—the media is paying attention.

News Rooms Decide What's News Several Times a Day

Newsroom personnel hold story or editorial meetings several times a day to determine what stories they will cover, what will lead, and what visuals they will need to support the story.

Most local TV newsrooms have their morning meeting at 9:00 a.m. (some have them at 8:00 a.m. or 10:00 a.m.). Afternoon meetings can be at two or three; but some stations don't have an afternoon meeting. For network news there is a conference call in the morning with executive producers and senior producers at 9:00 a.m. EST, 6:00 a.m. PST. The *Austin American Statesmen* holds story meetings at 10:00 in the morning and at 1:45, 3:45, and 5:30 in the evening.

It helps to know when story meetings are held, so you can make a timely pitch for coverage. After the evening news line-up is decided is too late to make a pitch (unless news is breaking).

Who's Who in a TV Newsroom?

Station Manager: Responsible for administration and financial management at large stations. At smaller stations, the station manager also sets policy on news coverage and supervises overall operation, but generally does not influence daily content.

Program Director: Manages different programming divisions and the "mix" of content (e.g., news, music or entertainment programming, and sports) at large stations. The program director is unlikely to be involved in daily news decisions at any station.

News Director: Depending on the format and size of a station, the news director can be an administrative manager, a daily assignment director, or on-air broadcaster. In general, the smaller the news department, the more influence the news director will have. For example, if there is an assignment manager at a major TV station, the news director is unlikely to read or respond to press materials.

Assignment Editor: At larger stations, the assignment editor makes day-to-day decisions on what breaking news to cover and who will report on it. At smaller stations, the news director takes the place of an assignment editor.

Executive Producer: Lead person for a particular program or a series of programs. Sometimes the on-air host of a program is given the executive producer title.

Producer: Responsible for the overall tone and content of a single news program. Producers book guests on TV programs and assign crews to cover particular stories.

Public Affairs Director: In charge of public service announcements, community outreach, and special local programming.

Reporter: Covers stories given by assignment editor or news director. The news staffs of TV stations are usually smaller than daily newspapers and beats are often less defined. At large TV stations, reporters will have traditional beats like politics, arts, and education—keep in mind, however, that they are likely to be pulled off those beats when breaking news happens.

The Scoop on TV News Operations

As we learned earlier in this chapter—news operations are downsizing, fewer reporters are being asked to cover more news and in more ways—on the air and on the Web. Be sensitive to the fact that they are being over-taxed and under-capitalized.

As a rule most local stations (especially in smaller markets) are under-staffed, under-funded, and have very high turnover rate as employees get a year or two of experience and move on to bigger markets. Be aware of this and know to be patient with reporters who may still be learning how to do the job. In small markets the reporter may even do his/her own camera work.

In addition, local stations generally do several broadcasts a day. All the reporters/ producers & cameramen at the station contribute to multiple broadcasts, and sometimes work on different stories for each show. As a result, potential interviewees should be prepared to provide a little background to the reporter, who may not have had time to figure out the whole story. Sometimes the reporter may not even go to the event being covered. There may be just a cameraman who will also conduct the interview.

In larger markets (especially at the higher rated stations), there are usually more resources and the journalists usually have more experience.

Networks are a whole different animal with methods all their own. The networks will generally show up with more people and equipment than any local station. (This is changing somewhat as the networks parent companies try to cut costs.) Also, because they have less airtime to fill and many employees who are dedicated to specific shows, networks have a little more freedom than local stations to be able to plan a day or two ahead. So unless an interview is related to a breaking news story, the interviewee may have a little extra time to prepare and practice. Unless your local issue receives national media attention, you are less likely to encounter a network.

Building Relationships with Reporters

You might know how to write a great press release, turn folks out to a media event, and even come up with a catchy idea—but the best way to guarantee that all of that hard work will pay off is to develop professional relationships with local reporters. This can take a bit of effort up front, but it will pay off in the end. Eventually, the reporters will call *you* when something important happens, instead of you having to track them down!

The first step is for you to build a comprehensive media list. A media list is something that you should constantly be revising. When you see a great article in your local paper—any article, for example, that covers something that could possibly be linked to homeland security, such as first responder training, or a good piece about businesses engaged in disaster mitigation efforts—you should make note of that reporter's name. Send an e-mail to that reporter mention the article and let him/her know who you are and what you do. Include your signature with contact info at the end of the email. Follow up with an intro call, just to establish contact with them. Later on, when you have a great, timely story to pitch to them, it will help to not have to make a cold call.

If you are a new or starting a new community-preparedness program in a new location, set aside some time to call through all the contacts on your list. Be friendly and inquisitive—inevitably, people will direct you to other reporters who may cover the issues. At papers where you have no contact name, ask for the assignment editor, and he/she can direct you to the person most likely to cover disaster management issues. Every time you make a contact, end your call by asking if there is anyone else that they think you should talk to about the issue; this is a great way to grow your list.

Sample Intro Call Rap:

"Hi, my name is _____ and I'm calling from the _____. Are you on deadline, or do you have a second? Okay, great! I just wanted to call and introduce myself because I know you sometimes write on disaster management issues, and I'm involved in a new disaster mitigation program in our community. I wanted to give you my contact information so that you can feel free to get in touch with me if you have questions about any emergency management issues. Also, I wanted to give you the heads up that we'll be starting up a disaster preparedness program in our community. I'll keep you posted when we kick things off, and wanted to see if you prefer to receive our press releases via email or fax. [note their preference]. Great. Are there other reporters at your outlet that you would recommend I talk to about this? Thanks!"

This technique is best for developing relationships with journalists who work at newspapers, rather than television or radio stations. If you are in a larger media market, your local TV stations may have a reporter who specializes in covering disasters, so that is worth calling around to find out if there is someone who has that beat. Your local NPR affiliate is likely to have someone on that beat as well.

It is also worthwhile to call through the radio stations on your list and find out the name of the person responsible for Public Service Announcements, or PSAs. You could also send out a typed announcement regarding an upcoming local public hearing, community forum, slide show, or educational event, and the station's announcer may read it. PSAs are unlikely to create turnout to your event (if you are lucky, one or two people might show up because they heard it on the radio) but they do help to create buzz and visibility for your program and activities. Finding out the name and fax number of the person at the station in charge of PSAs is a good thing to do in the beginning of your program. When you are a week away from your event, you will have too much else going on to make those calls.

Another important way to build relationships with reporters is to take them out for lunch or coffee. This gives you some more time to connect with them, and to give them more in-depth information about your campaign. While it may seem intimidating to invite a reporter out for lunch, the reporter will appreciate the chance to get away from the office and be able to focus on the issue (and hey, who doesn't like free lunch?). Before meeting with the reporter, make sure you spend some time putting together a few different compelling story pitches, from different angles. You should assemble materials such as fact sheets, reports, human interest bios of your activists or volunteers, past press clips on the issue at hand, and a list of upcoming campaign events, in a folder that the reporter can keep.

□ □ □

Television Equipment—What's What?

Camera: Generally larger and a little more intimidating than your average video camera, but it serves the same purpose; it records pictures and sound onto videotape.

The tapes used in TV are also shorter than your average tape, 20–30 minutes, so you may have to stop and wait while the cameraman changes tapes.

B-Roll: This is the video used while the reporter is talking (but is not on camera). It must be visually interesting and relate to the issue (i.e., a forest you are trying to protect or a factory polluting air/water in your area). Usually a reporter will "write to video," which means that they will look at what they shot and write their story according to what they have on tape. A common example is, "Say dog, see dog."

Microphone:

1. Camera mike: Mounted directly onto the camera; least sensitive, but very common when the crew consists of one person (common in small markets)
2. Stick mike: Handheld by the reporter, who will lean it toward you while you are speaking
3. Boom mike: Large microphone mounted on a pole and suspended above you
4. Wireless mike: Small microphone, which can be clipped to your clothes. It is connected to a small battery pack/transmitter (The cord connecting the two is generally run under your shirt)

IFB (Interruptible fold-back): This is the earpiece you sometimes see reporters wearing it. It is used when you are doing an interview with a reporter who is in a different location from you. It allows you to hear the questions the reporter is asking, as well as the responses of other guests you may be debating. What you

Continued

hear is the show's audio "folded back" to you. Don't be surprised/distracted if you hear your own voice a second or so behind you. The fold-back may also be "interrupted" by the show's producer or director if they wish to speak with you.

Lights: These can range from a single light mounted on the camera to several lights mounted on stands pointing at you or at the background. The crew may even put colored gels or cellophane on the lights to adjust for the color of your skin or the background.

Monitor: A small TV screen that is connected to the camera. It allows the cameraman and the producer to see what the shot will look like. It will generally face away from you so you don't get distracted by watching yourself on TV.

Microwave Truck: These are used to send video back to the station from the field. They have an antenna that can be raised when they need to microwave video. Their range is relatively small, generally just in the immediate viewing area of a given station. They are used to cover live events and press conferences, reporter live shots, and if a news event/story is too far away for the crew to return to the station in time for the broadcast.

If you are organizing an event where stations will be using microwave trucks, they will need plenty of room on level ground to park. They also need to be away from obstructions & most importantly power lines. Over the last couple of years there have been a couple of instances where microwave antennae have been raised into power lines and have resulted in sometimes fatal electrocutions.

Satellite Truck: Satellite trucks serve much the same purpose as microwave trucks, but their range is much larger. They have large satellite dishes mounted on the back or the top of the truck and can send video anywhere in the world via satellite. They are commonly used by national networks and sometimes by local stations when a story is out of the range of a microwave truck.

Communications Outreach: A Checklist

- Why communicate?
- Know why very specifically you are reaching out to the media
  - To promote the program
  - To communicate program content—what should you do to prepare for a disaster?
  - To recruit participants or volunteers
- What's the story?

Continued

- What's the headline or lead that captures your story?
  - Write it out
- What aspects of the program do you want to promote?
  - Its name
  - Its purpose and value
  - How to participate
- What's the most valuable piece of content could you put out there? Communicate that and then add to it if time allows
- Who do you want to participate and what do they have to do?
- What are the qualifications?
- What's the job/time commitment?
- How to sign-up/contact you?
  - Have 800 numbers or Web site available
- How to make your story memorable?
  - Reach and frequency
  - Being seen often enough by your target audience to be remembered
- Who's your target?—You do not want to pitch a program for seniors on rap radio
- There's more than one way to tell the story:
  - Connect to a national event or what's already on the news (piggyback)—use a hurricane in Florida, and to explain how would we prepare for a hurricane here, who's working on it? Comment on what they are facing here
  - Pitch content—how preparedness could save lives, businesses, and money
  - Participant profiles
    - Someone unique with a story to tell
    - Someone part of a national trend—businesses everywhere want to reduce disaster losses
    - Someone was part of historical event—profile survivors of a disaster and promote their common link—their efforts to disaster proof their homes and businesses
  - Milestones
    - One thousandth preparedness training held
    - Dollars saved by the federal government not having to rebuild communities that prepared
  - Appeals for participants
    - Peer to peer opportunities—business and civic groups
    - Public service announcements
    - Online social networks—use new tools
- Match up your story with the right outlet(s)

Continued

- Analyze your market
- Make a list of TV and radio stations and print outlets: Google them if you are not sure of their format and demographic (who watches, listens to, or reads them)
- TV stations? Local Cable stations?
  - Do they do news? Local news?
  - Who are the guests now on their community newsmaker?
- Inventory online news sites and blogs in your community
- Most Web sites and bloggers have a specialty—politics, sports, local events
- More communities now have online news sites that augment or have replaced local newspapers
- What radio formats make sense for you? News/Talk? Music stations that have new blocks? NPR?
- Print—the weeklies—including alternatives; suburban papers and shoppers are just as valuable as the daily papers—they are more likely to print what you provide, including photos
- Magazines—are there any?—City magazines are popular. Local trade magazines and new letters—AARP/Nurses/Elks/Knights of Columbus?
- What's the best format for your story?
  - TV—where most people get their information, 70% of Americans say local TV news is their primary source of information
  - Use cable to target demographically and increase frequency—women watch the Lifetime Channel; men watch ESPN
  - Print—more ways to tell the story, deeper—news—ties to national story, local, features, calendar listings
  - Radio—highly targeted, intimate, loyalty—news, talk shows
  - BL06—generate comments and invite citizen opinions

Source: Haddow Communications (2004).

So How do You Get Media Coverage?

Pitch the story—invite reporters to cover a story. Be prepared to "sell" the story with good visuals, interviews, and a compelling hook or angle.

Hold a news conference—gather a short list of speakers to present "news"—information that is timely and new—to the press.

Stage an event—invite reporters to cover rallies, permit reporters to go through the training, be part of a media tour and other active, creative events. These need to be highly visual and provide lots of activity for the camera.

Continued

Piggyback on another news event or news story—offer comments responding to a news event or remark from another source.

Generate copy yourself—news releases, stories, op/eds and LTEs (Letters to the Editor). This gives you ultimate control over the message, but minimal control over the time and location of their appearance.

Source: Haddow Communications (2004).

What Does TV Want?

TV stations generally conduct three types of interviews:

Stand-up interview at a rally/event: These interviews are generally short and low tech. The interviewee is pulled aside in the middle of the rally to answer a few questions. Because these types of interviews happen quickly and on short notice there won't be a lot of time. Talk to the reporter ahead of time and get an idea of what they are looking for. The best thing an interviewee can do is be prepared ahead of time. Know the issue, talk about what you know, and be ready to think on your feet. Volunteers and volunteer coordinators are likely to encounter this type on interview.

Sit-down one-on-one interview: This type of interview generally lasts longer and goes more in-depth than stand-up interviews. In addition, the interviewee generally has some time to talk to the reporter and prepare for this type of interview before the cameraman and reporter show up. But they should always be prepared for unexpected questions. Other than being prepared intellectually for the interview, they may want to clean their office, get a glass of water, and turn off the air conditioner before the reporter shows up. (If the air conditioning (a/c) kicks on in the middle of the interview it changes the audio levels for the rest of the interview. It makes it difficult if the reporter wants to use sound bytes from both pre- and post-a/c. They will sound different.) Program directors are most likely to encounter this type of interview.

Remote live-shot: Other than being live in the studio, this is probably the most high-tech and maybe the most intimidating type of interview. The interviewee will be conversing with someone they can't see. They will be talking to an inanimate object, the camera, which itself is wired to a satellite dish and beaming the pictures back to the show's location. They will be wired with a wireless microphone and an IFB (the cord you see dangling out of an anchor or reporter's ear). And they are often (but not always) on live television. Having said all that, there is nothing to be frightened of. Preparing for this type of interview is really no different than preparing for a regular sit down interview. The interviewee will be able to talk to the producer or the reporter ahead of time. They should just

Continued

know their issue and be comfortable discussing it. Sometimes this type of interview will be in the format of a debate. (This is commonly done on shows like *Nightline* and the Sunday morning talk shows.) If it is a debate, the interviewee should not get defensive or argumentative. Relax, stay on message, and smile.

How Do I Match My Story to Media Outlet?

Core question: Is it news—timely and new information or is a feature "timeless" or is it analysis—the grist for a think piece for a columnist?

Who do I call? There are several points of entry—generally call the assignment editor at a TV station. Pitch individual reporters at newspapers and magazines. If you are looking for a booking on a newsmaker show, call the show's producer.

If you are holding a news conference event, do the following:

- Send an advisory 5 days ahead by fax.
- Call to make sure it's arrived and been noticed.
- Make your pitch (work off a printed pitch memo).
- Get a NAME—always get a name.
- Send another advisory 2 days ahead.
- Call to make sure it's arrived and been noticed.
- Ask if they intend to cover.
- Call the day before the event and the morning of.
- Ask if they intend to cover.

In addition to the advisory, there are other materials to prepare to distribute: In your press kit—have a news release with approved quotes, a fact sheet about the problem and your organization, bios of the speakers, and visuals—photos the papers are free to reproduce, graphs/charts that help tell your tale/video—"B-roll" the TV stations can use to tell your story—shot of previous disasters or homeowners applying hurricane shutters.

If you are making a straight pitch for coverage: know what the reporter's beat is and the kind of story they like—do they like lots of interviews, dramatic footage, or do they like to cover stories about volunteers and community service? E-mail a pitch letter and call.

Keys to All Successful Media Outreach

1. Relationship building.
   - You will not be dealing with these news organizations just once
   - You have many stories to tell in many ways

- You want to be able to call this reporter again—and you want the reporter to call you for comment on news stories or for background information
- Never lie
- When you do not know an answer, admit it and tell the reporter you will get back
- Get back when you say you will

2. Tell the tale well.
   - Use compelling visuals—even for newspaper and magazines
   - Imagery, Action
   - Use credible, prepared and attractive messengers

3. Get the message out. A few strategic rules will help you get the message out:
   - Know the message. What one thing do you want the viewer to remember when you're finished? Say it out loud several times to get the words right before you're on camera. The goal is to go into an interview knowing the exact sound bytes you are going to get out. And no matter what is asked—get those sound bytes out. You are in control—they can't make you say anything—they can only write/play what you say
   - Start with your conclusion—that's usually your message. Most of us have been taught to build the case and then reach the logical conclusion—you will not be given enough time in a TV interview to do that
     - Wrong way: "The number of violent storms and extreme weather events are increasing. There are proven, inexpensive ways to save lives and property. That's why you need to take steps now to prepare for the next natural disaster."
     - Right way: "You need to take steps now to prepare for the next natural disaster." Then if time allows, you can give specifics. But leading with your conclusion will help ensure that the media doesn't edit out or cut short your message.
   - Keep it short
     - In the 1960s, the average sound bite was almost: 40 long
     - In the 1980s, it was about: 20
     - Now, it's about: 08

If you speak in sound bites longer than that, you increase the odds your message will be edited.

The law of diminishing returns applies here too: the longer you talk, the less attention the viewer pays. People remember what they hear first. Remember people want to know what time it is, not how to build the watch. Craft your message with the time constraints of broadcast in mind. What you create for TV and radio will work in print; but not the other way around.

4. Be consistent and disciplined.

   Seize all media opportunities as a chance to repeat yourself. You will be much more likely to cut through the clutter if you're consistent. Odds are people will remember a consistent message of "2222222" better than they will remember a random array of different numbers "3,12,15,99,62,7." That's the heart of message discipline.

5. Use everyday, value-laden language. Avoid jargon, acronyms and talking about process.

   Use the language and tap into the values of your target audience. People want to protect their loved ones, their homes, and businesses from disasters

6. Remember who you're talking to—and it's not the reporter.

   The reporter is not your friend or a debating partner to be convinced. Reporters are a means to an end—you must pass through them to have a conversation with a larger audience not normally available to you—people impacted by a disaster.

□ □ □ ▬▬▬▬▬▬▬▬▬▬▬▬▬▬▬▬▬▬▬▬

Interview Tips

Television Interviews

Whether you are on a live talk show or being taped for the local evening news, the following tips will help you make the most of a TV interview.

PICK THE RIGHT SPOKESPERSON—Your spokesperson must first and foremost be somebody who knows the angles of your program and issue well, and has had some experience talking about and debating the topic. His/her belief and commitment to the issue should be immediately apparent.

MASTER THE SOUND BYTE—A sound byte is a quote or succinct one-liner that summarizes an opinion in a colorful but simple manner. Since there is a lot of competition for airtime, it is essential that sound bytes be kept to 15 seconds. As with quotes in press releases, lead with the conclusion since that's the bite you want them to take. The less editing that must be done by the TV Producer, the better. Avoid jargon, use analogies, and be personal by explaining how the issue affects this particular audience. Be brief and direct.

KNOW YOUR SHOW—Before you have your interview you should watch several episodes of the talk show or news broadcast to familiarize yourself with the program and with the type of questions your interviewer might ask. Also talk to the booker or producer ahead of time about the overall format of the show, including whether your interview is taped or live and if there will be a studio audience. If you are on a talk show, find out if there are other guests and the order of appearance.

KNOW YOUR MESSAGE—Before the interview, know the main points you want to make. Anticipate questions but do not over-rehearse—you want to sound natural. Steer the interview toward the points you want to make before

Continued

time runs out. You can take notes with you to the set, but don't read from them on the air.

REITERATE YOUR POINTS—Make an effort to repeat your major point over and over, especially in taped interviews. Remember that portions of the interview may be edited, and you don't want to risk having your main point edited out. Take advantage of pauses in the interview to make your point. You have a right to complete your answers, so if you are interrupted, politely and firmly insist on finishing your answer. Request clarification if you are asked a question you do not understand, and do not fudge facts and figures. Bring visuals along if they will help make your point more memorable.

PAY ATTENTION TO BODY LANGUAGE—Avoid exaggerated hand movements, tapping your foot, saying "you know" and "uh" a lot and clearing your throat. If you are sitting, sit upright, lean slightly forward, and never cross your legs. Look at the interviewer, not the camera. Use moderate hand gestures, smile, and nod. Remember that everything you do will be magnified.

ASSUME YOU ARE ALWAYS ON CAMERA—Even if you think the camera is focusing on someone else, act like you are on camera at all times. Do not say anything, even jokingly, that could be taken out of context or picked up and used out of context. When you are in the studio, assume the cameras are always rolling.

DRESS CAREFULLY—Women should dress in solid-colored, simple suits or dresses. Avoid light colors, busy patterns, sparkling or noisy jewelry, and heavy make-up. If doing an in studio interview, men should stick with light blue shirts and dark suits. Otherwise dress accordingly, look professional but don't overdress. Ties should not have wild colors. Both men and women should avoid clothes that are uncomfortable or that rustle and make noise against a microphone. Contact lenses are preferred over glasses.

Appearing on Television

1. Television is visual! So be visually likable!
   - People make up their mind about you in the first 10 seconds—its appearance, personae. Being nice, polite, and likeable is the key.
   - Look presentable. Wear something appropriate to the location. Always wear a tie—unless out in the woods or in the rain. But it shows respect. Do not wear loud colors/prints (red is bad, light blue is good), large jewelry, or anything with small prints or narrow stripes (even ties). Wearing tans and drab colors is a downer. Look sharp, respectful, and like the good guy.

Continued

- Hair needs to be combed. No hats or caps.
- Make-up should be worn (men too), even if it is just a little powder to reduce shine or to cover a sweaty forehead. Some camera crews carry make-up with them, but don't count on it.
- If you wear glasses, try non-reflective lenses, otherwise the cameraman may ask if you can remove them. Do not wear sunglasses.
- Make sure you don't have a piece of lettuce on the front of your teeth.
- Posture: leaning back in the chair makes you seem pompous. Sitting on the edge of the chair makes you seem engaged. It forces you to sit up straight—which seems engaged. It also allows you plenty of air to speak loudly—so you have presence. It fixes many problems. If legs are under the table, don't cross legs.
- No moving around, bouncing, fidgeting, wiggling, or squirming. If hand gestures are needed, keep movements small & controlled.
- Be friendly—smile. And don't raise the tone of your voice. Imagine you're debating your grandmother. You are always nice and never condescending or angry or feeling like you have to pick up the pace. Once you turn slightly rabid, you lose no matter what. This also means no finger pointing. Would you try to intimidate grandmother? Smile, be polite, and very nice.
- Turn your torso towards the other person. This gives them your full attention and looks very respectful. Turning just your head can appear disdainful, sarcastic, etc.
- Make eye contact with and talk to the reporter. Do not look at the camera (unless you are participating in an interview via satellite). Don't lose eye contact with the other person. So if they're talking and you're framing your next answer in your head, the tendency is to be looking down or away. But this is rude. So keep eye contact at ALL times.
- Assume the camera is on you all the time. Don't be preparing notes, looking at your watch. When you're not talking still have your torso turned to who's speaking, on the edge of your chair, complete eye contact.
- Background: Don't stand in front of a blank wall. If you are inside, make sure there is a sign or a poster behind you. If you are outside, almost anything works as long as it relates to the issue. Wherever you are don't stand in front of another organization's signs.

2. **Sound and what you *say* is important too!**
   - Empathize with others. Frame answers so you show your empathy in a real way.
   - Slow down—a universal problem for almost all of us.
   - Anticipate the questions. Try to get the questions ahead of time. Have your sound bytes ready for response and know how you'll use the question to get your sound byte.

Continued

- Don't turn away from the reporter or microphone while speaking.
- Be prepared to stop/wait/repeat yourself if there is an interruption (i.e., plane, loud truck).
- Avoid um, er, like, etc.
- No one-word answers. If a reporter asks a question that can be answered with yes or no, repeat the question in your answer.
- Don't lecture, be conversational.
- Politely correct the reporter if they have their facts wrong.
- Speak with the reporter beforehand and craft the sound byte to fit what they need.
- You don't need to be right on top of the microphone, but don't turn away from it while speaking.
- Don't speak negatively about the other side; take the high road. You don't want the story to become about a feud you may/may not be having with the other side.

3. **Practice, practice, practice.**
   - Say it out loud, in front of the mirror.
   - Have other's role play with you—it will also help you anticipate the questions.
   - Tape and review the media work you do. It's the best way to improve.

Source: Haddow Communications (2004, May).

Building an Effective Disaster Communications Capability in a Changing Media World

Introduction

The world of emergency management is changing rapidly. The onslaught of major catastrophic disasters around the world and the projected impact of global climate change have forced the emergency management community to reexamine all of its processes, including communications. Managing information before, during, and after a disaster has changed significantly in recent years and emergency operations at all levels—local, state, and national—must recognize and acknowledge this change and adapt accordingly.

As we have noted throughout this book, the biggest change in disaster communications has come with the emergence of the "first informers"—citizen journalists—and their use of new, widely available, online, and digital technologies to gather and share information and images. No organization working in the emergency management field—government, nongovernmental groups, voluntary agencies, private sectors—can ignore the role that these "first informers" and their information networks will play in future disasters. On the contrary, it is incumbent that emergency management organizations embrace the "new media" much the way traditional media outlets (i.e., television, radio, newspapers) have done.

In the future, emergency management organizations must establish partnerships with both the traditional media outlets and the new media in order to meet their primary communications mission of providing the public with timely and accurate information before, during, and after a disaster. These new partnerships must be based on the communications principles detailed in this book and take full advantage of the various information sources, networks, and messengers available to emergency management organizations.

The purpose of this chapter is to detail the seven elements that we believe will comprise an effective disaster communications capability in the future. These seven elements include:

- A communication plan
- Information coming in

- Information going out
- Messengers
- Staffing
- Training and exercises
- Monitor, update, and adapt

A Communication Plan

Disaster communication plans can take several forms. Planning for communicating in disaster response focuses on collecting, analyzing, and disseminating timely and accurate information to the public. A disaster response communication plan will include protocols for collecting information from a variety of sources including citizen journalists, analyzing this data in order to identify resource needs to match available resources to these needs, and then disseminating information concerning current conditions and actions to the public through both traditional and new media outlets. The plan will identify trusted messengers who will deliver disaster response information to the public. The plan will identify how disaster communications will be delivered to special needs and non-English-speaking populations. The disaster response communications plan will include a roster of local, state, and national media outlets, reporters, and first informers. This roster will be contacted to solicit information and to disseminate information back out to the public. Finally, the plan should include protocols for monitoring the media, identifying new sources of information collection or dissemination, and evaluating the effectiveness of the disaster communications. This information would be used to update the plan.

A communications plan for the recovery phase will look very similar to the disaster response plan. The recovery phase plan must also include protocols for collecting, analyzing, and disseminating timely and accurate information. During the recovery phase, much of the information to be disseminated to the public will come from government and other relief agencies and focus on available resources to help individuals and communities to rebuild. The communications plan must place a premium on delivering this information to the targeted audiences and must identify the appropriate communications mechanisms to communicate these messages. Information collection from the field from a wide variety of sources must be a priority in the communications plan for the recovery phase. Community relations staff, community leaders, and first informers are good sources of information on the progress of recovery activities and can provide valuable perspective of the mood of the individuals and communities impacted by the disaster. These sources are also effective in identifying communities, groups, and individuals who have been passed over by recovery programs.

Communication plans for hazard mitigation and preparedness programs can be very similar and include the basics of a good communications plan including:

- Goal—what do you hope to accomplish. Preparedness campaigns seek to help individuals and communities to be ready for the next disaster while the goal of most hazard mitigation programs are to promote community actions to reduce the impacts of future disasters as was the case in Napa, CA with the Flood Reduction Program.

- Objectives—how will you achieve your goal? A common objective for a preparedness campaign is to help families to create a family disaster plan. A hazard mitigation program may seek the support of the voters to pass a bond issue such as the bond issues passed by voters in the City of Berkeley, CA to retrofit critical buildings and infrastructure to resist earthquakes.

- Audiences—to whom will your communications plan be speaking? Target audiences for both preparedness and hazard mitigation communications campaigns may include residents in specific geographic locations, groups of individuals, such as homeowners, small business people, or families, special needs populations such as children, elderly, disabled, and hearing impaired, low-to-moderate income groups and neighborhoods, and individuals who own pets.

- Tools—what communications mechanisms will be used to communicate with the targeted audience(s)? These mechanisms should include working with traditional media outlets (television, radio, newspapers, and the Internet), the new media outlets (Short message system [SMS], bloggers, and bulletin boards), and neighborhood communications networks.

- Messengers—who will deliver the messages? Potential messengers include elected and appointed officials, trusted community leaders, and, as is the case in communicating with children, animated characters.

- Timetable—the length of the communications program. Plot the various tasks to be undertaken to successfully implement the plan over a time frame including days, months, and years.

- Evaluate—how well did the communications plan work? Develop means for evaluating the effectiveness of the communications campaign. Success could be measured in terms of raising awareness, prompting action, or securing the votes needed to pass a bond issue.

In all four phases of emergency management, it is important to have a comprehensive communications plan.

Information Coming In

Information is the basis of effective disaster communications. In disaster response, receiving and processing regular information concerning conditions at a disaster site and what is being done by agencies responding to the disaster allows disaster communicators to provide timely and accurate information to the public. In collecting this information, no potential source should be ignored and all possible sources should be encouraged to forward relevant information. To be successful in this task, you should identify all potential sources of information and develop working relationships with these various sources before the next disaster strikes. You must also be prepared to identify and partner with new sources of information as they come on the scene in the aftermath of a disaster.

Potential disaster information sources include:

- Government damage assessment teams—government disaster agencies at every level have staff responsible for assessing damages in the aftermath of a disaster. For a major disaster, a damage assessment team may include representatives from local, state, and federal response agencies. The information collected will include deaths; injuries; damages to homes, infrastructure, and the environment; and other critical data.

- First responders—among the first on the scene at any disaster, equipped with the necessary communications devices and trained to be observant.

- Voluntary agencies—these groups often have members or volunteers located in the disaster areas trained in damage assessment who can make first and ongoing assessments. For example, the Red Cross has extensive experience in reporting damage to homes and the number of people evacuated and in shelters.

- Community leaders—trusted leaders who have their own neighborhood network or work with community-based organizations with networks into the community can be a valuable source of on-the-ground information.

- First informers—individuals in the disaster site with the wherewithal to collect information and images and to communicate information and images by cell phones, hand held devices, or laptops.

- New media—Blogs (Web logs), Google Earth, Google Map, Wikis (Wikipedia), SMS (text messaging postings—Twitter), Flickr, Picasa (photo survey sites), and YouTube (video sharing sites).

- Online news sites—aggregate of community news, information, and opinion (ibrattleboro).

- Traditional media—television, radio, and newspaper reporters, editors, and news producers can be good sources of information, especially if they have deployed news crews to the disaster area before or just after a disaster strikes.

Having identified the potential information sources in your area, you must reach out to these sources to develop a working partnership and to put in place whatever protocols and technologies are needed to accept information from these sources. It is important that all potential sources of information understand what types of information you need from any situation so that they are looking for the information you need to make decisions. Government response agencies and voluntary agencies practicing National Information Management System (NIMS) and Incident Command System (ICS) will know what information to collect. You must reach out to the nongovernmental, nontraditional information sources before the next disaster to let them know what information you need and how to communicate that information to you.

Ideas for developing these working partnerships with nongovernmental, nontraditional information sources include:

- Build neighborhood communications networks—partner with community-based organizations, churches, and neighborhood associations to build neighborhood communications networks. Local residents can be trained in information collection, maybe as part of community emergency response team (CERT) training, and local community leaders can be entrusted to collect this information and forward it to emergency officials. These networks could also be used to send messages from emergency officials to neighborhood residents through trusted community leaders.

- Create and distribute a disaster information protocol for first informers—list what information you will be seeking over the course of a disaster response and get this list out to the public. Make sure they know where to e-mail or post the information and images they collect.

- Establish a point of contact within your organization for information sources—designate staff that are accessible and will work with information sources during a disaster.

- Create an electronic portal for information from the field—wikis and Web logs (blogs) can accept and aggregate comments from users, set up a Twitter Web site that can be updated via text messages, and create a homepage on YouTube and Flickr (see Fig. 8.1).

- Include first informers and traditional and new media outlets in disaster response training and exercises—incorporate these information sources into your disaster exercises to identify issues and gaps and to update plans accordingly. Media are not always included in exercises nor are first informers,

FIGURE 8.1 Flickr Web page. Source: http://www.flickr.com/

but by including these groups in your exercises you make the exercise more authentic, you create an opportunity to identify difficult issues prior to facing them in the next disasters, and you can make appropriate adjustments. It is also a chance to get to know each other.

- Meet with traditional and new media types on a regular basis—another way to create personal relationships with these critical partners in any disaster response.
- Include information sources in your after-action debrief—their perspectives and experiences can be used to update the plan and operations.

Many of these information sources can be identified as part of hazard mitigation and preparedness campaigns. Working relationships can be developed during these non-disaster periods that will facilitate information collection and flow in disaster response.

Information Going Out

If information coming in is the basis for disaster communications, then information going out is the goal. Timely and accurate information can save lives in disaster response and in hazard mitigation and preparedness programs. In getting information to the public, you must use all the available communications mechanisms including:

- Traditional media—television, radio, newspapers, and the Internet
- New media—post new information on community Web sites, blogs, wikis, and bulletin boards; share timely photos and video online and tell traditional media that online outlets are being updated routinely
- Neighborhood communications networks—trusted community leaders who go door-to-door

Historically, emergency officials have disseminated disaster information to the traditional media by means of press conferences, briefings, tours of the disaster site, one-on-one interviews with disaster officials, press releases, situation reports, and postings on the Internet. Radio actualities, photographs, and videotape have also been provided to traditional media. In major disasters, emergency management agencies have used satellite uplinks and video and audio press conferences to reach traditional media outlets across large sections of the country.

Disseminating information through new media outlets is something new for emergency officials and will require patience and understanding of how these new media function with their audiences. Most of this work can occur during non-disaster periods. This is the time to learn more about Wikipedia, Twitter, blogs, Flickr, Face-Book, YouTube, and social networking sites, and to discover how you as an emergency manager can best use these new media to deliver preparedness and hazard mitigation messages as well as communicate with their target audiences in the disaster response and recovery phases.

Prior to the next disaster you might consider:

- Starting a blog—get your message out there about the risks your community faces; how to take action to reduce those risks and protect your family, home, and business; how to prepare for the next disaster; when to evacuate and how; what will happen when your organization responds; and how members of your community can become first informers. (See Eric Holdeman's "Another Voice" for comments on blogging.)

☐ ☐ ☐ ━━━━━━━━━━━━━━━━━━━━━

Another Voice: Eric Holdeman

Eric Holdeman, former director of the King County Office of Emergency Management, is a principal with ICF International.

Blogging

We are living in the information age. The rise of computers and the internet has provided the opportunity to now share information and knowledge like never before. Only the invention of the Gutenberg's printing press rivals the information availability explosion that we are currently living in.

The culture of professional emergency managers is to share information with other emergency managers and other professions. Emergency management crosses the entire spectrum of interests in communities. The private sector, public sector, and nonprofit sectors are all areas of interest to an emergency manager preparing a community for the next disaster.

With this in mind, it was only natural to begin blogging on the topic of emergency management and homeland security. It started innocently enough by establishing e-mail lists for the various disciplines. When I'd come across information that would be of interest I'd share that with the appropriate spectrum of people and organizations that I had on my e-mail list. There were some days when I was sending 10 or more e-mails a day. Maintaining a viable e-mail list in our mobile society was also a time consuming proposition. One of my staff who was administering our King County Office of Emergency Management (OEM) Web site suggested establishing an "Eric's Corner" Web link on our King County Web site and then inviting people to sign up to get weekly updates "pushed" out to them. Without knowing it I had "backed into" the world of blogging. Besides sharing facts and documents, I was also providing a bit of commentary if I had an opinion on the information being shared.

Putting the mechanics of a blog in place was not that difficult, but establishing a listserv to push updates out proved more challenging. I found that King County did not have the capacity to do another listserv and I was stymied for a period of time. Then through casual conversations with staff from other organizations, one of them, the City of Seattle's Information Technology (IT) Office,

Continued

offered to host the listserv that pushed the blog updates out—and for no charge, where in my own jurisdiction I would have had to pay for the service. This is a great example of the level of cooperation that is needed if regional enterprises are to thrive.

After leaving King County I was able to establish a new blog, "Disaster-Zone" that operates on my company's Web site. The advantage in having a company sponsored Web presence is that it enables me to tap into the technical expertise of Web professionals, which I would not have if I were blogging on my own. It also has enabled the establishment of another listserv function that again pushes out information to people in "Weekly Updates." There are currently almost 1000 people who receive weekly Disaster-Zone blog updates. Technology has also advanced so that people who want to be notified of updates as they occur can sign up for Really Simple Syndication (RSS) which is a blogging tool available to people who desire the updated blog postings as they happen (see Fig. 8.2).

Information is power. Some people chose to hoard it in order to maintain control over what gets done or doesn't get done. The opposite of that thinking, which I follow, is that if I share what I know with others, I empower them to become better informed and therefore more effective in how they prepare their organizations, communities, and regions. Sharing information in effect gives

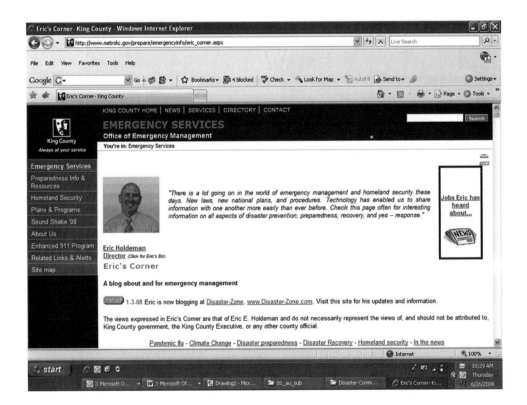

FIGURE 8.2 Eric's Corner Web page. Source: http://www.metrokc.gov/prepare/emergencyinfo/eric_corner.aspx

Continued

immortality to the person who is willing to share what they know. And, what you know should not die with you. It would be such a waste of a precious resource, years, sometimes decades, of experience which means hundreds or thousands of mistakes that you learned from.

People, when they have information, are empowered to make better decisions that may in some cases impact tens of thousands of people during disasters. I have found that blogging is a form of "mentoring" that allows a person to coach others in a profession that is still finding its way. If I can blog, anyone can! Try it and share what you know with others. Reap the rewards of knowing that together we are a stronger profession, and one that is known for collaboration.

- Create a bulletin board—this could serve as a link to community leaders involved in hazard mitigation and preparedness programs in the neighborhoods and could be accessed by all community members before, during, and after a disaster.
- Get on Wikipedia—load preparedness and hazard mitigation information and links for more information on the site. Understand that this site will grow with information added by readers.
- Start a YouTube site—that features "How To" videos on how to disaster-proof your home, office, and business. Post videos that explain how to survive the next disaster (how much water and food to have on hand, where to go for information).
- Create a Google Map—of the locations of designated shelters and evacuation routes.

When the next disaster strikes, consider:

- Regular updates on your blog—allows you a direct link to members of your community. Include time in your schedule to get interactive and answer questions and inquiries.
- Regular updates on your bulletin board—again another opportunity to talk directly to members of the community. Another opportunity to get interactive.
- Review and update Wikipedia—place your information in the Wikipedia file on the disaster and keep it regularly updated. Update disaster aid and shelter information, links to missing persons' sites, correct inaccurate information, and confront rumors.
- Post on YouTube—videos from informational briefings, from affected neighborhoods, and appeals for help.
- Update Google Map—to show locations of open shelters and hospitals.
- Display on Google Earth—locations of affected areas.

Maintain and regularly update all of these sites during the recovery phase.

Messengers

The person who delivers the messages plays a critical role in disaster communications. The messengers put a human face on disaster response and these people are critical to building confidence in the public that people will be helped and their community will recover. Public Information Officers (PIOs) regularly deliver information and messages to the media and the public. However, the primary face of the disaster response should be an elected or appointed official (i.e., mayor, governor, county administrator, city manager) or the director of the emergency management agency or both. These individuals bring a measure of authority to their role as messenger and, in the case of the emergency management director, someone who is in charge of response and recovery operations.

The public wants to hear from an authority figure and the media wants to know that the person they are talking to is the one making the decisions. Elected officials who served as successful messengers in recent disasters include California Governor Arnold Schwarzenegger during the 2007 southern California wildfires, New York City Mayor Rudy Giuliani during the September 11 attacks, Florida Governor Jeb Bush during the four hurricanes that struck Florida in 2004, and Oklahoma Governor Frank Keating during the 1995 Oklahoma City bombing. Successful emergency managers as messengers include former Federal Emergency Management Agency (FEMA) Director James Lee Witt and California Office of Emergency Services Director Dick Andrews in the 1994 Northridge earthquake and Craig Fugate with the Florida Division of Emergency Management during recent hurricanes, tornadoes, and wildfires in Florida. Former FEMA Director Witt and Former President Clinton worked very well together in delivering messages concerning federal relief programs in numerous disasters in the 1990s.

Prior to the next disaster, each emergency management agency should determine if an elected or appointed official will serve as the primary messenger alone or in tandem with the emergency agency director (see Fig. 8.3). It is best to work out in advance what types of information will be delivered by which messenger. Protocols for briefing books and situational updates should be developed. A determination should be made as to who will lead press briefings and news conferences, who will be available to the media for one-on-one interviews and who will be involved in communicating with the new media outlets. Again, all of these activities can be shared by the elected/appointed official and the emergency agency director.

Emergency management agencies should also designate appropriate senior managers who will be made available to both the traditional and new media to provide specific information on their activities and perspective. This is helpful in even the smallest disaster when persons with expertise in specific facets of the response can be very helpful in delivering disaster response information and messages.

Involving the designated elected/appointed officials and the agency director in hazard mitigation and preparedness communications will help them to prepare for communicating in disaster response and recovery and will make them familiar with the public as disaster communications messengers.

FIGURE 8.3 Tampa, FL, May 11, 2005—Under Secretary Michael D. Brown and Florida Governor Jeb Bush brief the media on FEMA's preparations for the 2005 hurricane season. FEMA photo/Leif Skoogfors.

Staffing

Not many emergency management agencies have a single communications specialist much less a communications staff. Federal agencies such as FEMA, Department of Homeland Security (DHS), Health and Human Services (HHS), and others involved in disaster have extensive communications staff (see Fig. 8.4). Most state emergency management operations have at least a communications director. The depth of staff support for communications varies widely. Emergency management agencies in major cities in the United States often have communications directors and in some cases extensive communications staff. Small to midsize cities and communities are unlikely to have a communications director or staff.

The time has come for all organizations involved in emergency management to establish an ongoing communications staff capability. For agencies in small to midsized communities this may require enlisting help from the local government's communications staff. One way to do this is to provide funding for a percentage of this individual's time each month. In this way communications activities required during non-disaster periods could be acquired on a consistent basis. This will also allow for the local government communications staff and director to become better informed of the emergency management agency's activities and be better prepared to work with the emergency agency director during disaster response and recovery.

FIGURE 8.4 Mobile, Ala., May 3, 2006—FEMA Deputy Federal Coordinating Officer Jesse Munoz addresses a press conference at the conclusion of today's public display of the National Oceanic and Atmospheric Administration (NOAA) Hurricane Hunter Research Aircraft. Photo by George Armstrong/FEMA.

For large cities and federal and voluntary agencies with existing communications staff it is now a matter of reordering priorities to meet the demands of working with the new media. Staff will be required to establish and maintain working relationships with new media outlets and to interact with various blogs, bulletin boards, social networking sites, and other new media outlets that serve their community. At minimum, there should be one designated staff person on the communications staff who is responsible for the day-to-day interaction with new media. Additional staff should be made available in a major disaster to work with these groups.

The new media designated staff would also work with new media outlets in promoting hazard mitigation and preparedness campaigns in the community and serve as the staff support for the establishment and maintenance of neighborhood communications networks working with trusted leaders in the community.

Training and Exercises

An effective disaster communications operation requires well trained messengers and staff and should be a vital part of all disaster exercises. Elected/appointed officials, agency directors, and PIOs should all receive formal media training in order to become comfortable working with the media to communicate disaster messages to the public. Media training teaches how to communicate a message effectively, techniques for fielding difficult questions, and provides the opportunity to practice delivery outside the crucible of a crisis. If possible, media training should be provided to senior staff who may appear in the media.

Staff training should come in several forms including:

- Media Relations—learning how to work with traditional and new media including meeting deadlines, responding to inquiries, scheduling interviews, and understanding what types of information each media outlet requires and how a news operation works.
- New Media—learn what a blog is, how social networking works, and how to establish and maintain a neighborhood communications network.
- Marketing—learn how to pitch a story idea for a preparedness program or hazard mitigation project to all forms of media, how to develop supporting materials for preparedness and hazard mitigation campaigns, and how to evaluate the effectiveness of such efforts.

Communications operations must always be included in future disaster exercises. It is highly recommended that these exercises include reporters from traditional media outlets and representatives from the new media, including bloggers and online news sites. Working with new media and online news sites should be included in exercises such as updating and correcting a Wikipedia site and posting information on a community bulletin board. Community leaders involved in neighborhood communications networks should also be included in the exercise.

Monitor, Update, and Adapt

Staff should be assigned to regularly monitor all media outlets. Summaries of news stories in the traditional media should be compiled regularly. Staff should routinely monitor new media outlets and provide regular summaries of news on these sites. This activity is especially important during a disaster response. Through monitoring, the media staff is capable of identifying problems and issues early in the process and can shape communications strategies to address these issues before they become big problems. This is also an opportunity to identify trends in how information flows through the media to the public and to identify areas for improvement of message development and delivery. Regular monitoring will identify rumors and misinformation and speed corrections.

The information collected as part of monitoring activities can be used to update communications plans, strategies, and tactics. This data can be used to determine how to allocate staff resources and to update training and exercise programs.

New media will continue to emerge as new technologies are developed and become widely accepted. Emergency management agencies must be constantly on the look out for emerging communications technologies and opportunities. Agencies must adapt to changing media constantly and strive not to become fixed to any one media.

Conclusion

The changing shape of emergency management in the coming years will demand that communications take a larger role in all emergency operations and programming. Incorporating new media forms and functions into communications plans and strategies and adapting to new technologies will be the order of the day for all emergency management agencies. Emergency officials can no longer avoid communicating with the media and the public. Emergency agencies must accept the expanded role of communications in all four phases of emergency management and embrace it as a valuable tool in meeting the needs of the public.

Resources

The purpose of this section is to provide additional information that practitioners can use to design, implement, and maintain an effective disaster communications capability. We have included the following:

Glossary of Terms—provides definitions for new media terms, emergency management communications-related terms, and television newsroom terms.

Innovations—summaries of recent innovations in disaster communications with weblinks to additional information.

Disaster-Related Newsletters—list of online and print newsletters focused on emergency management and business continuity issues, including communications-related issues.

Disaster Websites—list of websites for new media, general emergency management, response, preparedness, and media support. URLs are provided for all.

Bloggers—list of bloggers involved in emergency management issues with a long list of media and individual bloggers related to Hurricane Katrina. URLs are provided for all.

Special Needs Populations—information on communicating with special needs populations in all four phases of emergency management.

Preparedness Messages—papers and research reports concerning how best to craft and communicate emergency preparedness messages to the public.

Research Reports—list of academic and governmental research reports on disaster communications. Summaries/excerpts and URLs are provided for all.

Communications Plans/Guides—summaries and weblinks to several disaster communications guides to building a communications plan.

Case Studies—summaries and weblinks to five case studies prepared by FEMA focused or communications in disaster response and preparedness.

National Media Outlets—list of traditional national news outlets with weblinks to their new media operations.

Online News Services—examples of online news services serving communities across the country.

Books—list of books on new media and its use in disaster communications.

☐ ☐ ☐

Sources for the Resources Section

A variety of sources were used in compiling the information presented in this section including searches of the Internet by the authors and those books and reports listed below. It should be noted that the summaries provided for information sources identified in this section are most often taken directly from the reports and websites where the information was located so that the most accurate description of the information available is presented to the reader.

Assessing Your Disaster Public Awareness Program: A guide to strengthening public education, 2006, Emergency Management Accreditation Program, The Council of State Governments, through support from the Alfred P. Sloan Foundation, October 2006.

Social Media: Staying in Touch with Today's Online Community. 2008. Presentation by Jeremy Lasich, Deputy Director for Communications, Fairfax County Office of Public Affairs, Fairfax County, Virginia.

Wikipedia.org, 2008.

Working with the Media, 2004, Presentation by Haddow Communications.

Laituri, Melinda and Kris Kodrich, 2008, "On Line Disaster Response Community: People as Sensors of High Magnitude Disasters Using Internet GIS," Colorado State University, 2008.

☐ ☐ ☐

Glossary of Terms

Assignment Editor: At larger stations makes day-to-day decisions on what breaking news to cover and who will report on it. At small stations, the news director takes the place of an assignment editor.

Blog: (An abridgment of the term web log) is a website, usually maintained by an individual, with regular entries of commentary, descriptions of events, or other material such as graphics or video. Entries are commonly displayed in reverse chronological order. "Blog" can also be used as a verb, meaning to maintain or add content to a blog.

B-Roll: This is the video used while the reporter is talking (but is not on camera). It must be visually interesting and relate to the issue (i.e. a forest you are trying to protect, or a factory polluting air/water in your area). Usually a reporter will "write to video," which means that they will look at what they shot and write their story according to what they have on tape. A common example is, "Say dog, see dog."

Citizen Journalism: Also known as public or participatory journalism, is the act of citizens "playing an active role in the process of collecting, reporting, analyzing, and disseminating news and information," according to the seminal report "We Media: How Audiences are Shaping the Future of News and Information," by Shayne Bowman and Chris Willis.

Del.icio.us: Is a **social bookmarking** website—the primary purpose is to store your bookmarks online, which allows you to access the same bookmarks from any computer. You can also see the interesting links that other people bookmark.

Digg: Is a **user-driven social content news website**—everything on Digg is submitted by the community. After users submit content, other people read the submission and Digg what they like best.

Emergency Management Program: A jurisdiction-wide system that provides for management and coordination of prevention, mitigation, preparedness, response, and recovery activities for all hazards. The system encompasses all organizations, agencies, departments, entities, and individuals responsible for emergency management and homeland security *(EMAP Standard, April 2006)*.

Emergency Public Information: Information that is disseminated primarily in anticipation of an emergency or during an emergency. In addition to providing situational information to the public, it also frequently provides directive actions required to be taken by the general public *(NIMS, March 2004)*.

Executive Producer: Lead person for a particular program or a series of programs. Sometimes the on-air host of a program is given the executive producer title. If you are organizing an event where stations will be using microwave trucks they will need plenty of room on level ground to park. They also need to be away from obstructions and most importantly power lines. Over the last couple of years there have been a couple of instances where microwave antennae have been raised into power lines and have resulted in sometimes fatal electrocutions.

Flickr: Is an online photo management and sharing application in the world designed to help people make their content available to the people who matter to them and to enable new ways of organizing photos and video. Flickr gets photos and video from the web, from mobile devices, from the users' home computers, and from whatever software they are using to manage their content and pushes them out in as many ways as possible: on the Flickr website, in RSS feeds, by email, by posting to outside blogs, or ways we haven't thought of yet.

IFB (Interruptible Fold-back): This is the earpiece you sometimes see reporters wearing. It is used when you are doing an interview with a reporter who is in a different location from you. It allows you to hear the questions the reporter is asking, as well as the responses of other guests you may be debating. What you hear is the show's audio "folded back" to you. Don't be surprised/distracted if you hear your own voice a second or so behind you. The fold-back may also be "interrupted" by the shows producer or director if they wish to speak with you.

JIC (Joint Information Center): A facility established to coordinate all incident-related public information activities. It is the central point of contact for all news media at the scene of the incident. Public information officials from all participating agencies should collocate at the JIC *(NIMS, March 2004)*.

JIS (Joint Information System): Integrates incident information and public affairs into a cohesive organization designed to provide consistent, coordinated, timely information during crisis or incident operations. The mission of the JIS is to provide a structure and system for developing and delivering coordinated interagency messages; developing, recommending, and executing public information plans and strategies on behalf of the Incident Commander; advising the Incident Commander concerning public affairs issues that could affect a response effort; and controlling rumors and inaccurate information that could undermine public confidence in the emergency response effort *(NIMS, March 2004)*.

Lights: These can range from a single light mounted on the camera to several lights mounted on stands pointing at you or at the background. The crew may even put colored gels or cellophane on the lights to adjust for the color of your skin or the background.

Mashup: is a Web site or Web application that seamlessly combines content from more than one source into an integrated experience. The term derives from its similar use in pop music, where a mashup is a category of music where the tune from one song is combined with the vocals from another. Example: a Web site for an amusement park that contains a Mapquest page for visitors to get directions.

Microphone:

1. Camera mike: Mounted directly onto the camera; least sensitive, but very common when the crew consists of one person (common in small markets).
2. Stick mike: Handheld by the reporter, who will lean it toward you while you are speaking.
3. Boom mike: Large microphone mounted on a pole and suspended above you.
4. Wireless mike: Small microphone, which can be clipped to your clothes. It is connected to a small battery pack/transmitter. (The cord connecting the two is generally run under your shirt.)

Microwave Truck: These are used to send video back to the station from the field. They have an antenna that can be raised when they need to microwave video. Their range is relatively small, generally just in the immediate viewing area of a given station. They are used for to cover live events & press conferences, reporter live shots, and if a news event/story is too far away for the crew to return to the station in time for the broadcast.

Monitor: A small TV screen that is connected to the camera. It allows the cameraman and the producer to see what the shot will look like. It will generally face away from you so you don't get distracted by watching yourself on TV.

News Director: Depending on the format and size of a station, the news director can be an administrative manager, a daily assignment director, or on-air broadcaster. In general, the smaller the news department, the more influence the news director will have. For example, if there is an assignment manager at a major TV station, the news director is unlikely to read or respond to press materials.

PIO (Public Information Officer): A member of the Command Staff responsible for interfacing with the public and media or with other agencies with incident-related information requirements *(NIMS, March 2004)*.

Producer: Responsible for the overall tone and content of a single news program. Producers book guests on TV programs and assign crews to cover particular stories.

Program Director: Manages different programming divisions and the "mix" of content (e.g., news, music or entertainment programming, and sports) at large stations. The program director is unlikely to be involved in daily news decisions at any station.

Public Affairs Director: In charge of public service announcements, community outreach, and special programming.

Public Education: The process of making the public aware of their risks and preparing public information activities.

Public Information Systems: Processes, procedures, and systems for communicating timely and accurate information to the public during crisis or emergency situations (NIMS, March 2004).

Public Information: Messages and the delivery of messages to the public in anticipation of and during an incident. Public information is incident specific and includes the development and release of messages in real time as a key function in a jurisdiction's incident management system *(EMAP working group)*.

Reporter: Covers stories given by assignment editor or news director. The news staff of TV stations are usually smaller than daily newspapers and beats are often less defined. At large TV stations, reporters will have traditional beats like politics, arts and education—keep in mind, however, they are likely to be pulled off those beats when breaking news happens.

RSS: Meaning Really Simple Syndication, RSS is a simple system that allows users to subscribe to their favorite Web sites. It allows viewers to subscribe and then download newly published content to their computers automatically once it becomes available.

Satellite Truck: Satellite trucks serve much the same purpose as microwave trucks, but their range is much larger. They have large satellite dishes mounted on the back or the top of the truck and can send video anywhere in the world via satellite. They are commonly used by national networks, and sometimes by local stations when a story is out of the range of a microwave truck.

Second Life: Is a 3-D virtual world entirely **built and owned by its residents**. Since opening to the public in 2003, it has grown explosively and today is inhabited by approximately **6 million** people from around the globe.

Short Message Service (SMS): Is a communications protocol allowing the interchange of short text messages between mobile telephone devices. SMS text messaging is the most widely used data application on the planet, with already 2.4 billion active users, or 74% of all mobile phone subscribers sending and receiving text messages on their phones. The SMS technology has facilitated the development and growth of text messaging.

Social Media: Describes the *online* technologies and practices that people use to share opinions, insights, experiences, and perspectives with each other. A few prominent examples of social media applications are Wikipedia (reference), MySpace (social networking), YouTube (video sharing), Second Life (virtual reality), Digg (news sharing), Flickr (photo sharing), and Miniclip (game sharing). These sites typically use technologies such as blogs, message boards, podcasts, wikis, and vlogs to allow users to interact.

Social Networking Services: Are primarily web-based and provide a collection of various ways for users to interact, such as status updates, chat, messaging, e-mail, video, games, file sharing, blogging, discussion groups, and more. Common examples include: My Space, Facebook, Linkedin (for the business community), Eons (for the 50+community) and Club Penguin (for kids).

STARCC: Simple, Timely, Accurate, Relevant, Credible, and Consistent.

Station Manager: Responsible for administration and financial management at large stations. At smaller stations, the station manager also sets policy on news coverage and supervises overall operation, but generally does not influence daily content.

TV Camera: Generally larger & a little more intimidating than your average video camera, but it serves the same purpose; it records pictures & sound onto videotape.

The tapes used in TV are also shorter than your average tape, 20–30 minutes, so you may have to stop and wait while the cameraman changes tapes.

Twitter: Is a free social networking and micro-blogging service that allows users to send "updates" (or "tweets"; text-based posts, up to 140 characters long) to the Twitter web site, via the Twitter web site, short message service (SMS), instant messaging, or a third-party application such as Twitterrific or Facebook.

Video Blogging: Sometimes shortened to vlogging, is a form of blogging for which the medium is video. Entries are made regularly and often combine embedded video or a video link with supporting text, images, and other metadata.

Wiki: Is a collection of web pages designed to enable anyone who accesses it to contribute or modify content, using a simplified markup language. Wikis are often used to create collaborative websites and to power community websites. For example, the collaborative encyclopedia Wikipedia is one of the best-known wikis.

YouTube: Is a video sharing website where users can upload, view, and share video clips. In July 2006, the company revealed that more than 100 million videos were being watched every day, and 2.5 billion videos were watched in June 2006. Fifty thousand videos were being added per day in May 2006, and this increased to 65,000 by July. In January 2008 alone, nearly 79 million users watched over 3 billion videos on YouTube.

Sources:

- *Assessing Your Disaster Public Awareness Program: A guide to strengthening public education*, 2006, Emergency Management Accreditation Program, The Council of State Governments, through support from the Alfred P. Sloan Foundation, October 2006.
- Social Media: Staying in Touch with Today's Online Community, 2008, Presentation by Jeremy Lasich, Deputy Director for Communications, Fairfax County Office of Public Affairs, Fairfax County, Virginia.
- Wikipedia.org, 2008.
- Working with the Media, 2004, Presentation by Haddow Communications.

Innovations

VA Emergency Officials Launch YouTube Channel

Virginia Department of Emergency Management (VDEM) is launching the VA Emergency Channel on the wildly popular video-sharing Web site YouTube.com. Department officials say visitors will be able to see public service announcements from Governor Tim Kaine—and may be able to get critical information during emergencies. The site is a continuation of the Commonwealth's partnership with Google. The channel can be accessed at http://www.youtube.com/user/VAEmergency. VDEM is not alone. Old Dominion University, Roanoke County, the Virginia Department of Conservation and Recreation, the Virginia Tourism Authority, and the Library of Virginia all are building their own YouTube channels. Source: Associated Press, 2/27/08.

Full Article: http://www.wjla.com/news/stories/0208/499594.html

State Posts Clips About Preparedness On YouTube

Hoping to grab an audience it might otherwise miss, the Virginia Department of Emergency Management has begun offering clips on YouTube. "Just about everybody looks at YouTube nowadays," said Bob Spieldenner, VDEM's public affairs director. "But our big thing is to try to reach the young generation with our messages. We want the kids who are going out there on the Internet to see what we're doing." YouTube.com is the three-year-old Web phenomenon that allows people to watch and share videos—some serious, some sassy, some downright silly. VDEM's YouTube channel leans toward the serious side, focusing on the agency's bread-and-butter issue: emergency preparedness. "I'm Governor Tim Kaine," one clip begins. "Unexpected disasters can happen at any time with little or no warning. So act now to get ready, Virginia." Kaine (D) is seated in what appears to be an elegant room, with blue walls and an ornately framed painting. "Three simple low-cost steps will go a long way toward making sure your family is prepared for any emergency," he continues. "Get an emergency kit, make a plan, and stay informed. Three ways to make a difference in your family's life." Source: Washington Post, March 9, 2008, http://www.washingtonpost.com/wp-dyn/content/article/2008/03/05/AR2008030500201.html

Spanish Class Offered for First Responders

Covington resident Tommy Schubert never realized while growing up among the Hispanic culture in Killeen, Texas, that just learning Spanish and speaking both Spanish and English with friends in his neighborhood would provide him with skills to save lives in St. Tammany. But Schubert, 27, who has been in St. Tammany since 2003, has done just that each time he has been called upon to translate for first responders who do not speak Spanish. Schubert stepped in as translator first as a deputy sheriff in Criminal Control for the St. Tammany Parish Sheriff's Office, then as a volunteer for community Fire District 12. The need for all first responders to be able to communicate with everyone is so important that Schubert has created a "first responders" Spanish course." He is teaching the course to 45 firefighter and medical emergency personnel along with administrators and guests at Fire District 12. "The importance of being able to speak Spanish in this community now is vast," Schubert said. "There has been a huge influx since Hurricane Katrina of people from Mexico, Honduras, and other Hispanic countries. When a responder gets to a scene, the first thing we must do is make sure the scene is safe, then render aid to anyone who needs it. We must be able to ask questions. How can you help someone if you can't communicate with them?" Schubert has seen the problem first-hand. While working with the Sheriff's Office, he served as unofficial translator. Source: New Orleans Times Picayune, 2/7/08.

Full Article: http://www.nola.com/northshore/t-p/covingtonpicayune/index.ssf

Guard Has New Cellular System

The Louisiana National Guard, which lost much of its ability to communicate with its own personnel and other agencies for nearly three days after Katrina, has selected a communications system it says will survive the next disaster. The system uses basic Blackberry devices and broadband frequencies that about 300 senior-ranking Guardsmen are using on a daily basis through a commercial cellular phone service provider. During a disaster, if cell phone service is knocked out as it was after Hurricane Katrina, those devices remain operable through a temporary communications network that could be set up in the disaster area. The network, called Interoperable Communications Extensions System, or ICE-S, also lets troops communicate with local police, firefighters and other governmental agencies who need to talk to each other in coordinating the emergency response, said Army Col. Ronnie Johnson, the Louisiana National Guard's communications chief. "It is a tremendous system that gives you the ability to rapidly re-establish communications," Johnson said. Louisiana's is one of nine National Guards nationwide using the system, but it's the only one putting it to daily use, Rivada spokesman Dale Curtis said. While about 300 Guardsmen use the system daily at a cost of $700,000 annually, the Guard has more than 1000 Blackberries on hand that can be distributed as needed during a disaster to other Guardsmen or to civilian agencies, such as the New Orleans Police Department. Source: New Orleans Times Picayune, 12/30/07.

Full Article: http://www.nola.com/news/t-p/frontpage/index.ssf?/base/news-26/1198995684155080.xml&coll=1

Advanced Technology Helps Firefighters Talk to Each Other in Maine

The National Association of State Fire Marshals (NASFM) and the Maine Fire Chiefs' Association (MFCA) have embarked on a program to provide advanced technology to allow fire departments in strategic communities to achieve voice interoperability and improve incident commander operations at the scene of an emergency. The project is made possible by Assistance to Firefighters Grants (AFG) from the US Department of Homeland Security for the Regional Interoperable

Communications Initiative (RICI) launched jointly by NASFM and MFCA. The AFG program awarded two $800,000 grants to communities in Maine to implement the RICI program. Traditionally, interoperable communications has not been possible with communications devices used by public safety officials from different responding agencies, because their radios tend to operate on different frequencies and protocols. The RICI program was developed to seek technology alternatives to avoid the problem of replacing all communications equipment so that they are on the same system, which could run into the millions of dollars for a single community. The technology selected for the RICI program is BAE Systems' First InterComm system, which is new to the commercial market. Michael Greene, Director of Homeland Security Solutions for BAE Systems explained, "This system was initially developed for the defense industry and has been carefully adapted to serve the specific needs of emergency responders." The First InterComm technology is installed in first-responder vehicles and allows radios on different frequencies to communicate with each other at the incident scene without requiring major communications equipment replacements or investments. Source: PR Newswire, 12/27/07.

Full Article: http://www.forbes.com/prnewswire/feeds/prnewswire/2007/12/27/prnewswire 200712271615PR_NEWS_USPR____DC10657.html

Making the Call When a Crisis Hits

In July 2006, a storm cut off power to parts of Lower Providence Township for five days. Police went door-to-door, telling residents how to cope. A month later, officials got word that dynamite was buried in a local backyard. Officers knocked on doors, telling some neighbors to evacuate, others to stay. Should trouble strike again, don't expect a knock at the door, Township Manager Joseph Dunbar says. Instead, look for a new emergency notification system to call. "Hello, this is an important message from Lower Providence Township," a recording says. The voice of a township official goes on to explain the nature of the emergency. The tool is called Connect-CTY. It's a mass notification service for communities, marketed by the NTI Group in Sherman Oaks, Ca. The firm does business at 17,000 sites nationally. Its software is customized for military, academic, and municipal applications, spokeswoman Natasha Rabe said. The service consists of a Web site that township officials can access to dispatch messages. All hardware and software are owned and maintained by NTI. Lower Providence signed up early this month at a yearly cost of $15,500. It joins Upper Providence Township and West Chester Borough as the first Philadelphia-area governments to subscribe, NTI and township officials said. Though the decision to join flows from the atmosphere created by the Sept. 11, 2001, attacks, no **Homeland Security** money is involved, Dunbar said. Instead, the township pays out of its general fund. Source: Philadelphia Enquirer, 1/27/08.

Full Article: http://www.philly.com/inquirer/local/pa/montgomery/nabes/20080127_Making_the_call_when_a_crisis_hits_1.html

State Unveils 211 Phone Number for Storm Calls

There's a new phone number to call during storms or disasters in Massachusetts. It's 211. Officials at the Massachusetts Emergency Management Agency say 211 is designed to reduce the number of non-emergency calls made to 911. By dialing 211, people can get updated disaster information and post-disaster programs, as well as volunteering and donation opportunities. The 211 call center operates weekdays 8 a.m. to 8 p.m., providing information about social services. It can be staffed around the clock during emergencies. The state is operating the 211 system with the Council of Massachusetts United Way. Source: Associated Press, 1/22/08.

Full Article: http://www.boston.com/news/local/massachusetts/articles/2008/01/22/state_unveils_211_phone_number_for_storm_calls/

Alabama Tests Blimp for Disaster Communication Use

Today's standard response to Katrina-like catastrophes that wipe out telecommunications infrastructure relies on a 7th Cavalry-like rescue mission by trucks laden with high-tech satellite communications equipment. But today in Alabama, as part of a wider state homeland security response exercise, state and federal officials have been testing blimps to provide a backup infrastructure when normal telecom infrastructure services collapse. During the early morning hours of April 7 at Redstone Arsenal, a team of officials from several agencies lofted a 70-foot-long aerostat equipped with a camera and Wi-Fi transmitter to an altitude of 3000 feet. Their plans call for the blimp to hover steadily, except for nightly downtime, until mid-day Thursday. During the test, personnel from Alabama's Homeland Security Department as well as members of the state's Air and Army National Guard and the Army's Space and Missile Defense Command (SMDC) will test their disaster coordination plans. The blimp comes from an SMDC project aimed at creating high-altitude, long-endurance platforms for surveillance and communications. The airship project supports two missions: providing high-resolution imagery to ground installations and restoring communications to areas where natural or man-made disasters have disabled existing telecom facilities. Source: Government Computer News, 4/9/08.

Full Article: http://www.gcn.com/online/vol1_no1/46090

County EMA to Distribute 260 Weather Radios (Ledger Enquirer (GA), 5/18)

The memory of a tragedy 14 years ago in north Alabama has helped spawn a program that could possibly save lives in Russell County. The county Office of Homeland Security and Emergency Management will be distributing National Oceanic and Atmospheric Administration weather radios to recreation areas, churches, and schools in an effort to provide early warning when dangerous storm cells are crossing the county. Kathy Russell, the county's emergency management coordinator, said the office wants to prevent an event such as the tornado that hit a church in Piedmont, Ala., on Palm Sunday 1994, killing 22 people and injuring 90. Emergency Management plans to buy 260 radios and distribute them to groups where large numbers of people congregate. The church tragedy was one of the catalysts for seeking grant money to purchase the radios. "Unfortunately, this was a tornado that had been on the ground for 10 miles before it struck the church," Russell said. "They had no warning whatsoever. So what we want to do is place an NOAA weather radio in every church in the county. They will also go in every public building, every recreational facility, nursing homes... everywhere that we can find to place these radios, we're gonna have one there." The agency also plans to hold information meetings to explain why the radios are necessary and how they are maintained. The Rev. Johnny Rutledge of the Saint John AME Church in Fort Mitchell said the weather radios would be an indescribable asset for churches. "It's probably one of the greatest assets we can have, especially in our area where the population is steadily growing," he said. "It's really important, especially when we are (at church) on Sundays. Communications when dangerous weather is imminent is so important."

Full article: http://www.ledger-enquirer.com/news/story/325104.html

More Weather Radios for Sale in Wisconsin (Capital Times, 5/14)

A second batch of weather hazard radios is now available through municipalities across Dane County, but won't be available at Madison Fire Department stations until June because the department-run sale needs to be approved by the Madison City Council. Dane County Emergency Management bought 4500 radios this time around, after the initial batch of 6800 radios sold out. The fire department's initial order of 1500 radios was sold within 15 minutes at the city's 11 fire stations during a sale April 26. Fire Department Public Information Officer Bernadette Galvez said the next sale at the fire stations can't take place until the council OKs checks and/ or cash (no credit or debit cards) as payment for the radios. The fire department doubled its order this time, getting 3000 radios instead of 1500 radios. No date has been set for the sale. The radios sell for $22.68 each (plus tax), about half the price of comparable radios sold in stores, because the county bought them at cost and doesn't mark up the price.

Full article: http://www.madison.com/tct/news/286340

Illinois Distributes Emergency Radios to College Campuses

Officials from Governor Rod R. Blagojevich's administration today announced that Illinois will complete the distribution of more than 300 radios to 70 colleges and universities as part of his initiative to strengthen safety for students, faculty, staff, and visitors at Illinois institutions of higher education. The STARCOM 21 radios will help campus security officials communicate with other response agencies during emergencies on or near their campuses. Representatives from more than 20 colleges are meeting at the State Emergency Operations Center (SEOC) in Springfield today to pick up their radios and receive training on how to operate them. Forty-six colleges have already received their STARCOM radios and completed hands-on training during a similar session on August 28 at the University of Illinois-Chicago. "The

Virginia Tech tragedy showed us how critical communications are to enhance campus security. These radios will provide campus security with a critical communications link to law enforcement and other first responders whenever an emergency arises," Blagojevich said. "The Illinois Campus Security Task Force will continue their work to ensure the safety of our college students, faculty and visitors." On April 29, Blagojevich announced three college campus security initiatives, including $330,000 in grants from the Illinois Terrorism Task Force (ITTF) that was used to purchase 171 STARCOM21 radios. Schaumburg-based Motorola, Inc., developer of the network, agreed to contribute an additional 132 radios, valued at $294,000. Altogether, the state was able to purchase more than 300 radios for distribution to college campuses. The radios will provide colleges with the capability to access the interoperable communications network used by other responders during emergencies. Source: Government Technology, 09/13/07.

Full Article: http://www.govtech.com/em/articles/143162

Maryland Colleges Trying to Institute Text Message Systems to Send Emergency Alerts

After the shootings last April at Virginia Tech, many colleges instituted text message systems to send emergency alerts to the mobile phones of students, faculty, staff, or even concerned parents, no matter how far-flung. But those systems only work if the intended recipients are registered to receive the messages – and encouraging them to do so has proven to be a challenge, according to officials at local schools. "We can't seem to get them to sign up," said Robert M. Rowan, assistant vice president for facilities management and head of the University of Maryland, Baltimore's Emergency Management Team. "Sign-up for our program has been slower than we'd like," said Johns Hopkins University spokesman Dennis O'Shea. The reasons for the reluctance to register seem unclear, but whatever they are, the schools are determined to sign more users. Text messaging alerts became popular among higher education institutions after the Virginia Tech administration faced criticism for poor communication to students, faculty, staff, and parents during the shootings. The e-mail and Internet alerts, and even campus-wide siren systems, that most schools already have in place only reach people who are online or on campus at any given time. But sending out text message alerts in the event of an emergency reaches anyone with a mobile phone, anywhere, any time – as long as they're registered users, Rowan said. Source: Daily Record (MD), 11/5/07.

Full Article: http://www.oea.umaryland.edu/communications/news/?ViewStatus=Full Article&articleDetail=2995

Nonprofit Group Puts Web to Work for Emergencies

In a quiet brick building 17 miles west of the White House, Arthur Bushkin has prepared for disaster. Now the former telecom executive and Carter administration official is asking: Will you join him? Bushkin has tapped technology, much of it developed by his nonprofit Stargazer Foundation over the past eight years in Fairfax County, to help families and organizations plan for catastrophe, and communicate when one hits. His Web site, http://stargazer.org, aspires to be part personal command center, part meeting place. It uses Web- and cellphone-based tools to connect users of handheld devices with colleagues and relatives. It also seeks to give people an efficient way to tell loved ones or co-workers how they are, or what they need, even when cellphone networks fail under an onslaught of calls or people are away from their desktop computers. "Everybody's plan is: When something happens, I'm going to call everybody," Bushkin said. "The whole point of Katrina, 9/11, of snowstorms, of fires, is that things don't work the way you planned them…. The technology exists to make people safer today. How many more people have to die or be dislocated for this to spread?" One service lets people with Web-enabled cellphones that are equipped with a keyboard, such as a Treo or iPhone, create or respond to surveys. The results can be sent to a Stargazer Web page or to the cellphones of the people in a network you set up. "One form would be an 'I have' form, one would be an 'I need' form," Bushkin said, as in: have blankets, need food. In another service, provided through a partnership with the British company 2sms.com, users in the United States can text a message to 80911 describing their status, such as whether they are safe. Anyone with a computer can then type in the cellphone number to see the message. That is useful because cellular data networks sometimes stay up even after cellphone voice networks fail. Source: Washington Post, 11/22/07.

Full Article: http://www.washingtonpost.com/wp-dyn/content/article/2007/11/19/AR2007111901976.html?hpid=sec-tech

Wildfires Communications

http://findarticles.com/p/articles/mi_m0REL/is_n10_v94/ai_16182763

Many communications products are marginal improvements over existing technologies. They patch a few problems and cause a few of their own. Wildfire Communications has taken a fresh look at the act of communication and has created an elegant and useful speech-recognition interface that helps expedite and simplify phone use, yet is positioned to move beyond the telephone. It is one of the most creative designs of a communications interface that we have seen. Think of it as a glimpse into the future that isn't a wishware video.

National Cell Phone Emergency Alert System?

Davidson, Paul. *Nationwide Cellphone Alert System in the Works.* USA Today, April 8, 2008. At: http://www.usatoday.com/money/industries/telecom/2008–04–08-fcc-emergency_N.htm

Excerpt:

> "*Federal regulators as early as Wednesday are expected to take a major step toward development of a nationwide emergency alert system that would send text messages to cellphones and other mobile devices wherever a crisis occurs. Lack of a simple way to deliver vital warnings to residents has hindered emergency response in disasters such as Hurricane Katrina, recent college-campus shootings, and a spate of devastating tornadoes in the Southeast in February. The Federal Communications Commission is slated to establish technical*

standards and other requirements that for the first time would make such communication possible, two FCC officials say. The officials requested anonymity because commissioners have not yet voted on the plan. Although wireless carriers would not be required to upgrade their networks to accommodate the alerts, those that agree to participate would have to implement the FCC's standards. All four national cellphone providers — AT&T, Verizon, Sprint Nextel, and T-Mobile — said they almost certainly will take part if the FCC adopts an advisory committee's recommendations on how the system would work. The agency is expected to approve those proposals, which, among other things, would initially limit warnings to the English language and 90 characters in length, officials say.... The network is expected to be up and running by 2010. The FCC action is rooted in a 2006 federal law that ordered sweeping upgrades in the way emergency alerts are sent to mobile devices, land-line phones, and broadcast TV stations....

Today, many counties and law enforcement agencies can send warnings to mobile devices, but residents must sign up for the service. Plus, those who enlist receive alerts even if they're out of the affected area, while visitors who haven't joined don't get the news. Also, a separate missive must be sent to each resident, clogging the network and delaying the arrival of many alerts. Under the planned system, a county, state, or federal first responder would send an alert to a still-to-be-determined federal agency that would serve as a clearinghouse. That agency then would relay the alert to participating wireless carriers. The messages would be broadcast on a single pathway to many users in the affected region, like a radio signal, avoiding the congestion that now afflicts such warnings. Few cellphones today can receive such messages, but most will be able to in three to five years, says Verizon Chief Technology Officer Tony Melone. Consumers with compliant phones would receive alerts unless they opt out. The system could be used for a variety of incidents, such as severe weather, a terrorist threat or child abduction. A message could be sent to a county, region, state or the entire nation."

Note: The authors have already heard some internet buzz in emergency management circles asking to what extent emergency management entities have been communicated with concerning this planning.

Emergency Text Alerts to Cell Phones Approved

Federal regulators have approved a plan to create a nationwide text message emergency alert system that could be used to alert affected populations during natural disasters and other emergencies, the Associated Press has reported.

A 2006 federal law that requires the Federal Communications Commission to upgrade emergency alert systems and develop ways to better alert the public about emergencies led to the development of this project, which should be in effect by 2010.

Cell phone carriers' participation is voluntary, but the plan is receiving strong support from the industry, according to the Associated Press. Customers may not be charged for receiving alerts and will have the option to opt out of the program. Additionally, the emergency alerts would be delivered with a unique audio tone to distinguish them from normal messages. According to the plan, three types of messages are proposed:

1. *National Alerts from the President, including for terrorist attacks or natural disasters*
2. *Imminent threats like university shootings, hurricanes, and tornadoes*
3. *Amber Alerts, which are reserved for abducted children*

Read the Associated Press article at http://www.nytimes.com/2008/04/10/washington/10alert.html
Source: FEMA Emergency Management Higher Education Reports.

California Wildfires—Using New Media to Communicate In A Crisis

http://fleetstreetpr.com/2007/10/california-wildfires-using-new-media-to.html

Immediacy is one of the great things about new media/web 2.0. Nowhere is this more apparent than in the coverage of the devastating wildfires down in California recently. I'm fully aware that crisis communications must focus on traditional channels – TV, radio, print – in today's media environment. However, quick and responsive new media tactics provide the ability to communicate directly with citizens that those channels do not. Allen Stern at CenterNetworks wrote a great post about web 2.0-based coverage of the fires on Monday. His post provides a useful list of the ways some people have used new media to post up-to-the-minute information on the fires.

Firestorm 2.0—Using Social Media Services to Track The California Fires

Written by Allen Stern – October 22, 2007
    http://www.centernetworks.com/california-fires-social-media

Today my thoughts and prayers are with everyone affected by the fires in California. The pictures show a scene straight out of a war movie. I thought it would be interesting to look at how the popular social media services are being used to report on the fires. Putting the various sites together shows an almost live look at what's going on across the region. One thing I do notice is that there is no central keyword or search term to find everything, everyone lists their content in a different way. *An idea would be to create "crisis centers" and aggregate the content together for easy locating.*

Twitter Used By News Outlets and Emergency Services During California Fires

Wednesday, 24 Oct 2007
    http://www.hypergene.net/blog/weblog.php?id=P359

As the fires in Southern California rage out of control, the LA Times and KPBS—even the Los Angeles Fire Department—have started posting real-time updates and public service announcements on Twitter.

Disaster-Related Newsletters

Continuity E-Guide: A Wednesday Update by the Disaster Resource Guide

http://disaster-resource.com/newsletter/subpages/signup_page.htm

Based on the philosophy of "working together", the weekly Continuity e-GUIDE provides a concise seven-day snapshot of the business continuity and emergency management industry from around the world right down to the local level.

Attainium's Business Continuity NewsBriefs

http://list-manage.com/subscribe.phtml?id=81fedbfe33

These NewsBriefs are produced and delivered weekly by Attainium to keep our friends and clients current on topics relating to Business Continuity, Disaster Recovery, and Crisis Management.

Disaster Research

http://listproc@lists.colorado.edu

DISASTER RESEARCH (DR) is a moderated newsletter issued by the Natural Hazards Center at the University of Colorado at Boulder for creators and users of information regarding hazards and disasters. Questions for the readership and contributions to this e-newsletter are encouraged. Questions and messages should be indicated as such and sent to http://hazctr@colorado.edu. Publication of the DR is supported by the National Science Foundation (NSF). However, the information presented here does not necessarily reflect the views of NSF. Any opinions, findings, conclusions, or recommendations expressed here are those of the indicated author(s) or the Natural Hazards Center, University of Colorado. To subscribe or unsubscribe, send messages to http://listproc@lists.colorado.edu.

To SUBSCRIBE: Send this one-line command in the body of your e-mail message (do not include): SUBSCRIBE HAZARDS<Your Name>

Homeland Security Week

http://www.govexec.com/email/#sub

Published weekly by Government Executive Magazine and provides access to articles concerning government, non-governmental, and corporate activities in homeland security and emergency management.

FEMA Emergency Management Higher Education Reports

https://service.govdelivery.com/service/subscribe.html?code=USDHSFEMA_130

The FEMA Higher Education Project provides a daily update on activities in the program, among college and university emergency management education programs and emergency management news in general including information on new technologies, trends and practices in emergency management communications.

Disaster Websites

General

Disaster Center

http://www.disastercenter.com/

This site provides a variety of information including current warnings and advisories, current weather conditions, recent earthquakes, newspaper, radio and television links, links to tsunami warning centers, weather services worldwide, to the National Hurricane Center, US Drought Monitor, National Fire News, and others.

New Media

Flickr

http://www.flickr.com/

Flickr is an online photo management and sharing application in the world designed to help people make their content available to the people who matter to them and to enable new ways of organizing photos and video. Flickr gets photos and video from the web, from mobile devices, from the users' home computers, and from whatever software they are using to manage their content and pushes them out in as many ways as possible: on the Flickr website, in RSS feeds, by email, by posting to outside blogs, or ways we haven't thought of yet.

Del.icio.us

http://del.icio.us/

Del.icio.us is a **social bookmarking** website—the primary purpose is to store your bookmarks online, which allows you to access the same bookmarks from any computer. You can also see the interesting links that other people bookmark.

Digg

http://digg.com/

Digg is a **user-driven social content news website**. Everything on Digg is submitted by the community. After users submit content, other people read the submission and Digg what they like best.

Second Life

http://secondlife.com/

Second Life is a 3-D virtual world entirely **built and owned by its residents**. Since opening to the public in 2003, it has grown explosively and today is inhabited by approximately **6 million** people from around the globe.

Twitter

http://twitter.com/

Tweeter is a free social networking and micro-blogging service that allows users to send "updates" (or "tweets"; text-based posts, up to 140 characters long) to the Twitter web site, via the Twitter web site, short message service (SMS), instant messaging, or a third-party application such as Twitterrific or Facebook.

Wikipedia

http://en.wikipedia.org/wiki/Hurricane_Katrina

Wikipedia a multilingual, Web-based, free content encyclopedia project. The name Wikipedia is a portmanteau (combination of words and their meanings) of the words *wiki* (a type of collaborative website) and *encyclopedia*. Wikipedia's articles provide links to guide the user to related pages with additional information. Wikipedia is written collaboratively by volunteers from all around the world. Since its creation in 2001, Wikipedia has grown rapidly into one of the largest reference Web sites, attracting at least 684 million visitors yearly by 2008. There are more than 75,000 active contributors working on more than 10,000,000 articles in more than 250 languages. As of today, there are 2,408,858 articles in English; every day hundreds of thousands of visitors from around the world make tens of thousands of edits and create thousands of new articles to enhance the knowledge held by the Wikipedia encyclopedia.

YouTube

http://www.youtube.com/

YouTube is a video sharing website where users can upload, view, and share video clips. In July 2006, the company revealed that more than 100 million videos were being watched every day, and 2.5 billion videos were watched in June 2006. Fifty thousand videos were being added per day in May 2006, and this increased to 65,000 by July. In January 2008 alone, nearly 79 million users watched over 3 billion videos on YouTube.

Response

FEMA: Federal Response to the California Wildfires

http://www.fema.gov/hazard/wildfire/ca_2007.shtm

This site serves as a central node of information on the Federal Emergency Management Agency's role in the response to the California wildfires. Included on the site are specific responsibilities of other government agencies, information on donations and volunteering, and tips for recovery and rebuilding.

FEMA Hurricane Katrina Information

http://www.fema.gov/press/2005/resources_katrina.shtm

This Web page of the Federal Emergency Management Agency (FEMA) provides information on Hurricane Katrina, including evacuees and disaster victims, emergency personnel, volunteers, and federal sources.

EERI Kashmir Earthquake Virtual Clearinghouse

http://www.eeri.org/lfe/clearinghouse/kashmir/

This virtual clearinghouse developed by the Earthquake Engineering Research Institute (EERI) provides data on the earthquake in Pakistan for use by government agencies, nongovernmental organizations, and local builders in the reconstruction.

UN Emergency Response Humanitarian Information Centre for Pakistan

http://earthquake05.un.org.pk/

The Humanitarian Information Centre for Pakistan is a common service to the humanitarian community managed by the United Nations (UN) Office for the Coordination of Humanitarian Affairs. Their Web site includes situation and assessment reports, coordination and logistical information, photos and map products, and technical advice to organizations to help them manage data and information in earthquake relief efforts more effectively.

World Health Organization Information on the South Asian Earthquake

http://www.who.int/hac/crises/international/pakistan_earthquake/en/

This Web site of the World Health Organization provides situation reports and other information on the countries affected by the October 8, 2005 earthquake in Pakistan.

Floods and Landslides in Central America and Mexico

http://www.paho.org/english/dd/ped/ElSalvador-Floods1005.htm

This Web site of the Pan American Health Organization includes reports and photographs from the countries impacted by Hurricane Stan and the related floods and landslides.

The Global Disaster Information Network

http://gdin.org/

The Global Disaster Information Network is a voluntary, independent, self-sustaining, non-profit association and seeks to provide "the right information, in the right format, to the right people in time to make the right decisions" (http://www.gdin.org). It is a consortium of industry, government, education, and NGOs that develop unique information sharing procedures that augment the existing system and develop new disaster information management methodologies.

Unosat

http://unosat.web.cern.ch/unosat/

UNOSAT (http://www.unosat.org) provides the international community with "updated and accurate geographic information and to universalize access to satellite imagery".

Relief Web

http://www.reliefweb.int/rw/dbc.nsf/doc100?OpenForm

Relief Web (http://www.reliefweb.int) provides information (documents and maps) on humanitarian emergencies and disasters.

Asian Disaster Reduction Center

http://www.adrc.or.jp/

The Asian Disaster Reduction Center (ADRC) (http://www.adrc.or.jp/) builds upon a formal network between government, private interests, and industry to develop a state-of-the-art Internet GIS.

Warning

Ranet

http://www.ranetproject.net/

The RANET project (http://www.ranetproject.net/) uses Internet technology to disseminate early warning information, satellite imagery, weather, and climate data to rural areas. The RANET project seeks to share information, but builds on the existing capacity of the communities it serves where an Internet GIS may not be the most appropriate technology due to factors such as bandwidth, literacy levels, and data availability.

Preparedness

Ready.gov

http://www.ready.gov/

Ready.gov, a campaign of the U.S. Department of Homeland Security, provides disaster preparedness resources and information for families, businesses and kids. The site provides a listing of community and state resources for the entire nation and information about the risks associated with a wide range of natural and man-made disasters.

Ready Kids

http://www.ready.gov/kids

This section of the Ready.gov Web site provides kids an opportunity to plan for disasters, learn about disasters, and play games. Additionally, the site provides information and resources that parents and teachers can use to teach kids about disaster preparedness.

READYColorado Campaign

http://www.readycolorado.com/

READYColorado is a public awareness campaign supported by public and private partners concerned with raising awareness about the importance of disaster preparedness among Colorado citizens. The Web site includes tools, checklists, strategies, and information for preparing, responding, and recovering from natural and man-made disasters.

We Prepare

http://www.csc.ca.gov/familyplan/index.html

CaliforniaVolunteers educates Californians about the need to prepare for disasters that may strike our state. Whether they are natural—floods, fires, and earthquakes—or man-made disasters, we all must have a disaster plan that includes our family, friends, and neighbors. Since 1950, 255 states of emergency have been proclaimed in California. And since 1989, there have been 27 major declared disasters. Although these numbers are staggering, statistics show that less than half of Californians have a disaster plan.

CaliforniaVolunteers created a disaster preparedness pilot program in the greater Los Angeles area to encourage moms to prepare their families for disaster. CaliforniaVolunteers received a federal grant from the Office of Homeland Security for this pilot program. The initiative encourages moms to go online, identify their risk, develop a family disaster plan, practice their plan, and prepare their children for disaster.

Florida Division of Emergency Management Media Center

http://www.fdem-mediacenter.org

The Florida Division of Emergency Management's Interactive Media Center features numerous video public service announcements (PSAs), in both Spanish and English, on topics such as emergency supply kits, hurricane wind protection, pets and disaster, and family disaster plans. The site also presents videos of officials discussing lessons learned and a regular video blog from Craig Fugate, the director of the FDEM.

Orlando Sentinel Hurricane Survival Guide

http://www.orlandosentinel.com/news/weather/hurricaneguide/

The "Orlando Sentinel" has published this hurricane survival guide, which features 10 lessons learned from the 2004 hurricane season and additional information for local residents, including important phone numbers and a list of shelters.

Small Business Preparedness PSAs at Ready.gov

http://www.ready.gov/business/index.html

The U.S. Department of Homeland Security teamed up with The Advertising Council to create new public service announcements (PSAs) describing the ease and affordability of business continuity planning for small businesses. The PSAs are available here.

Media Support

FEMA Photo Library

http://www.photolibrary.fema.gov/

The Federal Emergency Management Agency (FEMA) has updated its online photo library, a collection of more than 9,200 images of natural disasters and terrorist events, including response and recovery activities, taken by FEMA's disaster photographers. The majority of photographs in the collection are in the public domain and may be downloaded, reproduced, and distributed for educational and informational purposes without further permission from FEMA.

FEMA "In the News" Website

http://www.fema.gov/media/

The Federal Emergency Management Agency (FEMA) has launched a new Web page for its Public Affairs News Desk. "In the News" features facts on emerging issues, official statements, background material, and downloadable high-resolution photos. The Web page provides the latest information on what FEMA is doing in the areas of mitigation, preparedness, response, and recovery.

Mapping

Google Earth

http://earth.google.com/index.html

Google Earth provides access to online satellite imagery.

Google Map

http://maps.google.com

Google Map provides imagery that has been used to develop maps of shelter locations and fire updates during the 2007 wildfires in California. Maps can be overlaid with satellite images of the same location.

http://maps.google.com/maps/ms?f=q&hl=en&geocode=&time=&date=&-ttype=&ie=UTF8&om=1&msa=0&msid=114250687465160386   813.00043d08-ac31fe3357571&ll=32.990236,-

GIS

Volunteer Groups

A further development in response to the multiple disasters has been the formation of volunteer organizations that provide hands-on expertise to develop location-specific, GIS applications. These organizations form in cyberspace to solicit assistance in times of need, development, and implementation of socio-technological networks for disaster response:

GISCorps

http://www.giscorps.org/

Operating under the auspices of the Urban and Regional Information Systems Association (URISA), GISCorps coordinates short term, volunteer GIS services to underprivileged communities worldwide. They provide GIS services that include: needs assessment and strategic planning, technical workshops, database modeling, disaster management, and remote sensing processing and interpretation. GIS allows relief agency staff to obtain critical information about how humanitarian support efforts are progressing to ensure appropriate response agencies are acting in a coordinated and efficient manner. Once in the field, the coordination can continue as new data can be added and disseminated via wireless applications and Internet/Intranet connectivity.

Mercy Corps

http://www.mercycorps.org/

Mercy Corps has created the Geospatial Relief & Development Team. A volunteer base of more than 50 GIS and remote sensing professionals in the Pacific Northwest has mobilized to apply geospatial technologies to expedite the flow of aid and accelerate recovery. They seek to establish a Non Governmental Organization (NGO) geospatial coordination team to reduce redundant efforts in emergency mapping, increase efficiency, detect change, transfer knowledge, and provide a geospatial data repository for all NGOs in collaboration with the United Nations Geospatial Initiative throughout all phases of recovery.

MapAction

http://www.mapaction.org/

Based in the UK, MapAction is an NGO dedicated to providing time-sensitive information during a disaster. They integrate geospatial technologies (GIS, GPS, and RS) to create maps developed by a cadre of volunteers. In addition, they provide training programs in developing countries.

Citizen Groups

A further component of Internet GIS for disaster is the rise of citizen GIS, participatory GIS, and civic web mapping. Existing systems managed by local and federal agencies were not strong enough to handle disasters of the magnitude of the twin hurricane events. As local and federal agencies struggled to respond to Hurricanes Katrina and Rita in 2005, two software engineers created Scipionus.com—a Google map of affected areas with site-specific comments provided by numerous individuals. Online grassroots disaster response demonstrated the power and speed in which people could disseminate information. Creating mash-ups by seamlessly combining data from other sources with Google maps do not necessarily require geospatial skills and GIS expertise.

Hurricane Information Maps

http://www.scipionus.com

Using Google's free API (application programming interface), this site presents information using Google maps with other data creating a "mash up" or a mash up of programs [9]. These maps were designed for people affected by Hurricanes Katrina or Rita who were trying to find information about the status of specific locations affected by the storm and its aftermath. This site explicitly asks for updated information and provides instructions for how to add new locations and their attribute information.

Source: Laituri, Melinda and Kris Kodrich, 2008, "On Line Disaster Response Community: People as Sensors of High Magnitude Disasters Using Internet GIS," Colorado State University, 2008.

Bloggers

In Case of Emergency

http://breakglass.wordpress.com/about/

In Case of Emergency is a blog dedicated to exploring public health preparedness efforts in the U.S. My primary interest is in communication, though I have a great interest in planning for public health emergencies in general. In the past, I have posted on new, or social, media use in disaster situations, crisis communications (or crisis and emergency risk communication, as the CDC calls it), homeland security, public health, and open access scholarly journals.

Eric's Corner—King County—http://www.metrokc.gov/prepare/emergencyinfo/eric_corner.aspx

"There is a lot going on in the world of emergency management and homeland security these days. New laws, new national plans, and procedures. Technology has enabled us to share information with one another more easily than ever before. Check this page often for interesting information on all aspects of disaster prevention, preparedness, recovery, and yes—response."

Katrina Blogs: (NOTE: Go to http://katrinahelp.info/wiki/index.php/Blogs to access this list of blogs)

News Organizations' Blogs

- WWL-TV (best N.O. authenticated radio-tv news blog) (*http://www.wwltv.com/*)
- Times-Picayune (best authenticated N.O. print news blog)(*http://nola.com*)
- 2theadvocate.com, WBRZ (*http://2theadvocate.blogspot.com/*), Baton Rouge, Louisiana
- CBS News Disaster Blog (*http://www.cbsnews.com/stories/2005/08/31/national/main807164.shtml*)

- Weather Channel's Blog (*http://www.weather.com/blog/weather/?from=wxcenter_news*)
- Weatherguide (*http://blog.myweatherguide.com/*) - Katrina from a meteorological angle
- The Infozone (*http://www.theinfozone.net*)—News, Updates and Information

Hurricane Blog Aggregators

- Part 1 (*http://homepages.cwi.nl/~cilibrar/projects/a/aggs/*), Part 2 (*http://homepages.cwi.nl/~cilibrar/projects/a/ag2/*), and Part 3 (*http://homepages.cwi.nl/~cilibrar/projects/a/ag3/*)
- Katrina Feeds (*http://www.katrinafeeds.org/*)
- The truth laid bear hurricane blog aggregator (*http://www.truthlaidbear.com/topicpage.php?topic=Katrina*)

Weblogs

- Help Bay St Louis (*http://www.helpbaystlouis.blogspot.com*) This is the Team Blog from First Presbyterian Church in Bay St Louis.
- Say Thanks to NOAA Slidell LA (*http://www.theinfozone.net/lifestyle.html*) This is the Team that helped spread the warnings for Katrina.
- KatrinaBlog.org (*http://www.katrinablog.org*) Lots of news and resources with a human touch. Damage caused by failure at every level of government: Human, Animal, Environmental, Economic.
- KatrinaCoverage.com (*http://www.katrinacoverage.com*) Hundreds of extensively-tagged posts about the politics and news reports of the hurricane: media bias, who did what when, etc.
- Kathryn Cramer (*http://www.kathryncramer.com/kathryn_cramer/2005/09/welcome_new_yor.html*) has a wealth of New Orleans related info in the Katrina hurricane affected areas.
- National New Orleans' House Party! (*http://www.theinfozone.net/lifestyle.html*) Help Raise Donations for Red Cross, Salvation Army and Bush Clinton Relief Fund
- Storms411.com (*http://www.Storms411.com*) - Pictures and videos; News and information about resources, aid, donations, and volunteer efforts for all hurricanes.
- Amateur Radio Watch (*http://www.arrl.org/news/stories/2005/08/25/1/?nc=1*)
- Apathy Online (*http://katrina.apathyonline.net*) - Providing free web hosting accounts for use by any project related to Katrina, and other help.
- HR Horizons (*http://www.nickroy.com/hrblog/*) - Nick Roy, special coverage on the recovery from Hurricane Katrina.
- Brainwidth (*http://www.brainwidth.net/blog*) - blogging from Lafayette, LA.
- Brendan Loy (http://brendanloy.com/)

- Bigjim.org (*http://bigjim.org/*) - First-person blogging from Mississippi.
- Cathouse Chat (*http://romeocat.typepad.com/cathouse_chat/2005/09/carnival_of_rec.html*) - Offering $5 donations for every comment on the Sept 1 post.
- Crooks and Liars (*http://www.crooksandliars.com*) - Nuggets from Broadcast TV coverage.
- Crossroads Dispatches (*http://evelynrodriguez.typepad.com*) Check new category "Resiliency." Resources and advice regarding psychological, spiritual, emotional healing for victims, family members, friends, and acquaintenances. Written by December 26th tsunami survivor, with help from clinical psychologist sister.
- Dancing With Katrina (*http://dancingwithkatrina.blogspot.com/*) - Ms. Gulf Coast hurricane blog.
- Deadlykatrina.com (*http://www.deadlykatrina.com/*) - News and information about Hurricane Katrina, including links to news stories with synopses.
- Ernie the Attorney blog (*http://www.ernietheattorney.net/*)
- Eye of the Storm Blog (*http://eotstorm.blogspot.com/*)
- Florida Cracker (*http://www.florida-cracker.org/archives/002284.html*)
- Florida Information (*http://thefloridamasochist.blogspot.com/*)
- Grace Davis (*http://gracedavis.typepad.com/katrinablog/*) All Mississippi all the time.
- Global Learning Initiative: Hurricane Katrina Information (*http://nlcommunities.com/communities/gli/archive/category/1098.aspx*)
- Hellicane (*http://hellicane.blogspot.com/*) - Poems written by, for, and about the victims of Hurricane Katrina.
- Huffington Post (*http://www.huffingtonpost.com/*)
- Hurricane Help Chicago (*http://www.hurricanehelpchicago.com/*) - How to help in Chicago.
- Hurricane Katrina Help News Blog (*http://www.hurricanekatrinahelp.com/*) - Information resources to help you help others!
- Hurricane Katrina and smart mobs (*http://stephensonstrategies.com/categories/hurricaneKatrinaAndSmartMobs/*) - Applies the smart mobs for homeland security concept to disaster relief, empowering the public as full partners.
- Hurricane Harbor (*http://hurricaneharbor.blogspot.com/*) - BobbiStorm, blogging from Miami, FL
- Hurricane Katrina Direct Relief (*http://gracedavis.typepad.com/katrinablog/*) - Coordinating direct shipment of supplies to shelters in the Gulf Coast.
- The Interdictor (*http://mgno.com*) - Live from a data center in the heart of New Orleans.
- JoshBritton.com (*http://joshbritton.com/*) - Info from Louisiana State University - Updated very frequently.

- Katrina Aftermath (*http://katrina05.blogspot.com/*) - Community blog and podcasting tool; anyone can add new entries or post podcasts from their phone.
- Katrina Help Blog (*http://katrinahelp.blogspot.com/*) Katrina help blog
- Katrina Stories Project (*http://www.katrinastoriesproject.org/*) - Pulling the stories together - volunteers needed.
- Kaye Trammell's Hurricane Katrina Blog (*http://hurricaneupdate.blogspot.com/*) - Dr. Trammel is blogging from Baton Rouge, Louisiana.
- Lake Vista Katrina Blog (*http://katrina.jp3.com/*)
- Michelle Malkin (*http://michellemalkin.com/*)
- New Orleans Met Blog (*http://neworleans.metblogs.com/*)
- NPR Katrina Web Log (*http://www.npr.org/news/specials/hurricane/katrina/*)
- Operation Eden (*http://operationeden.blogspot.com/*)
- Unapologetic (*http://www.unapologetic.com/blog/*) - One New Orleans blogger, fled to Florida.
- Paultwo (*http://paul2.net/?cat=5*)
- Prayer Vigil (*http://h2otheworld.blogspot.com*) - 24-Hour prayer vigil at the Houston Astrodome on Sat. Oct. 8th.
- RagingBlog (*http://www.ragingblog.com*) Scientific and political analysis, links to video and articles.
- Rebuild Green (*http://www.rebuildgreen.org/*) - New Orleans residents. Working through Global Exchange to make sure government and corporations don't determine the city's future without community participation.
- Rita Help Blog (*http://www.ritahelp.blogspot.com*) - Blog specific to Hurricane Rita.
- Savannah Katrina Help Blog (*http://katrinahelp.gatherat.com/*) - Events and resources for Savannah, Ga residents who want to help.
- Senate Democrats' Katrina Relief Plan (*http://www.democrats.org/reliefplan*)
- Slidell Hurricane Damage Blog (*http://slidell.weblogswork.com/*) - Info on damage in the Slidell, La area, blogged by Brian Oberkirch.
- Scientology Volunteer Ministers (*http://www.volunteerministers.org/eng/news/index.htm*) - Katrina News
- StormDigest (*http://www.stormdigest.com/index.php/category/hurricanes/*)
- Survival of New Orleans (*http://mgno.com/*) From a blogger still in New Orleans.
- ThinkDude (*http://www.thinkdude.com/*) Coverage on Katrina and now Rita, day and night.
- Update from Jack City (*http://www.geocities.com/badgerminor/index.htm/*)- One blogger from Jacksonville.
- View From Texas (*http://www.viewfromtexas.com/*)

- VatulBlog (*http://vatul.net/blog/*) - New Orleanian Maitri V-R blogs from Houston, Tx. - "on the ground" info, perspective for evacuees and the rest of the nation, resources for Shell employees and evacuees, neighborhood updates and some opinion.
- You Big Mouth, You! (*http://blog.simmins.org/2005/08/hurricane-katrina-lets-help-ourselves.html*) - Includes a list of aid agencies and phone numbers
- Where To Send Donations For Katrina blogspot (*http://wheretosenddonationsforkatrina.blogspot.com/*)
- Volunteer FD (*http://www.volunteerfd.org/katrina/*)

Source: KatrinaHelp.com, http://katrinahelp.info/wiki/index.php/Main_Page

List of Blogs, etc. from 2007 Southern California Wildfires:

The List: California Wildfire Coverage by Local Media, Blogs, Twitter, Maps and More—Mark Glaser. MediaShift. October 25, 2007

http://www.pbs.org/mediashift/2007/10/the_listcalifornia_wildfire_co_1.html

The last few days have shown that online resources, social media, and collaboration on the Net can make a huge difference in a natural disaster. As the wildfires have spread in Southern California, the evacuees and local residents have utilized the Internet not only to connect and get updated information; they have used it to tell their stories and share photographs and video of the fires with the outside world. Probably the most heartening aspect of the online coverage is the way that mainstream media and individual citizen journalists have worked together. Local media has been highlighting user-submitted photos and videos, and embedding new technology in their prime coverage. San Diego's public television station, KPBS, used Twitter to give its audience updates when its Web site went down, and the Twitter updates now have a prominent place on their home page. MediaShift associate editor Jennifer Woodard Maderazo put together a large collection of links, and we are asking that you add to the list by sending along any other resources you've seen online in the comments below. We'll update the list over the next week or so, and give you credit for any important sources you add.

Southern California Wildfire Resources—Bloggers Blog

http://www.bloggersblog.com/cgi-bin/bloggersblog.pl?bblog=1023071

This post contains a list of resource about the wildfires in Southern California. More coverage can be found in our 2007 California Wildfires section.

Message Boards and Web Portals

Nola.com

http://www.nola.com/forums/searching/index.ssf

Katrina message boards, such as NOLA.com (http://www.nola.com/forums/searching/index.ssf), were critical in providing information about shelter locations, family tracing, and missing persons.

Katrina Help

http://katrinahelp.info/wiki/index.php/Main_Page

Wiki software was used as an organizational tool to create Web portals (http://katrinahelp.info/wiki/index.php) to Web pages such as those identifying immediate shelter needs (ShelterFinder) and family tracing (PeopleFinder).

Special Needs Populations

Emergency Preparedness Initiative (EPI): A program of the National Organization on Disability

http://www.nod.org/index.cfm?fuseaction=Page.viewPage&pageId=1564

Compelled by the attacks of September 11, 2001, NOD launched the **Emergency Preparedness Initiative (EPI)** to ensure that emergency managers address disability concerns and that people with disabilities are included in all levels of emergency preparedness- planning, response, and recovery.

EPI Guide for Emergency Planners, Managers, & Responders

http://www.nod.org/index.cfm?fuseaction=Feature.showFeature&FeatureID=1034

National Organization on Disability's (NOD) first emergency preparedness guide highlights key disability concerns for officials and experts responsible for emergency planning in their communities. This guide is also designed to help emergency managers, planners, and responders make the best use of resources to include all citizens of the community in emergency preparedness plans.

National Organization on Disability

http://www.nod.org/index.cfm?fuseaction=Feature.showFeature&FeatureID=1136

This Web page includes guides, checklists, Web sites, and more information concerning people with disabilities and disasters.

Disability Preparedness Resource Center: The Interagency Coordinating Council on People with Disabilities in Emergency Preparedness

http://www.disabilitypreparedness.gov/

This disability preparedness Web site provides practical information on how people with and without disabilities can prepare for an emergency. It also provides information for family members of and service providers to, people with disabilities. In addition, this site includes information for emergency planners and first responders to help them to better prepare for serving persons with disabilities.

Lessons Learned from September 11. Claude L. Stout

http://www.nod.org/index.cfm?fuseaction=Feature.showFeature&FeatureID=847

Recommendations Offered for Improvements and Advanced Technology For Benefit Of People With Hearing Loss In Emergencies—In the aftermath of the tragic events of September 11 that shook the world, the staff at TDI reflected on their own personal experiences and reviewed reports from members throughout the country. Although unscientific, these anecdotal reports provided a rare opportunity for TDI to review where it looks like we have been successful in a particular area, and where there appears to be more work left that needs to be done.

Special Needs Populations. Brenda D. Phillips, Ph.D. Center for the Study of Disasters and Extreme Events. Oklahoma State University. 2007

http://www.vaemergency.com/newsroom/events/pdf/vema2007/Brenda_Phillips.pdf

Power Point presentation discussion of Populations at Risk, Warnings, Evacuation, and a Practical Approach to communicating with special needs populations including ideas for individual, household, community, and agency strategies.

Disabilities Websites

The following list of sites, offer good starting points from which other information on emergency preparedness for people with disabilities can be located.

(Source: EPI Guide for Emergency Planners, Managers & Responders - http://www.nod.org/index.cfm?fuseaction = Feature.showFeature&FeatureID = 1034)

- **www.nod.org/emergency**: National Organization on Disability links and information about disaster information and people with disabilities.
- **www.ready.gov**: Department of Homeland Security's emergency preparedness information Web site.
- **www.preparenow.org**: California site but general links on disasters and special needs.
- **www.easter-seals.org**: s.a.f.e.t.y. first evacuation program.
- **www.jan.wvu.edu/media/emergency.html**: Job Accommodation Network emergency evacuation for employees document called Employer's Guide to Including Employees with Disabilities in Emergency Evacuation Plans.
- **www.nbdc.com**: Emergency evacuation checklist for people with disabilities in the workplace. (Search bar on left of homepage; type emergency evacuation checklist.)
- **www.aoa.dhhs.gov**: U.S. Department of Health and Human Services Administration on Aging information about the senior population.
- **www.cdihp.org/evacuationpdf.htm**: The Center for Disability Issues and the Health Professions' guide for people with disabilities and other activity limitations called Emergency Evacuation Preparedness: Taking Responsibility for Your Safety. For publication visit Web site or call (909) 469–5380, TTY (909) 469–5520.

Preparedness Messages

Talking About Disaster: Guide for Standard Messages

http://www.redcross.org/images/pdfs/code/Complete_Guide.pdf

The purpose of this guide is to assist those who provide disaster safety information to the general public. The information presented is based on historical data for the United States and is appropriate for use in the United States and its territories. Some of the information may not apply to other countries. Users of this guide may include emergency managers, meteorologists, teachers, disaster (natural and human-caused) educators, public affairs/public relations personnel, mitigation specialists, media personnel, and communicators. If you would like more in-depth or scientific information, please contact your local emergency management office, local National Weather Service office, local American Red Cross chapter, state geological survey office, state foresters office, or local fire department.

Public Perceptions of Disaster Preparedness Presentations Using Disaster Damage Images

http://www.colorado.edu/hazards/publications/wp/wp79.pdf

This paper discusses the level of preparedness of 4,739 persons who attended education presentations intended to heighten awareness and cause individuals to take action to prepare for disasters. The results of this nationwide survey on the use of disaster damage images about tornadoes, flood, and earthquakes are presented herein. It is argued that the use of disaster damage images diminished the purpose of these presentations; the data here demonstrate significant lack of action among members of the public after attending presentation using such images.

The Twelve Cs of Disaster Preparedness Education. 2007. Rocky Lopes, PhD, Manager, Homeland Security, National Association of Counties

http://www.rockylopes.com/publications.html

Educating the public about hazards such as tornadoes, earthquakes, hurricanes, fires, and floods, among other natural and technological events, not to mention a deliberate attack on human life such as a bombing or intentional release of a biological agent, is always a challenge. People generally do not want to believe that anything bad can happen to them. They are usually in a state of what risk communicators call *denial.* They want to decline acknowledgment of negative consequences that may result from impact of natural hazards because they either believe firmly that the hazard can not happen *to them*, where they live, or they rationalize about the impacts of the hazard to believe (or want to believe) that such events can only happen elsewhere, will not be "that bad," or attribute to the fates and say to themselves, "If it is that bad, there's nothing I can do about it anyway." Worse, some are under the misconception that the government, the Red Cross, or insurance will provide funds to restore their household to its pre-disaster state.

In order to be more successful in engaging the public in meaningful activities toward being prepared for disasters and disruptive events, those who desire to do this work should keep twelve points in mind which research has shown to improve the effectiveness of disaster preparedness education. These "twelve Cs" are: Community Focus, Consistent Messages, Cost-effectiveness, Coalitions, Conciseness, Compel Action, Clear Messages, Constant Repetition and Reinforcement, Common Language, Children, Citizens, and Conversation.

Research Papers

Early Warning— From Concept to Action: The Conclusions of the Third International Conference on Early Warning

http://www.ewc3.org/upload/downloads/Early_warning_complete2.pdf

This document (33 pp.) is an outcome of the Third International Conference on Early Warning (EWC III) hosted by the government of Germany under the auspices of the United Nations in March. The major objectives of the conference were to showcase innovative early warning projects for potential financial support and implementation; to identify unused potential in early warning; and to facilitate multidisciplinary scientific debate on latest practices and research. Other outcomes include "A Compendium of Early Warning Projects" (47 pp.), which consists of project proposals from all parts of the world, and a tool for practitioners, "Developing Early Warning Systems: A Checklist" (13 pp.), which are both available at http://www.ewc3.org/.

Communicating with the Public Using ATIS During Disasters: A Guide for Practitioners

http://ops.fhwa.dot.gov/publications/atis/index.htm—U.S. Department of Transportation, Research, and Innovative Technology Administration, Federal Highway Administration. April 2007.

Advanced Traveler Information Systems, ATIS, can play an important role in communicating essential information to the public during disasters. Variable message signs, 511 telephone systems, highway advisory radio, and Web sites are some of the dissemination devices of systems that collect, process, and disseminate information about travel conditions to the public for day-to-day transportation operations, and these same systems need to be effectively used during disaster situations. This document provides advice on use of ATIS during disasters and is intended not only for state and local transportation agencies but for their partners in public safety and emergency management agencies. Five case studies of actual disasters in Georgia, California, Nevada, Utah, and Washington State show the role that traveler information has played in current practice and provide lessons for others. A concept of operations is presented that characterizes the flow of information among the people, organizations, and technologies comprising traveler information dissemination during disasters.

Quick Response Research Report 189—The Emergency Management Response To Hurricane Katrina: As Told by the First Responders—A Case Study of What Went Wrong & Recommendations for the Future

Henry W. Fischer, Kathryn Gregoire, John Scala, Lynn Letukas, Joseph Mellon, Scott Romine, & Danielle Turner, Center for Disaster Research & Education, Millersville University of Pennsylvania, Millersville, Pennsylvania, 2006. http://www.colorado.edu/hazards/research/qr/qr189/qr189.html

Excerpts:

Mass Media: Part of the Solution and Part of the Problem

Media as Helper. Without the television broadcast media calling attention to the plight of those stranded at the Superdome and the Convention Center, the misery of these evacuees would undoubtedly have been unnecessarily lengthened even further. The media were extremely helpful in calling attention to problems that needed to be redressed, in providing information to evacuees and survivors, and in providing information to responders as well—in some cases the media were the only source of information for an extended time (radio and then television for those who could obtain electricity via generator or service restoration). A responder comment indicated the dependency on the media in the absence of communications when he said, "I had a ten-gallon can I filled with gasoline before impact that enabled me to run my home generator, and that gave me access to radio and some television I could capture off the antenna that was on one of my small televisions. This is all the communication I had for the first six or seven days. It was impossible to travel with all the debris. I could not do anything except help survivors in my own immediate area. For all I knew, the world ended. All I knew was from the mass media when I turned it on, which I did sparingly in order to preserve my gasoline as long as I could. That is how I eventually knew how big the event was and how long it was taking, and going to take, to get help to all of us."

Media as Part of the Problem. There was also the usual problematic aspect to the mass media reporting, exhibited by the following responder's experience. "I saw (on television) how people were really acting out in New Orleans—it scared me. I knew we were going to need police and military help to get control." Another responder indicated "it was through television that we knew about the looting, raping, and killings in New Orleans; we had some of the looting here (Mississippi), but nothing like those crazies."

A volunteer medical responder in New Orleans shared, "we drove over the infamous bridge one evening to go to see who may need some medical attention and we were immediately surrounded by scary people pounding on the ambulance. We locked our doors; they had a crazed look in their eyes. We didn't get out, we just slowly backed up until they stopped, then we turned around and left. The next day we went in with some support (National Guard) and then helped them. We then realized what was going on. Those pounding on our vehicle the night before were going through drug withdrawals. They saw the ambulance and assumed we would have something they could shoot themselves up with to get high and stop the withdrawal symptoms. They weren't intending to harm us; they were desperate for the drugs they could not now buy since they were cut off from their dealers. Everything here is just one hell of a mess. Reporters see some things, make assumptions, and come to the wrong conclusions about what is really going on, which only makes it worse."

Rumor, as is noted in the research literature, was often reported as fact. "We kept hearing (from media reports) about the shootings at helicopters by marauders in the city; we were afraid to go in because we didn't want to get shot trying to help these damn ungrateful people." Later, it was determined that these alleged shootings never occurred; rumor reported as fact suppressed responder action, which prolonged misery. Others indicated they "were afraid to go in because we felt uncomfortable. I'm not prejudiced, but in this situation we were only a few whites surrounded by many blacks. We had to be prudent." Fear of what deviance may occur had a restraining effect on how quickly help was provided. The desire for police or National Guard protection was frequently articulated as a precondition for feeling comfortable to provide assistance to the victims. The nature of the mass media reporting was the primary source of perceptions of the dangers of advancing into large populated areas with minority populations.

Media Convergence. Responders indicated they "need more training in how to deal with the mass media when they converge in such large numbers, are pushy and rude. The media were in sooner than anyone else. We would have liked to have had some control on the media's ability to move around in such large numbers. Perhaps a media pool would be less bothersome when we are trying to complete our mission. Prevent them from wandering around the city; instead, give them information periodically from press meetings."

Quick Response Report #117—Hurricane Georges: The Experience Of the Media and Emergency Management on the Mississippi Gulf Coast

Henry W. Fischer III, Department of Sociology, Millersville University of Pennsylvania, Millersville, Pennsylvania 17551. 1999. http://www.colorado.edu/hazards/research/qr/qr117.html

A content analysis was conducted on news stories published in the print media and broadcast on local and network television during the pre-impact, impact, and post-impact periods of Hurricane Georges. Media and emergency management personnel were interviewed. The research focus was to determine if the media reporting had changed in any way since a similar study was conducted ten years earlier (Hurricane Gilbert). The researchers found most of the reporting content and patterns to be very similar to the Gilbert findings. Reporting content was largely accurate, except for some tendency to dwell on deviance such as looting and price gouging (part of the disaster mythology). Local reporting patterns varied from network broadcasting and national print media in that the local media sought to serve the local population by disseminating mitigation and response information. On the other hand, national and network reporters constructed news stories that conformed to their expectations of what they perceived normally occurs. A notable exception, however, was the reporting of one NBC news reporter. Robert Hager replaced the entertainment norm with an educational norm. His reporting could serve as a model of how the media can effectively serve the public.

Communities that implemented an effective public information plan, which anticipated media and community needs, were much more effective in maintaining a good relationship between the media and emergency management than those which did not have or effectively implement such a plan. More importantly, communities with effective public information plans were far more effective in disseminating mitigation and response information to their constituents than the other communities. The former communities received praise from local officials and citizens, while the later received sever criticism.

The Role of the Media in Disaster Mitigation: Roundtable on the Media, Scientific Information and Disasters

Fred H. Cate, ed., *International Disaster Communications: Harnessing the Power of Communications to Avert Disasters and Save Lives* (Washington, D.C.: The Annenberg Washington Program in Communications Policy Studies of Northwestern University, 1994). http://www.annenberg.northwestern.edu/pubs/disas/disas32.htm

Complementing the focus of earlier meetings and publications on the importance of technical communications systems, disaster site communications, and organizational communications in disaster preparedness and response, the World Conference on Natural Disaster Reduction and the Roundtable on the Media, Scientific Information, and Disasters addressed the vital roles of communications among and between scientists, engineers, government officials, disaster response officials, and particularly the media and the public in disaster mitigation.

The Roundtable participants sounded two themes that dominated the entire conference: disaster prevention, rather than merely response, and the importance of individual action to mitigate the impact of natural hazards. The participants stressed that "timely, accurate, and sensitive communications in the face of natural hazards are demonstrated, cost-effective means of saving lives, reducing property damage, and increasing public understanding. Such communications can educate, warn, inform, and empower people to take practical steps to protect themselves from natural hazards."

The Media and Disaster Reduction: Roundtable on the Media, Scientific Information, and Disasters at the United Nations World Conference on Natural Disaster Reduction–

Fred H. Cate. Fred H. Cate, ed., *International Disaster Communications: Harnessing the Power of Communications to Avert Disasters and Save Lives* (Washington, D.C.: The Annenberg Washington Program in Communications Policy Studies of Northwestern University, 1994). http://www.annenberg.northwestern.edu/pubs/disas/disas3.htm

In the face of extraordinary and increasing human and economic costs of natural disasters, the United Nations designated the 1990s as the International Decade for Natural Disaster Reduction (IDNDR). Initiated by Dr. Frank Press, then-president of the U.S. National Academy of Sciences, the IDNDR explicitly recognized that humankind possesses the means to reduce the impact of disasters— to save lives and reduce damage to property.

Effective, reliable communications are vital to disaster reduction and an important focus of the IDNDR. Communications technologies, skills, and media are essential to link scientists, disaster mitigation officials, and the public; educate the public about disaster preparedness; track approaching hazards; alert authorities; warn the people most likely to be affected; assess damage; collect information, supplies, and other resources; coordinate rescue and relief activities; account for missing people; and motivate public, political, and institutional responses.

Natural Disasters and the Media: Relevance of Mass Media for Disaster Management

Hans Peter Peters, Research Centre Juelich, Program Group Humans, Environment, Technology 52425 Juelich, Germany. http://www.chmi.cz/katastrofy/peters.html

Communication is an important part of disaster prevention and management. Many channels are used before and during a disaster—e.g. visible or audible signals, leaflets, announcements by speaker cars and public events. An important channel are the mass media: Newspapers, television, radio and - increasingly important - the internet. Mass media have certain characteristics that make them advantageous for disaster communication: they provide easy access to large publics and some of them constitute a robust communication system which remains working even in cases of a partial breakdown of the infrastructure (battery-powered radio). On the other hand sources dealing with the media know that media can be difficult channels. There is no direct control over the content and form of information transmitted. Sources who want to communicate with the public have to deal with journalists who do not form a passive "information channel" but act as gate keepers, interpreters and commentators. Hence, media can support or obstruct the disaster management of government agencies and relief organizations.

Communications Plans/Guides

Assessing Your Disaster Public Awareness Program

http://www.emaponline.org/?299

The Emergency Management Accreditation Program (EMAP) has created a guide for strengthening public education. The material in this guide provides supplemental content and program considerations to the professionally accepted emergency management standards. This guide also serves as a checklist of activities deemed important for having a successful disaster awareness program.

The Five Pillars of Emergency Communications Planning

http://www.idsemergencymanagement.com/Common/Paper/Paper_142/The%20Five %20Pillars%20of%20Emergency.htm

This white paper discusses the five pillars of emergency communications planning. The term "pillars," suggests these activities support emergency communications planning, which can fail if any one of them is not in place. These pillars are best practices to ensure your planning initiatives pay off when incidents occur. Successful communications planning depends on your ability to: Develop a modern communications plan; Ensure executive collaboration and decision-making; Conduct frequent training and testing; Compose your message carefully; and, Choose the right technology.

The Five P's of Crisis Communications

http://www.redorbit.com/news/health/1304030/the_5_ps_of_crisis_communications/ index.html.

If your company is facing a crisis, do you know how to communicate with your clients and the general public? One expert says it's as easy as following the "five P's" of crisis communications. In an article on the Red Orbit Web site, consultant Jane N. Abitanta says in the midst of a crisis, the last thing many people want to do is talk to another panicked client. But that, she says, is exactly what you should do. "In a crisis, the natural propensity is to stick one's head in the sand, far, far away from the phone. There may be many deep psychological reasons for this: maybe you don't want to face conflict, perhaps you worry that you've made mistakes, or it is possible that your father was distant and your mother didn't tell you she loved you," she says. "But for now, who cares about all that mumbo-jumbo? This is no time to confront those issues - you just have to deal with the crisis at hand... Procrastination and avoidance will come back to bite you: so make the calls." Using the example of a financial advisor during the current economic turmoil, Abitanta offers what she calls the "five P's" of crisis communication to help get through the tough times. They include: Be proactive; Be prompt; Offer perspective; Be prepared; Pool the calls.

Terrorism and Other Public Health Emergencies: A Field Guide for Media

http://www.hhs.gov/emergency/mediaguide/field/

The U.S. Department of Health and Human Services (HHS) created this guide to provide the important information that media professionals might need in the field while covering a terrorist attack or other public health emergency. This field guide is mainly aimed towards individual reporters, but may also be useful for newsroom managers and other media professional.

Small Business Administration (SBA) Disaster Recovery Media Guide

http://www.sba.gov/idc/groups/public/documents/sba_homepage/serv_da_media_ guide.pdf

The media's role in post-disaster recovery is as vital as the federal agencies providing that assistance. Disseminating accurate information quickly allows disaster victims to take that first step toward rebuilding their homes and businesses. This media guide will help provide a basic understanding of the SBA disaster loan process. From details on the different disaster loans available to homeowners, renters, and businesses, to how loan funds are disbursed, the facts in this guide will provide practical information to the reporter. The idea is to then get this information out—clearly and quickly—to disaster victims, so they can begin the process of rebuilding their lives.

Nigeria—National Emergency Management Agency (NEMA)
The Media and Disaster Management

Charles Agbo. Ph.D. http://www.nema.gov.ng/Media/Article/Article_5.htm

Information management is very critical in disaster management. This is so because any major accident or disaster is an issue that concerns the general public and is therefore newsworthy. It is therefore important to develop and adopt crisis communication policies that would ensure proper media coverage of disasters. As events unfold in disaster situations, the media would seek information and would raise questions for disaster managers, it is therefore important that adequate preparations be made to handle media relations. A media relations coordinator of a disaster management agency must therefore alert the appropriate authorities of the immediate need to entertain questions from the media in disaster situations. The spokesperson of the disaster management agency should be briefed on how to respond to media questions.

Pandemic Influenza Preparedness, Response, and Recovery Guide For Critical Infrastructure and Key Resources, 2006

U.S. Department of Homeland Security. September 19, 2006. http://www.pandemicflu.gov/plan/pdf/cikrpandemicinfluenzaguide.pdf

Chapter 7 of this guide discusses communications during a pandemic flu outbreak, "Effective risk communication is essential to inform your employees and mitigate panic. As you prepare for the pandemic, it is critical for your company to develop a coordinated and streamlined information framework that facilitates, not impedes, communication to your employees, the public, government officials, and the media."

How to Develop a Communications Plan
Article by Nancy Rathbun Scott, Dumfries, VA

What is a communication plan? When should it be developed? Where does the information in the plan come from? How do you write one, and why should you bother?

Overworked and under funded communicators (Are there any other kind?) have a right to ask whether the work involved in developing a plan is worth it. The answer is yes because a written communication plan will:

- give your day-to-day work a focus,
- help you set priorities,
- provide you with a sense of order and control,
- help get the chief staff executive and staff to support your program,
- protect you against last-minute, seat-of-the-pants demands from staff and members, and
- prevent you from feeling overwhelmed, offering instead peace of mind.

What Is a Communication Plan?

A communication plan is a written document that describes:

- what you want to accomplish with your association communications (your objectives),
- ways in which those objectives can be accomplished (your goals or program of work),
- to whom your association communications will be addressed (your audiences),
- how you will accomplish your objectives (the tools and timetable), and
- how you will measure the results of your program (evaluation).

Communications include all written, spoken, and electronic interaction with association audiences. A communication plan encompasses objectives, goals, and tools for all communications, including but not limited to:

- periodic print publications;
- online communications;
- meeting and conference materials;
- media relations and public relations materials;
- marketing and sales tools;
- legal and legislative documents;
- incoming communications, including reception procedures and voice mail content;
- committee and board communiques;
- corporate identity materials, including letterhead, logo, and envelopes;
- surveys;
- certificates and awards;
- annual reports;
- signage;
- speeches; and
- invoices.

When to Develop the Plan

The best time to develop your plan is in conjunction with your annual budgeting or organizational planning process.

Where to Get Information

Grist for the plan generally comes from five sources:

1. your association mission statement,
2. a communication audit,
3. membership surveys and focus groups,

4. committee and leadership input, and

5. discussions with other staff and departments.

How to Develop the Plan

Take the following steps to develop an effective communication plan:

Conduct a research-communication audit. Evaluate your current communications. Some associations hire firms to do this, but the price for the objectivity of an outside auditor can be high. To conduct your own audit, find out:

- what every staff person is doing in the way of communication,
- what each communication activity is designed to achieve, and
- how effective each activity is.

To get the answers you need,

- brainstorm with communication staff,
- talk to other departments,
- interview the chief staff executive,
- interview the board,
- talk to communication committee members,
- survey the membership,
- host focus groups, and
- query nonmembers.

Define objectives. Armed with information from your audit, define your overall communication objectives-the results you want to achieve. These might include:

- excellent service to members,
- member loyalty,
- centralization of the communication effort,
- increased employee teamwork,
- improved product delivery,
- visibility for the association and the industry or profession it represents, and
- influence on government, media, consumers, and other audiences.

Define audiences. List all the audiences that your association might contact, attempt to influence, or serve. Included on your list may be:

- members;
- nonmembers;
- consumers;
- related associations;
- adversarial associations;
- educators;

- federal, regional, and local governments;
- related industries; and
- the media.

Define goals. With stated objectives, and considering available human and financial resources, define goals—in other words, a program of work for each objective. Goals include general programs, products, or services that you will use to achieve stated objectives. For example, if the objective is to improve member service, goals might include improved training for the member-service function, special communications directed at first-time members, a reference manual for handling complaints, and ongoing information for members.

Identify tools. Decide what tools will be used to accomplish stated goals. These tools can be anything from a simple flyer to a glossy magazine. Don't overlook less obvious tools such as posters, report covers, Rolodex cards, and Web sites. Brainstorm ideas with your staff.

Establish a timetable. Once objectives, goals, audiences, and tools have been identified, quantify the results in a calendar grid that outlines roughly what projects will be accomplished and when. Separate objectives into logical time periods (monthly, weekly, etc.).

Evaluate the result. Build into your plan a method for measuring results. Your evaluation might take the form of:

- a monthly report on work in progress,
- formalized department reports for presentation at staff meetings,
- periodic briefings of the chief staff executive and the department heads, and
- a year-end summary for the annual report.

Developing a written communication plan will take effort. Plan on three or four days the first time you do it. Once in place, the written plan will smooth your job all year long, earn you respect from the CEO and other staff, help set work priorities, protect you from last-minute demands, and bring a semblance of order to your chaotic job.

Case Studies

Emergency and Risk Management Case Studies Textbook

FEMA Higher Education Project, http://training.fema.gov/EMIWeb/edu/emoutline.asp

Case Study 6.1: Risk Communication During the Washington D.C. Sniper Crisis

Washington, D.C. metropolitan area residents were confronted with a heightened sense of vulnerability in the year leading up to the Sniper crisis. On September 11th, 2001, during the worst terrorist attack to take place on American soil, the city became the target of two hijacked airplanes. Three weeks later, anthrax-laced letters mailed to federal government offices arrived, resulting in building closures, mass pro-phylaxis, and the death of several postal workers. Ever increasing security became the norm, including disruptive street closures and military vehicles with mounted machine guns. Meanwhile, the media continued to report that despite these measures, Washington, D.C.'s emergency response capabilities would be severely deficient should a mass casualty event occur in the near future (Ward 2001).

Case Study 6.2: The Homeland Security Advisory System

The Homeland Security Advisory System (HSAS) is a color-coded rating system consisting of five threat levels, administered by the Department of Homeland Security (DHS), that indicates a nation-wide risk level for the threat of terrorist attack. A change in threat level prompts the implementation of protective measures by government agencies and public safety officials to reduce the likelihood or impact of an attack. The purpose of this case study is to provide an understanding of the history and components of the Homeland Security Advisory system and to examine certain shortcomings of the system in an effort to provide suggestions for improvement. This case study details the evolution of the HSAS including the history of the assigned national threat levels; the process for changing the current threat level; and HSAS notification procedures. This study also examines public awareness of the HSAS and adaptation of the private and public sector to the system.

Case Study 6.3: A Comparison of Leadership Between Two Outbreaks of Smallpox in the United States: New York City, 1947, and Milwaukee, 1894

Epidemics, whether the result of natural or intentional (terrorist) origin, are frightening events. Historically, **epidemics** and **pandemics** have proven to be the most devastating of all disasters, as illustrated by the staggering mortality figures from the 1918 Influenza Pandemic. During the single year that the pandemic lasted, between 20 and 40 million people died of the illness—more than all those killed in World War I. Furthermore, unlike natural disasters, technological disasters, or even chemical terrorist attacks, there is little indication that an epidemic is occurring until after many people are infected, making these events all the more difficult to predict and identify.

Unlike many other kinds of disasters, however, epidemics are preventable once they have begun, through effective public health activities. At the forefront of these activities is communication. Only information, and solid communication mechanisms, can control an outbreak of disease and reign in public panic and fear. This case highlights two outbreaks of the same deadly disease. Both of these outbreaks had catastrophic potential in regards to the number of people that may have been killed. Only one led to an epidemic. Clearly, through comparison of the two cases, strong leadership emerges as the cornerstone to effectively managing the emergency.

Case Study 2.1: TsunamiReady—An Effective Tsunami Preparedness Program

TsunamiReady is an initiative that promotes tsunami hazard preparedness as an active collaboration among federal, state, and local emergency management agencies, the public, and the NWS tsunami warning system. This collaboration functions for the purpose of supporting better and more consistent tsunami awareness and mitigation efforts among communities at risk. Through the TsunamiReady program, NOAA's National Weather Service gives communities the skills and education needed to survive a tsunami before, during, and after the event. TsunamiReady was designed to help community leaders and emergency managers strengthen their local tsunami operations. (NOAA, N/D) The TsunamiReady program is based on the NWS Storm-Ready model (which can be viewed by accessing http://www.stormready.noaa.gov/). The primary goal of TsunamiReady is the improvement of public safety during tsunami emergencies. As stated above, TsunamiReady is designed for those coastal communities that are at known risk of the tsunami hazard (tsunami hazard risk maps can be seen by accessing http://www.pmel.noaa.gov/tsunami/time/).

Case Study 2.2: Washington State Emergency Management Division—Comprehensive Public Disaster Preparedness Campaign

The Washington State Emergency Management Division considers public disaster education to be one of its highest priorities, and encourages participation in disaster education programs throughout the state. Their vision, in accordance with these beliefs, is to have the best-prepared public in the nation. The principal goal of the Public Education Program is to encourage, support, and empower local governments, state agencies, volunteer organizations, businesses, and other privately sponsored groups who desire to increase their level of preparedness or engage in preparedness programs. The ultimate goal is individual self-sufficiency for at least three days (72 hours) following a disaster.

The focus is all-hazard disaster preparedness. This is accomplished through presentations; by assisting schools, businesses, and government agencies; conducting train-the-trainer classes; facilitating neighborhood preparedness courses; development of awareness and preparedness materials; outreach to multicultural and special needs groups; coalition building and public-private partnerships. Each of these tasks is focused upon assisting citizens in preparing for emergencies and disasters, thereby saving lives, minimizing property damage, and reducing the impact on the environment and the economy.

National Media Outlets

CNN - http://www.cnn.com/
iReport - http://www.cnn.com/ireport/
NBC News - http://www.msnbc.msn.com/id/3032619/
MyNBC Community - http://my.nbc.com/

MSNBC - http://www.msnbc.msn.com/

First Person - http://www.msnbc.msn.com/id/16712587/

CNBC - http://www.cnbc.com/

CBS News - http://www.cbsnews.com/

Blogs - http://www.cbsnews.com/stories/2007/01/03/blogs/main2327516.shtml

ABC News - http://abcnews.go.com/

iCaught - http://ugv.abcnews.go.com/

FOX News - http://www.foxnews.com/

MYNEWS - http://www.foxnews.com/mynews/index.html

U Report - http://www.foxnews.com/studiob/ureport/

The Weather Channel - http://www.weather.com/

User Video - http://uservideo.weather.com/?from=hp_video_upload

National Public Radio (NPR) - http://www.npr.org/

Submit Ideas - http://www.npr.org/about/pitch/

PBS News - http://www.pbs.org/news/

Online Local News Sites

Driven by the economic downturn in the newspaper business, the desire to present opposing points of view other than those offered in the dominant local newspaper or to offer more granular information about discrete communities than can be covered in a big city daily, an increasing number of online new sites are becoming go-to information sites for communities across the country. Below are several examples:

Creating Community Connections, Chicago, http://www.creatingcommunityconnections.org/

Crow News, Crow Agency, Montana, http://www.rnnonline.org/crownews/2008/06/peregoy-wins-de.html

Dutton Country Courier, Dutton, Montana http://www.duttoncc.org/

The Forum, Deerfield, New Hampshire, http://www.forumhome.org/

iBrattleboro, Brattleboro, Vermont, http://www.ibrattleboro.com/

MyMissourian, Central Missouri, http://mymissourian.com/

New Castle Now, Chappaqua, New York http://www.newcastlenow.org/

Twin Cities Daily Planet, Minneapolis and St. Paul, http://www.tcdailyplanet.net/#

WestportNow, Westport, Connecticut, http://www.westportnow.com/

Books

Bowman, Shayne and Chris Willis, 2003, "We Media: How Audiences are Shaping the Future of News and Information," The Media Center at the American Press Institute, 2003.

Friedman, Thomas, 2007, "The World is Flat," Picador, 2007.

Gillmor, Dan, 2006, "We the Media: Grassroots Journalism By the People, For the People," O'Reilly Media Inc., 2006.

Gillmor, Dan and Sanjana Hattotuwa, 2007 "Citizen Journalism and Humanitarian Aid: Boon or Bust?" ICT for Peacebuilding, http://ict4peace. wordpress.com/2007/07/30/citizen-journalism-and-humanitarian-aid-bane-or-boon/, 2007.

Hattotuwa, Sanjana, 2007, "Who is afraid of citizen journalists?," Communicating Disasters, TVA Asia Pacific and UNDP Regional Centre in Bangkok, 2007.

Jenkins, Henry, 2006, "Convergence Culture: Where Old and New Media Collide," 2006.

Keen, Andrew, 2007, "The Cult of the Amateur: How Today's Internet is Killing Our Culture," Doubleday, 2007.

Laituri, Melinda and Kris Kodrich, 2008, "On Line Disaster Response Community: People as Sensors of High Magnitude Disasters Using Internet GIS," Colorado State University, 2008.

May, Albert L., 2006, "First Informers in the Disaster Zone: The Lessons of Katrina," The Aspen Institute, 2006.

Schellong, Alexander, 2007, "Increasing Social Capital for Disaster Response Through Social Networking Services (SSN) in Japanese Local Governments," National Center for Digital Government, 2007.

Shirky, Clay, 2008 "Here Comes Everybody: The Power of Organizing Without Organizations," The Penguin Press, 2008.

Tapscott, Don and Anthony D. Williams, 2006, "Wikinomics: How Mass Collaboration Changes Everything", Portfolio Hardback, 2006.

Index

Note: Page numbers followed by 'f' indicate figures.